SHARK ATTACKS

OF THE

JERSEY SHORE

A HISTORY

PATRICIA & ROBERT HEYER

THE
History
PRESS

Published by The History Press
Charleston, SC
www.historypress.com

First published 2020

Manufactured in the United States

ISBN 9781467144995

Library of Congress Control Number: 2019956032

*Maybe the time for hero worship is ending. Those singular souls cannot carry all the weight. We must **each** step into being heroes in our own community.*
— Kerry Washington, on Twitter.

The Six Steps of Overthrowing Apep

The Bremner-Rind Papyrus, c. 300 B.C.E.
The British Museum, London, England
Image used with permission.

CHAPTER ONE

The knock was gentle, but the Airstream's flimsy aluminum door rattled like it was about to fall off the hinges.

"Felicity? You in there?"

She yelled her answer over the cacophony of mewling cats. "Where else would I be?"

Felicity's lifelong best friend poked her carefully coiffed head inside the trailer, a cheerful smile on her face. "Are you busy?"

"Nope." She nearly laughed. What did Tasha think she was up to in here? Negotiating a peace treaty? Splitting the atom? Felicity pulled a pint of milk from the mini fridge and gave it a sniff. After all she'd been through, it would be anticlimactic if expired milk was the thing that finally took her out. She imagined her obituary, if those things still existed…*Felicity Renee Cheshire, 52, lifelong resident of Pine Beach, Oregon, has died after a brief battle with lactobacillus.*

"Got a sec to chat?"

"I haven't fed the cats yet."

"It'll just take a minute."

Felicity sighed. "Sure. Want some coffee?"

Tasha blinked rapidly, searching for a polite way to refuse. Felicity didn't blame her. These generic freeze-dried crystals made an elixir that tasted like liquified armpit hair.

"I'll pass." Tasha scanned the trailer interior, seeking out the latest damage, no doubt, or judging whether the litter boxes had overflowed.

Tasha was entitled to be as judge-y as she wanted, since the trailer and all things in it were hers. Except for the clothes, books, CDs, and litterboxes, anyway. And the cats, who belonged only to themselves, as all cats did. Everything else—from the whistling kettle to the TV and the electricity it required—was hers.

Tasha frowned as her eyes darted from cat to cat. "How about we sit out front?" She screeched when Mojo and Alphonse escaped between her legs into the wilds.

"They're cats, Tash. Not rattlesnakes. Go ahead. I'm right behind you."

Felicity dumped a spoonful of coffee into a cracked cup, added boiling water, and splashed some iffy milk into her creation, then stepped out to the stoop. Boudica escaped before she could shut the door.

"Everything OK?" Felicity plopped into the aluminum folding chair next to her best friend, and the two women settled in on the six-by-four rectangle of rickety metal mesh that served as the Airstream's front porch.

The sky was unusually blue for an early summer morning on the Oregon coast. Felicity couldn't help but notice how the direct light did no favors to the ramshackle house and five acres, wedged between a dairy farm and a junkyard, that Tasha had inherited from her parents. The place looked better in rain and mist, like an aging movie star through a Vaseline-smeared camera lens.

She knew she was partly to blame for the yard-sale ambience of the spot. Last year, Tasha had offered Felicity use of her grandparents' 1966 Airstream Overlander, now propped on cinderblocks in the side yard, hooked to water, septic, and power. Parked next to the trailer was Felicity's rusty Saturn sedan, with its cracked windshield and duct-taped exhaust pipe.

"Yes and no." Tasha folded her hands in her lap and avoided eye contact.

They'd known each other since kindergarten, and Felicity was all too familiar with her friend's mannerisms. This chat was about to veer off into late rent territory. Again. Nothing soothed Tasha's accountant soul like a tidy balance sheet.

"I'll catch up as soon as Rich accepts an offer on the house. It won't be long now. I appreciate everything you've done for me... are *doing* for me."

Tasha nodded, biting her bottom lip. "It's not that."

The bad coffee churned in Felicity's belly. "Then...?"

"It's Jim." Tasha looked sideways at Felicity. There was embarrassment in her expression. "He says he can't deal with the cats anymore. Turns out he's so allergic he can't even have them on the property. He gave me an ultimatum. Either the cats go, or he does."

Felicity froze, a cornucopia of delicious snarky responses ready to be served piping hot:

1. *I'll help him pack.*
2. *You just dodged a bullet, sweetie.*
3. *Fuck Jim and the Harley he rode in on.*

Lucky for Tasha, Felicity could say nothing with her mouth hanging open the way it was.

"I'm sorry about this. Really I am." Tasha picked at a ragged cuticle.

"I don't understand. We agreed…"

"That was before I met Jim."

The words stung. A metal-on-metal screech rose from the junkyard, and Felicity chose not to shout over the noise.

Well, *shit*.

It took a minute for the racket to cease, and Tasha jumped in before Felicity could.

"I know you see your cats as friends."

"Family, actually."

"It's just too much. I was planning to talk to you about it even before Jim."

"You knew I had several cats, Tasha. You said…"

"The word *several* means *three*. What's the total now? Twenty?"

Felicity laughed. "Don't be ridiculous." Her elbow jerked, shooting coffee across the front of her old chenille robe and onto her cat hair-covered slippers.

"Fifteen?"

"Nowhere near."

Tasha pursed her lips, waiting.

"Fine. Twelve cats."

Tasha's sigh was heavy and lasted a dramatically long time. Her shoulders drooped. "This is hard for me. I don't want to be cruel, but I have to consider my own needs along with yours. You can appreciate that, right?"

Felicity said nothing. It was probably a rhetorical question, anyway.

"I know you're in a bad place. You don't deserve the avalanche that's come down on you—the fertility stuff, getting laid off, Rich's affairs, the divorce, the breast cancer, the bankruptcy…"

"Gee, sounds bad when you string it all together like that."

Tasha smiled gently and placed a hand on Felicity's coffee-stained knee. "You are such a good person, with the kindest heart, and I love you to death. It's not fair what you've gone through."

Boudica padded up the rickety stairs to rub against Felicity's ankle. The one-eyed tortie's purr vibrated through her body.

Tasha recoiled. "Ew. What happened to its other eye?"

"No idea. She doesn't like to talk about it."

"Right. So here's the thing, Lissie." Tasha took a deep breath. "I'm madly in love with him."

Sweet suckling baby Jesus.

"Can you try to understand where I'm coming from?"

It was Felicity's turn to sigh. "You barely know the man, Tash. You let him move in after two dates, for crying out loud."

"It was four dates and sometimes you just know, you know?"

"Oh, I know." Felicity knew Hair Gel Jim was a slime bucket, leaching off her best friend. Not only was he not a great guy, he wasn't even a decent guy. But Tasha couldn't see it because she chose not to.

"He looks a little like DDL, don't you think?"

Oh, God. Not the Daniel Day-Lewis thing again. Since *Last of the Mohicans* hit the movie theaters nearly thirty years before, Tasha had convinced herself that every man in her life bore a striking resemblance to the tall, dark, and intense actor. None had, of course.

"I'm thinking his *Gangs of New York* period."

Felicity rubbed Boudica behind her ears, feeling a lump that had not been there yesterday. Great. Another cyst. Or tick. Or infection. Another vet bill.

"I'm not getting any younger, Lissie. I feel like this is my last chance for any kind of happiness. Please be glad for me and find homes for the cats."

Sadness expanded in Felicity's chest, pushing into her throat and stinging her eyes. How ridiculous would it be if she chose that moment to crack? She'd cried just twice in the last six years, and the first time barely even counted. Back then, losing her teaching job to budget cuts had seemed like the end of the world, the absolute worst thing that could ever happen to a person, and she'd sobbed and sobbed and sobbed.

She should have saved her energy.

Felicity decided to point out the obvious. "Nobody wants these cats, Tasha. There *are* no homes for them; that's why they're here. It's me or the kill shelter."

"I'm sorry." Tasha stared down through the mesh to the weeds below.

"I won't do it." Mojo came galumphing up the steps and jumped into Felicity's lap, bumping the coffee cup, which she placed under the chair so she could stroke the full length of his blue-black fur. "It'll be a death sentence for them. I can't."

"If you don't ditch the cats, you'll have to find somewhere else to live."

Felicity noted the curve of her friend's spine and how she continued to pick relentlessly at the spot where her fake nails sprouted from her real nailbed. The crescent of fragile skin looked red and sore.

How many years had passed since their hot tamale days? Thirty-five? The two of them used to hold court at the beach, oiled and posed on their blankets at the edge of the Pacific Ocean. Boys would trip over plastic buckets as they gawked at the expanse of hard, tanned flesh between their bikini tops and string bottoms. Tasha and Felicity had ruled the world back then, or at least a sandy slice of it. One day, a group of boys followed them to the taco stand and bestowed upon them their nickname: "The Hot Tamales."

They'd been filthy rich in those days—their currency strong arms, firm thighs, perky breasts, and the dimples displayed at the base of their spines. They called the shots with just a twitch of their hips or a flick of thick, glossy hair.

Tasha's had been a rich dark brown, stick straight. Felicity's had been strawberry blonde and curly.

And look at them now.

Beneath the stained chenille, Felicity's body was more puff pastry than hot tamale. Her hair had turned a lovely shade of... what? Beige? Taupe? Khaki? There were probably a thousand names for the blandness her hair had become, gray-streaked frizz pulled back by a headband.

Tasha's hair had gone stark white in her late thirties, like her mother's before her, and she'd invested a great deal of time and money into hiding that fact. Every few weeks, like clockwork, a blaze of white would appear along the center part of Tasha's scalp. She seemed to be forever chasing that stripe of doom with another touch-up.

And Tasha still preferred a heavy sweep of eyeliner, thick mascara, and bright lipstick, though it did nothing but point a big flashing arrow at her missing left incisor. She didn't seem to mind.

Tasha was desperate to stay in the fight. She wanted so badly to be worthy of love, for a man to want her, that she would settle for the likes of Hair Gel Jim, fifteen years her junior and as many IQ points shy of three-digit territory.

Allergic, my ass.

Felicity didn't feel superior to Tasha or think herself above the drama of dating and lipstick and love. Not at all. She was simply too damn tired for it. Even if she weren't bankrupt, jobless, scarred, and living in a tin can, the math didn't add up. Any benefit a man might bring to her life was not worth the effort needed to acquire him. Maybe simple biology was a factor, too. Tasha hadn't yet gone through menopause, while Felicity's was brought on by the chemotherapy.

Tasha still cared.

Felicity was out of fucks.

In fact, Felicity was proud to dwell within a designated fuck-free zone. Her world was fantastically fuckless in every way a middle-aged woman's life could be devoid of fucks.

"I was thinking two weeks."

She jolted from her thoughts. "For what?"

"To get rid of the cats."

Her heart dropped. "You can't be serious."

Tasha stood, placed a hand on Felicity's shoulder, and side-stepped between the railing and folding chairs. She clunked down the steps in her platform sandals, adding, in case Felicity missed it the first time: "Two weeks or you'll have to leave. I'm really sorry."

Tasha had already turned away, walking across the patchy weeds and gravel toward the front porch of the cottage. She called over her shoulder, "Let me know how it goes with Rich!"

Felicity was stunned. For the first time ever, she couldn't count on Tasha. The betrayal stuck in her windpipe like ground glass.

But hold up… if Rich accepted an offer on the house, none of this would matter. She could get her own place. She could keep the cats. She could afford to hire a lawyer to finalize her medical bankruptcy. All this weirdness with Tasha would become a non-issue, and one day they would look back on this and laugh.

Right?

Dark clouds rolled in, putting an abrupt end to their sunny morning. It happened so fast it was as if God had hit the light switch. "What the…"

Mrrrraaaow! Mojo jumped off her lap and raced down the

steps like flames singed his heels. Boudica followed, and both scurried under the cinderblocks. Before Felicity could even register what was happening, she felt something pummel the top of her head.

Plop.

"Huh?"

Plop.

Plop-plop-plop-plop-plop…

Tasha covered her head with her arms and made a break for her front porch, screaming the whole way. "What the fuck is going on? Are you seeing this?"

Felicity covered her head with the hood of her robe and glanced up, marveling at how the black clouds churned. They looked alive.

Splat! Something landed in the center of her forehead. Sound swelled from every direction as things crashed to the metal porch, the Airstream roof, the dirt. Felicity was surrounded by a chorus of croaking and pounding and thudding.

"What is *happening?*" Tasha shrieked from the cover of her front porch, her eyes wide in horror. "They're everywhere!"

Jim burst through the front door. "Fuckin A, man! It's the apocalypse!"

One frog plunked into Felicity's abandoned coffee mug, shooting coffee everywhere.

She grabbed the door handle and ducked inside the trailer, suddenly aware that something squirmed inside her nightgown. "Auugghh! Get off me!" She ripped open the chenille robe and flung the creature aside, then stomped her slippered feet on the linoleum to shake off the panic—and any clinging frogs.

Then it stopped. The pounding on the roof and dirt just ended. The dark clouds parted. But the ground writhed, covered with a light-gray layer of amphibians. Plenty had plummeted to their deaths, but some were alive and hopping.

Felicity poked her head out the door and stared across the yard at Tasha, too stunned to speak. Tasha's mouth hung open in shock. Jim laughed and strolled out to the yard, then bent down to snatch one of the visitors.

"A Great Basin spadefoot toad," he announced.

"That's nice, but what the hell are they doing falling from the damn *sky*?" Tasha hugged herself.

Jim shrugged. "Fuck if I know, babe. I'll get the rake."

From their respective spots, Tasha and Felicity stared at one another in silent confusion. Felicity had lived her entire life on Oregon's North Coast, and never once had she experienced anything like this. The closest she'd come was that weird locust swarm she and Rich saw out at the…

Rich.

Felicity perked to attention. "Hey, Tash? What day is it?"

She laughed. "End-of-the-World Day?"

"No, seriously. What's the date?"

Tasha pulled her mobile phone from her pocket. "Wednesday the sixth."

"What time is it?"

"Seven-fifty."

"Thanks." Today was her appointment with Rich. Felicity was supposed be at her ex-husband's office at nine. Maybe her luck was about to change.

Boudica, Mojo, and Alphonse ran back inside before she could shut the door. She turned to find twenty-three eyeballs staring at her.

"Don't even ask. I have no idea what that was. And I realize we're off schedule, so just gimme a sec to pull it together." Felicity nearly tripped over Valkyrie, who lounged in the center aisle near the

single-burner propane stove.

"Beep, beep." She nudged the fluffy, white she-devil with her slipper, got no reaction, then stepped over her, careful not to wrench her bum knee. "You can be a giant butt sometimes, you know that?"

She began the morning feeding routine with a lump of dread stuck in throat.

Two weeks? There's no way I can find good homes for all of them in two weeks!

She filled eight bowls with two brands of dry food, one brand of canned, then prepared two medicine dosages, one for roundworm and one for feline rheumatoid arthritis.

How could Tasha do this to me?

She made sure Mojo dined alone, quarantined in the tiny bathroom with the folding door latched tight. As the only as-yet-unneutered male on the premises, he did not tolerate onlookers. Alphonse, who could not wrap his head around the fact that he no longer had balls, ate outside on the metal stoop. It was best for everyone.

Why in God's name were frogs falling from the sky? And why did Hair Gel Jim claim to be allergic; what have I ever done to him?

She fed the tabby brothers, Scratch and Sniff, at the opposite end of the trailer, by the daybed. Valkyrie had taken on the role of surrogate mother to the weaned-too-soon feral kittens, and they all shared a bowl.

Rick James and Teena Marie were a bonded pair, and they shared everything, including the bowl they liked to have positioned near the bedroom privacy curtain.

Boudica, the one-eyed hellcat, had teeth problems and ate veterinary-grade soft food from a dish on the counter near the sink. Gumbo and Melrose nibbled from two bowls under the dining booth.

P. Diddy Kitty and Circe were spaced five feet apart down the center aisle, each with their own dish, because, for reasons known only to them, they hated each other's guts.

Felicity leaned against the counter while the crowd crunched, planning what she would wear to Rich's office. When everyone was done, she retrieved the food bowls, released Mojo from solitary confinement, and heard P. Diddy's distinctly irritating yowl, part voice-cracking male adolescent and part jackhammer.

M-m-m-m-r-r-uh-uh-uh-uh-ow!

The male tuxedo cat's latest obsession was to bat his favorite squeaky mouse under the daybed and complain until Felicity retrieved it for him.

"Just once, big guy. I've got somewhere to be this morning." Felicity carefully lowered herself to all fours and contorted her body to reach under the built-in seat, her cartilage-deprived knees throbbing against the linoleum. She stretched, wiggling her fingers. "You do this just to watch me do cat yoga, don't you?" She swept her arm back and forth. "What should we call this pose? Downward Diddy? *Got it!*"

She snatched the mouse, blew off some of the dust and cat hair, and flicked it down the length of the trailer. Diddy and Melrose went flying in pursuit. Felicity gripped the daybed to haul herself to a stand, then limped to the booth. "Beep, beep, Valkyrie."

Nothing.

Felicity stepped over the obstinate blob and slid across the vinyl leatherette booth. She switched on the tabletop black-and-white TV and adjusted its coat hanger antenna, checking whether the local news station made any mention of the apocalyptic frogs.

Nothing yet.

She turned to national news.

Oh, *hell* no. She switched it off.

If she wanted injustice, random catastrophe, and hopeless despair, all she had to do was open the mail scattered in front of her, obscuring her *Hardest Crossword Puzzles on Earth* paperback and the half-completed, two-thousand-piece puzzle of a tone-on-tone Tibetan sand mandala.

Inside those envelopes were helpful "reminders" from hospitals, surgeons, residents, attending physicians, and technicians. There were notices from attorneys representing MRI, CAT scan, and X-ray services, along with infusion clinics. There were passive-aggressive payment demands for operating room charges, pharmacy billings, outpatient biopsies, and follow-up visits.

There were thoughtful nudges from the credit card company, too, along with those from a former landlord and the parking enforcement division of the Pine Beach Public Safety Department.

That was a crap-ton of reminding.

Felicity parted the plastic shade and peered out the trailer window. Her little garden needed weeding again because gardens always did. She worried that her beets and chard weren't getting enough sun in the shadow of the Airstream and that her green beans were droopy. The catnip was going gangbusters though, which was the only bit of good news on this shit-show of a morning.

She'd take it.

Felicity marched down the sidewalk, tugging the panty hose twisting into her groin. What had she been thinking? Nobody cared what she wore, but she'd wanted to project the *je ne sais quoi* of a woman who meant business, and the old blouse, slightly tight pencil skirt, and wobbly heels comprised the best her anemic closet had to offer. She paused to examine her reflection in the bakery window.

As feared, she didn't look all-business. She looked all sweaty, fidgety, and uncomfortable in her own skin, which was probably due to the wrenching of her tender parts. She spied a clump of calico fur clinging to the front of her skirt and swiped at it, perusing the selection of goodies in the window. Maybe she'd pick up a cruller for herself on the way back to her car…

"*Ooomph!*" Her forehead slammed into the plate glass window. Her knees buckled and sparks swam in her vision.

"Jesus! Hold on a sec."

A young man stood next to her. She reached for him, grabbing at his shirt for balance, but he pushed her away.

Felicity blinked at him, waiting for her eyesight to clear.

He held his mobile phone away from his ear and inspected her with loathing. "I didn't even *see* you, lady! Watch where you're going, and…" he paused, giving her a quick inspection, "you might wanna skip the sweet rolls."

He stalked off, phone already reattached to his earlobe, his conversation back on track. "Some pudgy old bag just ran into me on the sidewalk! Yeah, totally, bro."

"Jerk." Felicity rubbed her forehead, sure that the impact would leave a mark. With another discreet tug at the crotch of her pantyhose, she walked on toward Rich's office at the corner. She should be taking calming breaths to prepare for this get-together, but instead found herself replaying the sidewalk collision in her mind, getting madder with each step.

She'd been standing perfectly still, dreaming of baked goods she couldn't afford, when he nearly bulldozed her over! *He* was the one who needed to watch where he was going!

And he hadn't made the slightest effort to avoid plowing into her. He didn't apologize. In fact, he'd blamed her. Called her names. Just for existing! What was *wrong* with the world?

Felicity paused beneath her ex-husband's shingle:

RICHARD P. HUME, ATTORNEY AT LAW
PERSONAL INJURY, MEDICAL MALPRACTICE, AND WRONGFUL DEATH
"YOU HAVE A RIGHT TO BE HAPPY!"

Felicity placed her hand on the brass door handle, remembering how she'd tried in vain to get him to choose a different slogan for his practice.

"It sounds like you're promising to make people happy," she'd observed.

"Exactly!" He'd pinched her bottom. "I make *you* happy, don't I?"

"But not all your clients will get the settlement they want, especially the wrongfully dead ones. And what if someone sues you because you didn't make them as happy as they wanted to be? How do you even define *happiness*?"

He'd frowned, then kissed her. "You crack me up sometimes."

The morning he'd hung that shingle, she'd held the ladder for him. She helped him decorate the office, too. But before any of that, she'd helped him pay for law school.

The bell jingled when she pulled open the heavy wooden door. There was no one at the reception desk, causing her to wonder whether yet another young woman had quit. Rich must go through three a year, but, of course, that had nothing to do with him.

"Another entitled brat from the participation trophy generation," he'd once said of a young assistant who went to lunch and never returned.

Felicity stood on the waiting room carpet, clutching her worn purse. What was the etiquette for an ex-wife who once had roamed freely through this very establishment, dusting every stick of furniture, cleaning the toilets, running the vacuum, and watering the plants? Since she no longer held the honorary title of Mrs. Richard Hume, Esquire, she supposed she'd stand there like anyone else and wait.

After a few minutes, she cleared her throat.

Rich's head popped into view. He was at his desk in the adjoining office, on the phone. He kept talking while pantomiming broadly, as if she could not discern for herself that he was on a call.

Still chatting, Rich pointed his index finger at her, angled it downward, and twirled it clockwise through the air. This could mean any number of things. Perhaps he wanted her to take a seat in the waiting room. Maybe he expected her to fetch him a well-stirred coffee with one cream and one sugar. Or maybe he wanted her to pirouette like a music-box ballerina.

She chose option one, sat down, and immediately heard the unmistakable *rrrrrip* of fabric. She reached around to find she'd busted the zipper of her skirt.

"Hey, Felicity. I didn't see you come in."

It was Rich's new wife.

Felicity's face burned. Oh, this was just *fabulous*. She'd eventually have to stand. And when she did, her panty hose-encased ass would be on full display to her ex-husband and his recently acquired spouse, Bethany, the woman now standing in front of her, the woman so young she gave off a whiff of new car smell, the woman who'd just become the second person in five minutes to deem her invisible.

Felicity nodded toward the front door. "There's a bell. It jingled…" She froze, mid-snark. Bethany had begun to stroke her belly absently, the way pregnant women do.

Felicity nearly choked. She and Rich had spent 15 years and most of their savings trying to have a child. Yet here was Bethany, married just a month and already succeeding where Felicity had failed.

The irony was brutal.

But it made sense; Bethany must have been pregnant when Rich married her. Maybe that was *why* he married her.

"Oh, my gawd, did you hear about the frogs?" Bethany's eyes flashed and her cheeks pinked. The girl positively bounced. She was a fresh-faced, fertile, bouncing ball of youth, the perfect counterpoint to Felicity's barren, shriveled existence.

"Well, did you?"

"Did I what?"

"Hear about the frogs! It was raining frogs from the sky this morning. Isn't that wild? The weatherman said it was a waterspout or something, but if you ask me, it's way freakier than that. It's an *omen*."

Bethany continued to smile down at Felicity, like they were friends, like her favorite thing in the world was chatting about weather anomalies while being all young and beautiful and pregnant and happy.

"Felicity!" Rich sounded thrilled to see her, though he surely was not, which meant he was about to serve up a steaming platter of bullshit. It was his signature dish.

He inserted himself between his two wives, as if protecting Bethany's shine from Felicity's dinge.

"Great to see you!" Rich bobbed on his toes like a boxer in the ring. He must be frantic about how to break the baby news to Felicity. Did he fear she'd fly into a mad, jealous rage? Embarrass him? Tell his current wife what a douche canoe he really was? Surely, Bethany would figure that out eventually, since Rich's douchery was as plain as the...

"What's that thing on your face, honey?" Bethany squinted, leaning close to inspect her husband. She pulled a clean tissue from her jeans pocket and began to wipe at a spot on Rich's cheek.

"Nothing. Just some kind of bump. Stop, Bethany."

She wasn't done with her ministrations. She pursed her plump lips with just the right mix of concern and pity, and Felicity suddenly imagined the young mother cooing over a baby fresh from the bath. Her stomach clenched.

"Gross, Rich. It's not a bump. It's a *boil*, like deep under your skin. You should probably..."

"*Stop.*" He grabbed her wrist, pushing her hand away. "I said I'm fine."

It was just a flash, a fraction of a second, but Felicity saw the irritation in Rich's eyes and the hurt in Bethany's.

Rich kissed her on the cheek as if to soften the dismissal. "It's all good, sweetie. Really." He turned back to Felicity. "Let's head into the conference room. How's trailer park life?" Rich got halfway down the carpeted hallway and turned toward the kitchenette. "Want some coffee? Tea? Soda? Water?"

What Felicity wanted was to keep her butt in the chair and get out of there as soon as humanly possible. "I'd rather talk here if you don't mind, and I don't live in a park. I live out at Tasha's place, as you well know."

For some reason, Bethany had not budged. She remained standing, staring down at Felicity, frank curiosity in her sparkly eyes. The tissue dangled from her fingers.

Felicity managed a pleasant smile. "How far along are you?"

"Just three months. How'd you know?"

"You're glowing!" And rubbing. And bouncing. "I wish you all the best."

Rich was out of breath when he returned, shoving a can of soda in Felicity's face. "Here you go. Is orange OK? We're out of everything else."

Felicity noted two things. First, Rich clutched an open Coke in his other hand, so they had not, in fact, been out of everything else. And second, for each of the thirty-two years they had known one another, Rich had been aware that she hated orange soda. Absolutely loathed the stuff.

She accepted the can and placed it on the empty chair next to her. "What's the status with the house, Richard?"

He glanced at Bethany and shrugged as if to say, *The ex-wife, what's a fella to do?* Bethany gave a quick smile. "I'll be in the filing room."

Felicity watched her go, wondering whether there was already trouble in paradise. "Is she working here again?"

"Just until I can find a replacement for the one who quit on me last week." He collapsed in a nearby reception room chair and fiddled with his salt-and-pepper goatee. "Look, Felicity, I know you don't pay attention to these things, but it's a buyer's market right now."

"Oh, really?"

"Absolutely."

He was lying. It was the exact opposite. She'd been tracking real estate closings and pricing trends from the computer at the public library, and single-family homes were in high demand throughout Tillamook County. Young professionals were being priced out of the Portland market and heading toward the coast.

"We can do better than this latest offer, Felicity. Trust me on this."

She snort laughed. "*Trust* you? Just take the offer, whatever it is. I don't even care. I need my half."

He shook his head and sprawled, legs wide, as if attempting to occupy as much space as possible. Mojo and Alphonse did the same when they wanted to look intimidating. Rich's manspreading was just another hint of the undercurrent of oblivious self-importance that flowed through his life.

He gulped the entire can of soda without taking a breath.

Once upon a time, Felicity had found his alpha male confidence appealing. Sexy, even. It was hard to pinpoint the exact moment when she began to feel differently, but it was probably the day she found the economy-sized box of condoms in the glove compartment of his car—while she was undergoing her last of seven rounds of in vitro fertilization treatments.

For reasons unclear to her still, she stayed with him for another eight post-condom years. It had been a merry-go-round of promises and lies and begging for forgiveness. In the end, Rich admitted that he hadn't loved her for most of their twenty-year marriage, but he'd needed time to get his finances in order before he filed for divorce.

Felicity later learned that "order" was douche-speak for hiding assets, taking payments under the table, and cooking his law office books to show a history of business debt. During mediation, he'd stonewalled her with overly complicated alimony formulas and opaque settlement wording that gave him wiggle room and left Felicity with nothing.

Her lawyer, the one she could afford, had tried his best but was no match for Tricky Dick Hume. She should have hired a forensic accountant, but she'd been distracted. Doctors had just found a six-millimeter tumor in her left breast that had metastasized into her lymph nodes.

The divorce was finalized two years ago. They'd agreed to sell the house that first year and split the proceeds fifty-fifty. And yet...

"Look." He held his hands palms up in front of him. "I'm only trying to do what's best for us both. Let's wait it out a little more."

The house was Felicity's only asset, and he knew it. He also knew she'd gone broke fighting cancer.

Rage roiled in her gut, so hot and fierce that she half expected it to shoot up through her cranium and blow a hole in the drop ceiling of his waiting room. She leaned forward. Her voice was hoarse and shaky.

"Enough of the endless bullshit, dick. Accept the offer. You're keeping me from what is rightfully mine. You're in violation of the divorce agreement. Do it. *Now*."

He tipped his head, as if puzzled by her assertiveness. "I prefer *Rich*, as you know."

"Oh, I know."

He laughed. "Unfortunately, your ignorance isn't funny. You'd be cheating us both if I take this offer. And is that really fair to me? Should I have to pay the price of your ill-informed impatience?"

How easily the twisted dishonesty rolled off his tongue. How had she ever loved him? How had she *ever* believed a word he uttered?

An image of Hair Gel Jim flashed in her mind. Welp, there was her answer. For twenty-plus years, Felicity had been as blind as Tasha. Not anymore.

"Whatever offer's on the table, take it."

"Or what?" His smile sickened her. "You gonna hire the best attorney money can buy and take me to court?" He scanned her up and down like she was a clearance rack of day-old donuts, from beige ponytail to cat-hair skirt to wobbly heels. She wanted to claw his eyes out.

"In other news, you should know I'm announcing my campaign for mayor of Pine Beach, which means there will need to be some changes. I'd like you to find somewhere else to live, somewhere out of town. Outside Tillamook County entirely would be better."

Wut?

"Look, I'm willing to help you out. I'll pay for your move and then when the house is sold, I'll take it out of your share of the profit. You know, like a bar tab."

Wuuuuut?

"My campaign is all about how I'm a fresh option for this town, a new kind of leadership, the best of both worlds. On one hand, I'm an established business owner, but on the other, I've got a young wife and a baby on the way, which means I care passionately about good schools and shit."

He paused, as if waiting for her to congratulate him.

"Look, all I'm saying is having an ex-wife who's..." He adjusted his position in the chair. "It'd just be better if you weren't part of the picture, OK?"

"Ohmigod."

She heard the dull shock in her whisper. Her brain buzzed in panic. Her vision grayed out. She gripped the arms of the waiting room chair like she was about to fall over the edge of the universe.

"You OK or what?"

Certain this was either an anxiety attack or a stroke, Felicity stood and headed for the door, her body alive like lightning, her flesh thrumming and rumbling like she was about to spontaneously combust. Now, *that* was an idea! As a human torch, she could incinerate his place of business.

Burn it down.

Down to the ground.

With her hand on the door handle, she glanced out the window. It was dark and menacing again. And now it had started to rain, hard.

Behind her, Rich chuckled. "You've got zipper issues, old gal."

She spun around, the worn soles of her pumps allowing for a smooth turn on the carpet, just like a music box ballerina.

She pulled her shoulders back and straightened. "Do you know what's kept me going, Rich?"

He shrugged. "Your stupid crossword puzzles and your fuckin' cats?"

She took a deep breath. "It's knowing that I'll be around to see you get everything you deserve."

He laughed. "Ooooh, a threat! Let me run down to the courthouse and file for a crazy-cat-lady restraining order!"

Thunder cracked outside. Felicity spied a raincoat hanging on the coat tree near the door. She snagged it and left.

"Hey! That's my coat!"

"Put it on my tab, dick." She looked back over her shoulder. "By the way, that's dick with a small *D*. Tiny, really."

CHAPTER TWO

Felicity scurried down the flooded sidewalk, holding the raincoat over her head. It was nice to have cover from the stinging rain, and as a bonus, she got a little thrill out of stealing something from Rich. Unfortunately, she was now trapped in a fog of her ex-husband's aftershave.

She might be sick.

She got to the car, fished her keys from her purse, and promptly dropped them in a puddle. She bent down, shoved her hand into the water to search for them, and the seam her skirt split, extending southward toward the hem.

You have a right to be happy!

She snagged the keys, opened the driver's side door, and jumped in. It took three tries for the engine to turn over. She took a deep breath and blew it out.

What in the world was she going to do? She needed a lawyer to force Rich to sell the house, but she couldn't afford to hire one until she had the proceeds from selling the damn house!

Tasha wanted the cats gone.

Rich wanted *her* gone, to another county, no less.

She had no money. No job. And if she managed to find one, her car was on death's door, leaving her with no reliable way to get there.

You have a right to be happy!

She'd survived cancer, but she'd had to drain her retirement savings and go into debt to do it—and that was *with* insurance!

She balled her fists and banged the steering wheel.

Fuck Rich.

Fuck Tasha.

Fuck Jim.

Fuck the sidewalk guy.

Fuck the rain.

Fuck cancer.

Fuck this fucking car.

Fuck a healthcare system that leaves sick people bankrupt.

Fuck my ripped skirt and my beige hair and every other ridiculously fucking-Felicity-like thing about me!

She backed out of the parking spot and steadied her breath.

The rage had subsided, thanks to the power of the F-word, even in silent-scream form. She felt only a simmering unease low in her belly now, but she worried that if one more thing happened today— the smallest little irritation or setback—she might shatter into a million pieces.

She drove through the rain to the grocery store. She found herself filling a handbasket with eggs and milk, made her way to the cashier, glad she'd had the presence of mind to steal her ex's raincoat since it was the only thing between her and misdemeanor indecent exposure charges.

Taking her place in line, she absently shoved her hand in the coat pocket, then jolted at what slid between her fingers. She pulled out two twenty-dollar bills, and stared in wonder at Andrew Jackson's bushy eyebrows and foppish hairdo. It had been years since they'd met.

This was real, cash money—Rich's money! Money that should have been hers! Which made it all the sweeter because she wouldn't have to risk having her Oregon Trail SNAP card declined; the balance was dangerously close to zero.

Maybe today wouldn't be a complete debacle after all.

With one Andy clutched in her palm and the other safely returned to the pocket, Felicity willed herself not to make eye contact with the candy display while the young man in front of her made small talk with the cashier.

"That was super weird, right?"

"Totally." The steady *beep!* of the bar code scanner kept time with the cashier's words. "It was bizarre, even for the Oregon coast, like God was pissed off or something."

"I half expected to see the mothership come down from the clouds." The customer laughed, then flung his hand behind him to grab something from the belt and smacked Felicity across her cheek.

"Oh, my God! I am sooooo sorry!" The man clutched Felicity's forearm. "Are you OK? I didn't see you standing there."

Felicity rubbed the side of her face, then worked her jaw back and forth.

"Please accept my apology. I feel terrible."

At least this latest assailant was polite.

"Let me do something for you. How about I carry your groceries to the car so you don't have to struggle with them?"

Struggle? Felicity eyed her two items and then the customer. "Thanks, but I got this."

His face fell, offended that his charity had been rebuffed. "Whatever you say." He paid for his groceries, grabbed his bag, and was gone.

The cashier gave her a dutiful smile. "Find everything OK?"

"Yes, thanks."

"Do you have your senior…?"

"Stop right there."

The cashier froze, his eyes wide and confused, like he'd missed part of the exchange. "Uh, I'm supposed to ask our older customers if they have a…"

"Don't say it."

He shrugged. "I'm cool with that." He completed the order, gave her the change from the twenty, and handed her the receipt. "Have a nice day, ma'am."

Felicity picked up the paper bag and was about to head for the exit, then turned back. "Wait. Excuse me."

The cashier rolled his eyes. "So *now* you want to use your senior save…?"

"Stop."

"Sorry."

"I'm not a senior citizen. I don't have a senior saver card."

"Is that what you came back to tell me?"

"No." Fortunately, no one was in line. Felicity stepped closer.

"I couldn't help but overhear your conversation with the guy ahead of me."

The cashier's eyes bugged. "I know! The frogs! The clouds!"

"Yeah, I saw them out at my place."

"Seriously? Because that was some completely whacked shit, you know? Frogs just falling from the sky! And just before it suddenly got super dark—like a rando eclipse or something—and this giant hole

27

opened up over town square and *bam!* Buckets of rain. Like a waterfall! It was straight out of an alien invasion movie or the Bible or something."

Felicity switched the bag to her other hip, curious. Frogs had been the only precipitation they'd experienced out at Tasha's. "So…you're saying it rained in town?"

"Not just *rained* like it's doing now." He gestured to the wall of windows. "*This* is normal. What happened earlier was super weird."

"Gotcha." Felicity backed toward the door. "Thanks."

She walked to the car, glancing up at the sky. Heavy, gunmetal gray clouds roiled overhead, and rain stung her face. Dreary, sure, but not as ominous as the cashier described.

Felicity went to unlock the car door, when out of the corner of her eye she noticed something odd. In the center of the parking lot, a line of large scorpions cut across the asphalt. A couple dozen of them marched as a group, equally spaced, like they were headed to a rendezvous point.

She'd seen scorpions around here before, of course, especially near the forest. But an arachnid parade? Smack in the middle of town? No. Never.

"Weird. Today is just weird."

She climbed into her car, put the slightly soggy grocery bag on the passenger seat, and put the keys in the ignition. This time, it took five tries to get the engine to catch. She had no idea what was wrong with the car—starter, alternator, ignition, fuel line, old age—not that a diagnosis would matter. Whatever it was, she had no money to fix it.

As she turned south on Highway 101, the morning sky went midnight-black again, cracked open, and dumped the rain in sheets. Though it was just a few miles to Tasha's, she'd be white-knuckling it the whole way. Her night vision was terrible. Her windshield wipers were shredded. Her tires were bald, too.

Marching scorpions? Pitch-dark skies? This can't be right.

She drove slower than the speed limit and kept her eyes on the yellow line along the right shoulder. A tractor trailer passed her, its driver laying on the horn. A tsunami of rainwater hit her windshield, and, for an instant, she was completely blind.

Her car began to slow, even as she pressed the gas to the floor. Forty-eight miles per hour. Forty-six.

"Oh, no. Please don't do this to me. Just hang in there a little longer."

Forty-five.

Her heart thudded in her ears. The rain pounded the car roof. The windshield wipers swung back and forth, leaving opaque smears on the glass.

Forty.

She checked the gas gauge—running on fumes, as usual, but she'd put three dollars' worth in the tank just the other day!

Thirty-five. Thirty.

She was barely moving when she saw a flash in her peripheral vision, a sparkle of something shiny along the roadside, then a dark, indistinct blur, low to the ground and lurching. Was that an animal?

She steered the now-crawling car to the shoulder, tires crunching on gravel as angry horns blared. She turned off the engine and moved her groceries to the back seat so she could exit from the passenger side, away from traffic. She swung the door open and stood, her eyes searching past the scrim of rain for the poor creature. Had she imagined it?

There it was! The form staggered away from the road, toward a field. Was it a dog? A fox? Whatever it was, she could tell by the way it moved that the poor thing was terribly injured, likely struck by a car.

She edged closer, peering through the rain and fog.

"Oh, God. No."

It was a cat. A large one. The flash she'd seen was some kind of gaudy collar around its neck. This kitty was someone's beloved pet, hurt, wet, and alone by the highway. Felicity ran toward it, knowing it would probably scamper away in fear and pain, and she wouldn't blame it. She forced herself to slow down, to become as gentle and nonthreatening as possible while still edging closer. She crouched down. Spoke softly.

The heel of her right shoe plunged into a hole and snapped off. She toppled forward, landing on her hands and knees in the gravel, just as a truck whizzed by and threw water directly into her face. Ignoring the throbbing pain in her knee, she scrambled to a stand, spit out the dirty road spray, and wiped her eyes. She hobbled toward the cat, hissing through her teeth, only then noticing that her knee bled through her shredded panty hose and her palms were scraped raw.

Felicity crouched as low as her injured knee would tolerate, inched forward, and held out her hands.

"You poor thing. You're really hurt."

The cat stumbled into the tall grass, its spine hunched and its tail hanging limp. It kept its face turned away from her. Even from this distance, Felicity could see a gaping wound on its side. It looked fresh.

"Let me help you, kitty. Will you let me help you?"

She inched closer still, not sure the cat could hear her reassuring words over the roar and rush of the rain-battered state highway. Had the cat even noticed her? It might be locked inside itself with agony, oblivious to anything else. If she were that cat, she'd be looking for somewhere quiet and dry to tend to her wounds. The last thing she'd want was a crazy lady chasing her into the weeds.

Felicity stopped. She stood tall and raised her voice above the *whoosh* of cars and trucks. "You will die if you don't let me help you. This is your only shot at staying alive."

The cat stopped and turned toward her then, its eyes connecting with Felicity's. She gasped. The animal looked like it had been through a meat grinder. Its head was sliced open and its face was coated in blood. The cat's slanted eyes were partially closed, but she could see that its pupils were huge. Even in the gloom she noticed the irises were different colors.

That wasn't what stunned her, though. Never in all her days had she seen a cat with such a soulful, wise face and an expression of such absolute defeat.

She took another uneven step forward, now doubting her ability to help this poor creature. She couldn't expect the vet to give her another emergency surgery on the house. The front office staff would see her pulling into the parking lot and close the blinds.

Was she collecting this cat only to watch it die? Would her interference only extend its suffering?

Felicity couldn't say how long the injured cat held her gaze, but she knew it was making up its mind. Finally, having weighed the pros and cons of putting its miserable life in her scraped-up hands, it stumbled toward her.

"You are so brave. The bravest cat ever." She crouched down again and encouraged the cat to come closer, all the while peeling the soaked raincoat from her body. "I promise I'll try to be as brave as you."

She wondered why the raindrops felt hot on her chilled cheeks, only to realize those were tears. She'd finally done it. She'd hit that wall of too much—too much random suffering in this world, always dumped on the most defenseless and innocent of creatures. She took a deep breath and focused. She could be despondent later. Right now, she had a nearly dead cat to get off the side of the highway, even if the only thing she could do was keep it company while it died.

Felicity scooped the creature into the coat, then gathered it in her arms, putting as little pressure against its body as possible. She'd seen it was a male, a breed she wasn't familiar with, gray with striking markings visible beneath the blood. It was a majestic sort of feline, well cared for and well loved.

Only to end up here, hanging by a thread, in the arms of an unqualified stranger.

She slid in the passenger side of the car and scooted over behind the wheel, gingerly placing the bundle on the seat next to her. The cat had buried itself fully inside the coat, and she couldn't tell if it still breathed.

She turned the key in the ignition. Nothing.

She turned it again.

Nothing.

Again.

Nothing.

Again and again and more nothing.

"Un-fucking-believable."

Her hands dropped to her lap, limp with surrender. She stared out the driver-side window at the smear of headlights and taillights in the steady rain. It was funny, really. She'd often wondered what the moment would feel like, the instant when she finally reached her limit, and by God, here it was. And it felt... hollow. Nothing special. Just more of the familiar numbness and empty ache.

But there was good news in giving up. She didn't have to keep trying. She was free. She could just sit back, put up her feet, and relax for the first time in six years. She finally had permission to look around and think, *Fuck it, I'm done.*

What a relief to admit the truth. That there was no "reason" for everything. That something good did not always come from something bad. That life might be nothing but a string of random occurrences, dissolving into chaos, and if that were the case then so be it.

Felicity let her head fall back against the seat. She took a great gulp of air, squeezed it in her throat, and readied herself for the explosion, the sob to end all sobs. She gave herself permission to let go.

She waited, eyes fixed on the rust spots on the upholstered car ceiling, mouth opening, pressure building...

Not a peep. Not another tear. Talk about anticlimactic.

Mmmmmroooooo-aaaaaow.

Felicity jerked. She'd forgotten she had company, and glanced down to the passenger seat, wondering how a cat in such terrible shape could produce such a rich and resonant complaint. The coat rustled, and from the folds of fabric a single cat eye appeared, unblinking and desperate.

Rrrrrowwwwww.

She sniffed, wiped her nose and eyes, and let go of the breath she'd been holding. "This is the last time, understand? The last cat, the last battle, the last day I give a rat's ass about anything or anyone, because after this, it's over and *I fucking mean it!*"

Rrrrop.

"We're in agreement, then."

She reached down to remove her right shoe, then beat it against the dashboard until the heel dislodged. Once both wet, equally flat shoes were on her feet, she grabbed the grocery bag from the back seat and carefully gathered the raincoat-covered cat to her chest.

She had no choice but to walk. It was a little over a mile to the trailer, less if the shortcuts weren't a flooded mess. She kept her head down against the rain and wind and walked, favoring her swelling left knee with each step.

Minutes later, the waterlogged grocery sack ripped, so she shoved the eggs into the center compartment of her purse and slipped the shoulder strap through the handle of the plastic half gallon of two percent.

She could feel the cat's breath rumble against her chest, ragged and irregular. He was alive, and that was all the information she could process at the moment. She didn't peel the coat back to get a closer look because if this was just a futile errand, she'd rather not know.

No one stopped to offer her a ride, but that wasn't exactly a shocker. Only a dangerously unbalanced individual would be staggering through the rain along a state highway with her ass hanging out, a milk jug swinging from her purse, and a balled-up coat in her arms. That coat could be hiding anything—a severed human head, a rancid Butterball turkey, or even a mostly dead cat. You couldn't be too cautious in this day and age.

Felicity cut through the dairy farm next to Tasha's. The route shaved a few minutes from the trek but required a lot of cow-patty dodging. All the while she trudged on, the cat breathed and the rain came down. Her back and neck throbbed; the creature had to weigh close to twenty pounds.

Eventually, she stumbled in the front gate of Tasha's property and headed for the house. She planned to use Tasha's phone to call the vet and ask for... what, exactly? Help? Advice? Her vet was a lovely woman, dedicated and kind, and she'd provided thousands of dollars of care for Felicity's strays and rescues over the years. But Felicity was well aware that the Pine Beach Veterinary Clinic wasn't a charity. And yet, she had no choice but to beg for one last favor.

Jim slouched on the porch swing, smoking a cigarette and staring into the rain. He acknowledged her only when she stood directly in front of him, dripping. Felicity let her purse slip to the decking, careful not to break the eggs.

"That better not be another fucking cat you got there."

"It's milk and eggs."

"I mean what you're holding in your arms."

"I need to use the phone."

"Tasha's not here."

"That's OK. I know where the phone is. It's been in the same spot on the kitchen wall for forty years."

She reached for the doorknob and Jim was on his feet, blocking her way.

"Maybe Tasha don't want you nosing around when she's out."

Felicity squeezed her eyes shut. Precious seconds had been wasted on this doofus, seconds she didn't have. She opened her eyes and glared at him. "I'm going inside to use Tasha's phone. If you try to stop me, I'll…"

"What?" He gave her a lopsided grin and leaned against the front door. "You gonna kick my ass? Is that what you're gonna do, cat lady?" Jim's gaze flicked above Felicity's head. He deflated, then sulked back to his spot on the swing. Tasha had pulled in. Felicity ran for the phone.

"Pine Beach Veterinary Clinic. How may I help you?"

"Hi. This is Felicity Cheshire. I have an emergency."

The line went silent.

"Hello?"

"Hey, Felicity. It's me; Ronnie."

Her knees wobbled with relief. The sweetest vet tech in the world had answered the call. "Ronnie, listen, I've got a cat—terribly injured. I don't know if he's been hit by a car or in some kind of horrendous fight with a wild animal. He's barely hanging in. He's…"

"Dr. Nguyen is in surgery right now. She can't come to the phone. I can..."

"He's going to die if I don't get help."

"*Felicity?*" Tasha and Jim stood behind her, frowning at the puddle of water and cow poop on the kitchen floor. Tasha glanced at the bundle Felicity carried and shook her head. Only then did Felicity realize that her arms had gone numb. This cat was *heav-eee*.

"Ronnie, he's got gaping wounds. I haven't had a chance to get a good look at him, but it's really bad. Is there anything you can do?"

Ronnie put her hand over the receiver and spoke to another office employee. Felicity heard her say something about covering the desk while she ran an errand.

Thank God. Thank God there were decent human beings left in the world.

"I'll be there in half an hour."

"Do you know where I live? I'm in the Airstream on a friend's property. Do you need an address?"

"Uh..." Ronnie cleared her throat. "I do the billing, so..."

Of course.

Felicity hung up, ran back outside, and grabbed her purse from the porch floor. Tasha and Jim ran after her.

"I can't talk right now, Tash. Let's talk tomorrow."

"Hey, cat lady! Your damn ass is hangin' out!"

"Nice of you to notice, Jim!"

Felicity pushed open the Airstream's aluminum door to find twelve cats lined up like toy soldiers upon the booth benches and tabletop—an unbroken semicircle of feline sentries. They sat at attention, facing the door, heads held high and paws tucked neatly before them. They looked as if they'd been waiting.

It was the strangest thing she'd ever seen.

"OK, guys. I need some room. Get down."

They did as they were told, which, in itself, was unusual. They hopped from their posts and reassembled on the daybed at the opposite end of the trailer, still on alert, not a complaint or demand from any of them. Their eyes tracked her every move.

Bizarre.

She set down her purse and turned on all the lights, including the mini wagon wheel fixture suspended above the booth. She carried the coat-wrapped cat to her bed and placed it on the comforter while she stripped. Off went the sopping wet blouse, skirt, pantyhose, bra, and underwear. She quickly toweled herself and changed into a hoodie sweatshirt, sweatpants, and her slippers, then piled her wet hair into a clip. She grabbed her only spare bedsheet and draped it over the tabletop, then turned on the electric kettle. The water would need to be hot but not boiling. She gathered clean towels, soap, and her first aid kit, and set everything on the vinyl bench. She returned to the bedroom. Felicity took a steadying breath and pried away the folds of the raincoat.

He was alive. One eye was shut. Blood was absolutely everywhere. He shivered. Wet and cold, obviously, but probably in shock too. Felicity didn't even know where to begin.

She lowered to her sore knee and leaned onto the bed, stroking the only spot on his head that was not bloodied. "You are beautiful, and strong, and worth saving, but you'll have to help me. You'll have to fight along with me. Do you understand?"

His blue eye focused on her.

"Good. I apologize in advance because I know I will hurt you trying to help you. Please forgive me."

Mrawpt. The reply was shaky and weak.

Felicity reached under his trembling body and carried him to the table, directly under the light. For the first time, she got a good look at her patient, and her eyes opened with wonder. What kind of cat *was* he?

It was hard to be sure, but his coat looked to be a smoky blue-gray adorned with thick black stripes and even a few spots. He was an elegant creature, muscular but sleek, with a refined neck and prominent, upright ears. He had the most majestic feline head she had ever seen.

"What a special tomcat you are!"

She fetched a bowl of warm water, got the syringe from the first aid kit, and dabbed soap on the wet cotton gauze. She stood over him, which would give her some semblance of control if he tried to bolt. And *of course* he would bolt; this was going to sting like a son of a bitch, and she had no sedative or anesthetic to give him. She wished she could place a washcloth between his teeth and tell him to bite down hard, like in the old cowboy movies.

As if a cat would ever agree to something like that.

His muscles flinched with her first cautious touch. She had to clean him before she could assess the extent of his injuries, and it was a painstaking process. But the cat did not attempt to run away. Instead, he turned to stare out the trailer window toward her now waterlogged garden, and Felicity swore the cat willed his body to calm so she could tend to him. What a strange creature he was.

She took advantage of his compliance, and quickly but gently cleaned his fur of mud and blood. She gasped at what she saw. He'd been cut on both sides of his body and on the back of his head. The head wound had begun to fester. She now knew he'd not been in a fight with another animal or hit by a car. It almost looked like he'd been chopped with an axe.

"What have they done to you?"

No. She wouldn't go there. *No one* was so evil that they'd take a hatchet to an innocent pet. Right? And anyway, that kind of attack would surely have killed a cat. Which brought her to the most pressing question...

How was this guy even alive? And how had the deep gashes not sliced through his muscle and hit the internal organs?

"You're a mess, Tom."

She used the syringe to flush out his wounds. Over and over she squirted warm water into the gaping slashes in his flesh, and he just lay there, staring out the window, even as she moved him to get every spot. He never made eye contact, as if he didn't want her to know how much he suffered.

The cat would need stitches. He would need antibiotics. He would need intravenous fluids. All things she could not provide.

With the utmost gentleness, she placed her fingertips beneath the cat's chin and turned his face to hers. She examined the closed eye—caked shut by blood but otherwise uninjured, thank God. She cleaned it with care, and only then did Felicity dare examine the head wound. She'd rescued enough cats to know that these kinds of infections were killers, and that once an abscess took hold, the cat's chances of survival were slim.

She flushed it, over and over. It was a gash like those on his sides but swollen and oozing.

The cat finally looked at her with his blue and gold eye. The intelligence in his expression startled her. The sorrow made her shudder.

Felicity had always known that humans couldn't grasp the emotional complexity of animals. This guy was proof of that. He was young, but those eyes told a long and complicated story.

"We should get this collar off you." Felicity brushed her fingers along the surface of the fanciest cat collar she'd ever seen. It was plastic molded to imitate gold and embedded with jewel-shaped colored glass. From it hung a little gold-plated bell, shiny and intricately carved with symbols.

"Do you belong to the Queen of Sheba or something?" Felicity smiled, then immediately scowled. "What the...?" There was no buckle or clasp on the collar. The unbroken loop fit snug around the cat's neck and had no give whatsoever, which meant there was no way to slip it off. Her brain scrambled. That wasn't even possible given the laws of physics. How did it get there to begin with? Did it grow as the cat grew?

The Airstream door banged.

"It's open!"

It was Ronnie Davis, the vet tech, and as soon as Felicity saw the young woman's determined face, she knew the cavalry had arrived.

"What do we have here?" Ronnie stepped into the trailer and stopped dead. She took one look at the cat, then looked to Felicity, then back at the cat. "Not good."

Felicity nodded. "I know."

"People are so shitty."

"Tell me about it."

"This is nothing but bottom-barrel human cruelty. Makes me puke."

Ronnie was an odd duck. Felicity didn't know her personally—only through her frequent flyer visits to Pine Beach Veterinary Clinic—but she'd always struck Felicity as an intense person, a sad person. She was shy. She was one of those young women with piercings, spooky-looking jewelry, and black lipstick, a defensive display that warned others to keep their distance. Her dark skin was covered in barely visible tattoos. Her tight, black curls had been pulled into two puffs on either side of her head, and her bangs had been straightened and whacked into purposely uneven lengths. Her T-shirt, cargo pants, and clunky boots were all a lovely funeral-hearse black. Goth, it was called. Gloom and doom was more like it.

"I'll be right back."

It took Ronnie two more trips to bring everything inside. She had IV bags and antibiotics and bandages and a kit for stitching. She got right to work.

She broke out the handheld chip scanner, which stayed silent. "If you decide to keep him, get him chipped when he's neutered."

Felicity snorted. "I can't keep this cat; he clearly belongs to someone. Besides, another cat is the absolute last thing I need."

Ronnie shoved a needle through the top of a small vial of clear liquid. "This will numb him. Hold him still."

Felicity did as she was instructed, though the tomcat continued to stare out the Airstream window, barely flinching when Ronnie pierced his flesh with the needle. She hissed when she was done.

"What?"

"He's real dehydrated. Worse, he's nonreactive. We may be too late."

"But he's conscious. His eyes are open, and he's staring out the window. He's staying as still as a statue!"

Ronnie shook her head. "Either he's a Zen master or he's about to die because cats don't go still like this until right before death." She gave him another numbing shot.

Felicity felt her heart plummet. "What can I do? Can I do anything?"

"Just hold him. Antibiotics incoming." Ronnie was fast and no-nonsense, switching out vials and going about her work with efficiency.

"You're calm under pressure, Ronnie."

"Yeah, well, I was a medic in the Marines."

Felicity's shock must have been obvious because Ronnie laughed. "Lance Corporal Veronica Davis. Out two years now. This cat's head's a fucking mess, which is our biggest issue. Let's see what we can do."

It took half an hour, even with Ronnie rushing. She cut away chunks of matted fur, drained and rinsed the head abscess, then left it unstitched. "It'll heal better that way." Next, Ronnie tended the gashes in the cat's sides, which she said were deep enough to require stitching. In addition to the numbing injection and antibiotics, she gave him a pain reliever and inserted the IV needle in his rear left foot.

"Let's be practical about this, Felicity." She rested her fists on slim hips. "If he survives, he'll rip out the IV as soon as he's feeling better. I just hope that by then he's out of dehydration danger. You'll need to feed him by hand, OK? He won't be strong enough to eat by himself."

Felicity nodded, still astonished by Ronnie's history. With her height and trim build, Ronnie looked more runway model than Marine. And a medic, to boot! So why was she working as a vet tech?

"You good with all that, Felicity?"

"What? Yes. Of course. I've got kitten formula and a dropper left over from Scratch and Sniff."

Ronnie smiled, gathering up the sharps and trash and putting everything in a bag. "Good. Try to get something in him every three hours, and be sure to keep the other cats away. You should probably take him into your bed and close the door."

That'll go over well.

Felicity and Ronnie turned their heads at the same time to see a dozen felines bundled together on the daybed. None were lying down. All were ramrod straight and at attention.

"Damn, Felicity." Ronnie chuckled. "You should take that show on the road. All right, I gotta go. I'm going to catch hell as it is. Here." She grabbed a pen from the counter and scrawled her number on the back of an envelope. "That's my cell. Call me if he gets worse, but I'll call to check in with you tonight." She was halfway out the door.

"Ronnie?"

She turned.

"You can't call me. I don't have a phone."

She tipped her head to the side. "Then...?"

"I use the phone in my friend's house."

She nodded. "I'll get you one. It's not safe for you to be cut off like that."

"What? No! I couldn't ask you to..."

"Hey, no big thing. I'm always taking electronics apart and putting them back together so I have a whole mess of extra phones. I'll bring you one, and we can hook you up with a prepaid service, OK?"

Felicity swallowed hard, emotion overtaking her. "I promise I'll pay you eventually, for the supplies, the phone, your time. I know I put you in a bad position. I can't thank you..."

"You're trying to save an animal's life. Pay me back when you can. No worries."

"One more thing." Felicity stood by the table, her fingers lightly touching the cat's fur. "Do you know what kind of breed he is? I've never seen markings like this."

She shrugged. "Something exotic and expensive, but I know one thing for sure—he's one lucky-ass cat."

CHAPTER THREE

The alarm went off at midnight, but Felicity had been lying awake for three hours now, watching the cat's sides rise and fall with each breath. He didn't seem to notice the IV dripping saline into his veins. He looked a bit better—it was hard to tell with cats—but she kept thinking about what Ronnie had said.

Cats don't go still like this until right before death.

He'd not moved. Sure, he was full of drugs and no doubt exhausted from his ordeal, but he hadn't even twitched since his last feeding. And he hadn't yet used the litter box she'd relocated to the bedroom. Felicity supposed she had no choice but to trust the process. Ronnie knew what she was doing, and this cat surely knew that he needed to heal. Felicity was just a conduit.

She left the tiny bedroom area, latched the accordion door, and was about to prepare the next eyedropper when…

The cats! What the hell was *wrong* with them? They were still gathered as a group on the daybed, perched tall and still. No one lounged. No one slept. No one played or groomed or fought or acted cranky or territorial. It was like they were in a trance.

She sat in the booth and called them. They swarmed. Some went to her lap, some her shoulders. Gumbo rubbed his face to her cheek. Melrose repeatedly bumped his head against her arm, insisting that he get all the attention. Teena Maria was a broken record of *Mrow, mrow, mrow, mrow....* Scratch and Sniff rolled together across the tabletop, an orange-tabby tumbleweed.

"What's going on with you guys?"

They purred and mewled, and Felicity sensed they were immensely relieved, thrilled to be allowed to come near her. Sure, introducing a new cat to the group was always a challenge, especially when it was an intact male, but never had she seen cats behave so strangely because of an interloper. Not one of them had attempted to approach Tom, let alone sniff him. Not even Mojo.

"It's OK, gang. I promise." Felicity wished she had four arms, like the goddess Shiva, so she could embrace everyone at once. "We just need to let him rest. Thank you for being such good kitties."

P-p-p-prrrrowpt.

Mmmmroooooow.

Rrrrrp.

The cats eventually relaxed and went off to their preferred sleeping spots. Felicity stepped over Valkyrie to mix the warm slurry of kitten formula, then carried it and the eyedropper to the bedroom. She slipped a hand beneath Tom's body, careful not to touch any of his stitches, and cradled him in a semi-sitting position. She double-checked that the IV line wasn't twisted. "It's time to eat again, handsome man."

His eyelids parted. He was drowsy, but there was a hint of recognition in his gaze. He allowed her to squirt small amounts of formula on his pink sandpaper tongue. He swallowed. The effort exhausted him, so once she got close to an ounce in him, she let him go back to sleep.

They repeated the routine at three a.m., six a.m., and nine a.m., and by then, the junkyard was in full swing and sleeping was no longer an option, no matter how tired she was. Felicity staggered out of bed and greeted the other cats. "Who wants breakfast?"

After she'd finished her routine, Felicity decided to work in the garden for a bit. She opened the screened bedroom window so she would hear if Tom woke or complained, then got down to the business of her plants. With the warm air delicious on her bare arms, she pulled weeds by their roots, tidied the rows, and checked on the bean and tomato supports. The heavy rain had left the ground loose and wet, and the plants teetered between happy and drowned.

"Hey, Felicity."

"Hey, Tasha." She peered over her shoulder to see her friend all dressed up in her best black pants, a colorful top, and her gold hoop earrings. "You look gorgeous. Is this an office day?"

"No. Just headed into town."

Felicity could smell... something. Was it the septic system after the rain? Her eyes watered against the sickly sweet and sweaty metallic odor, then realized it had arrived with Tasha. She tried to smile. "New perfume?"

"Yes." Tasha seemed a teensy bit defensive. "Jim gave it to me. It's called Passion's Fire and he loves it." Her eyes swept over the little garden and quickly changed the subject. "It's doing a lot better than last year, huh?"

"Absolutely. The butter lettuce is nearly ready. I'll bring you some. And help yourself to any of the herbs whenever you want. I've got dill, parsley, basil, and oregano. Just don't get it confused with the catnip."

"Thanks. Um…" Tasha produced a sound somewhere between a sigh and a whine. "Hey, did you really go out and get another cat yesterday? After our conversation? Please tell me that's not what you did."

"You're correct. That's not what I did." Felicity flipped onto her bottom so she could look directly at her friend. She tugged on her sunhat to block the glare and let her gloved hands hang over her knees. "He was injured on the side of 101. Almost dead. I was driving and caught a flash of…"

"Seriously, Felicity?"

"…his collar. So I got out of the car and called to him and he came to me, like he knew I was his only shot at survival."

Tasha wheeled around. "And where's your car now?"

"The Pine Beach impound, most likely. It died on me, so I had to leave it."

"You *walked* back? By your*self?* In the *rain?* God, you make me so mad!"

Felicity pushed herself to a stand, grunting with the effort. Her left knee was *killing* her after yesterday's ordeal, but scabbing over nicely. Same with the scrapes on her palms.

"Mad?"

"You're the most stubborn human being I've ever known! I told you to get rid of the cats you already had, not add to your collection."

"I just told you…"

"Get rid of this new one by the end of the day. *Please.* And get yourself a goddamn cell phone, for Chrissake! You can't be walking alone like that! Oregon is a breeding ground for serial killers! Frogs are falling from the sky!"

Felicity peeled off her gardening gloves finger by finger and dropped them on the large, flat rock beside the garden, all the while studying Tasha. Clearly, her outburst had nothing to do with Felicity or the cat. "You're my best friend, Tash. If something's going on with you, I'm here to listen, like always. But do not yell at me like that."

"Huh?" Tasha picked at her fingers and glanced back at the house.

So this was about Hair Gel Jim. "Why are you headed into town?"

"No reason."

"Oh, there's a reason."

"Look, we're just at the exploratory stage, not ready to commit."

Felicity felt her eyes pop wide as Tasha's words found purchase in her brain. "Are you thinking of *marrying* that idiot?"

"Of course not. Not yet, anyway. And he's not an idiot. He's far more complex than he seems—very into conservation and wildlife, even volunteers with a nonprofit. It's just that... well, I got an offer on the property and we're meeting with the real estate agent today. You know, to look at our options."

Felicity froze. "I didn't know you wanted to sell your family's land."

"I'm not! I don't! I didn't even list it! Somebody reached out to us, and we figured we'd at least hear what they have to say."

"*We?*" Felicity stepped closer to Tasha. "*You* own this land outright, Tasha. This is *your* inheritance. Jim has nothing to do with it. You're clear on that, right?"

Tasha laughed. "Pardon me if I don't jump at your real estate advice, since you've basically allowed Rich to steal your half of the house."

Felicity's jaw unhinged.

The front door of the house slammed. Tasha waved to Jim. "Be right there!"

Honest to God, Tasha had just yodeled. She sounded like *Mayberry's* Aunt Bea or Snow White with her twittering birdies. Tasha turned back to Felicity. "Why are you looking at me like that?"

"I'm worried about you."

"Yeah? I'm worried about *you*. That cat probably has hantavirus or something. It needs to go."

Tasha and Jim left a moment later, with Jim behind the wheel of Tasha's car. He waved to Felicity as he drove through the gate, a smirk on his gel-framed face.

The alarm clock went off inside the trailer. Eyedropper time again.

Felicity washed up at the outdoor hose, then left her muddy Crocs on the landing. Once inside, she found her cats in a clump, pressed tightly to the bedroom divider. Fear slashed through her. Had something happened to Tom? Had he died while she was tending to the butter lettuce?

"Beep, beep, kitties. Come on now, let me through."

All scattered as she opened the divider, everyone but Diddy, who charged into the bedroom, jumped on the bed, dropped his squeaky mouse at Tom's feet, and exited as quickly as he'd entered.

Tom was not dead. In fact, he stood on all fours on the bed, wobbly as a toddler. His back foot was twisted in the IV line. He turned his face toward her.

Mmmmraaaaaooooow.

"Tom!"

He toppled over, landing softly on the comforter. That's when Felicity noticed that his sutures had leaked, leaving watery blood all

49

over her bedclothes.

"No worries, my man. This comforter is ancient. What's a few more stains?"

She sat on the edge of the mattress to tend to him. Fresh bandages were the first order of business. He allowed her to remove the old gauze, keeping as still as he had yesterday, which made her decide his stillness was not a sign of impending death but a personality trait. His wounds were healing, definitely looking less raw.

His eyes were clear and alert too, and she smiled with relief. He was going to pull through, no doubt about it.

"You in a rush to get better, Tom? Got a hot date? A big presentation to the board of directors?"

Felicity moved the squeaky mouse, amused that Diddy had shared his precious toy. She scratched Tom on the unwounded spot on his head, then lay on her side next to him. He met her gaze, daylight dancing in those mesmerizingly mismatched eyes. The left was a startling turquoise blue, like you'd find on the cover of a Tahiti travel brochure, and the right was a rich amber, flecked with bits of emerald green.

He blinked those eyes slowly and scrutinized her, his gaze unafraid but full of questions. He must have been as curious about her as she was about him.

"I bet you're thinking... *How did I end up with this chick?*"

Felicity had never been one of those woo-woo New Age-y types, but she had to admit that this cat gave off a peculiar vibe, intense and tingly. During one of last night's feedings, she swore she felt electricity jump from his body into hers, zipping up her spine to the back of her neck.

She felt it again now, and shivered.

Felicity brushed her fingers along his collar. "Someday, you'll tell me all about this Frederick's of Hollywood choker, all right?"

Rrrraaow. His whiskers rose and fell with his response.

"And I mean the *whole* story—like how it got there, how to get it off, and why anyone thought it was a good idea to put something this clunky around a cat's neck. It can't be comfortable, amirite?

Rraow.

She scratched behind his ear, then moved on to the underside of his chin and to his chest. He didn't melt with pleasure at her touch, but he tolerated it. She stroked one of his front paws, intrigued by his onyx-black pads and sharp, shiny claws.

"Where in the world did you come from?"

She tapped the golden bell attached to his collar and heard it tinkle, clear and high. It was an odd accessory, with intricate carvings covering the plastic. Or metal. Or whatever it was made of. She jiggled the bell back and forth in the light, seeing no lines or divots from a mass-production mold. She'd need a magnifying glass to get a good look at those tiny markings.

"Too bad this getup isn't real. I'd take it to the pawn shop and buy treats and medicine and toys and fluffy cat beds out the yin-yang. I could get my car fixed, too. Maybe even hire a lawyer to deal with my dick of an ex-husband!"

Rraaooow.

Tom slept off and on through the afternoon and evening. After his nine o'clock feeding, Felicity crawled into bed, exhausted, and somehow managed to sleep through the midnight and three a.m. alarms. She woke at first light to find Tom curled up asleep against her side, the cat version of spooning. It was the first time he'd sought physical contact with her, and it made her smile.

Later that morning, Tasha came by the Airstream to make sure the hantavirus carrier was gone.

"Absolutely," Felicity lied.

"Really?" Tasha was suspicious.

"Yep." Felicity stepped out onto the front stoop, pulling the door shut behind her. "The vet tech took him."

"Are you telling the me the truth?"

"Have I ever not? How did it go at the Realtor's?"

Tasha shrugged. "I had no idea the land was worth so much. Apparently, it's a real seller's market right now; custom home builders are looking for large lots."

"You don't say?"

Tasha folded her arms over her chest and smiled. "Well, anyway, I'm glad you got rid of the cat. Only twelve more to go!"

That afternoon, Felicity was busy in the garden when an odd sensation swept over her. She glanced out to the tree line not ten feet away, fully expecting to see someone standing in the shade, staring at her. Nobody. She checked the Airstream windows. Sometimes the cats kept an eye on her. No cats. Twigs snapped, and she scanned the tangle of maple, ash, and alder. Eventually she detected movement, low to the ground.

Just bunnies and squirrels, no doubt.

A bit later, she heard someone drive through Tasha's gate. She squinted into the sun to see a Pine Beach flatbed tow truck carrying... *her Saturn?*

She wiped dirt from her knees, dropped her gloves, and greeted the truck driver as he pulled to a stop on the gravel drive. Whoever had been riding shotgun had already jumped out and started lowering the tow platform.

"Felicity Cheshire?"

"Yes."

"Sign here, please." The driver reached down through his window to hand her a clipboard.

Her eyes darted to the young man backing her car down the ramp. Wait—that wasn't her car. It was much nicer than hers, though the exact same color. Saturn had called it "gray bronze," if she remembered correctly.

"I'll just need you to sign."

"For what?"

"Release from impound. Sign and date on the X at the bottom."

"But that's not my car."

The driver cracked his neck. "Lady, you just told me I had the right address."

"No, I told you my name was Felicity Cheshire, but *that* is not my car." She raised a stiffened arm and pointed to the vehicle now pulling alongside the tow truck. "To begin with, it's too clean."

He laughed. "That's a first. Most people bitch and moan that we got their cars dirty."

"And the windshield's not cracked."

When the clipboard was shoved toward her a second time, she took it, then walked around the sedan. She needed more proof that this was all some kind of strange mistake, and she found it. The radial tires were right off the rack—they had visible tread and everything! The wiper blades weren't shredded. The exhaust was rust-free and not held in place with duct tape. The glass and mirrors sparkled. The exterior paint had been touched up and polished to a high shine. The inside was spotless—the dash buffed, the carpet shampooed, and the seat upholstery revived.

No way is this my car.

But when she circled around a second time, she saw her

customized Oregon license plate: CATITUDE. And centered directly below it was her signature bumper sticker:

Husband and Cat Missing
Reward for Cat

"Here you go, Mrs. Cheshire." The young man who'd driven the Saturn now held the keys out to her.

"*Ms.* Cheshire." The keys fell into her open palm. "How did you even get the engine to turn over?"

"Huh?" The kid shot a helpless look to the driver, who opened his door and jumped down, sighing loudly.

"Is there another problem?"

"Yes!" Felicity waved the clipboard. "My car was a shit can two days ago—cracked windshield, broken exhaust, bald tires, and covered in cat hair! And that doesn't even get to the mechanical issues. It died on me in the middle of a rainstorm on 101."

"Yeah, that alien cloudburst thing." The kid shook his head. "That was freaky shit, man, and the frogs? Damn, I wish I'd seen that."

"You didn't miss much." Felicity examined the paperwork she held in her hand. "It doesn't say who paid for any of this."

"Lady…"

"Who paid the impound fees?"

"I have no idea."

"Don't you people have recordkeeping rules? That's the problem with the world today; nobody follows the rules anymore!"

"Do you want your car or not?"

"Yes, I want my car! But this isn't my car!"

"Let's look at the VIN." The driver grabbed the clipboard and ran a greasy fingertip down the page. "Right here. That's your vehicle

ID number. It's like car DNA. Check it against your auto insurance policy."

"Be right back!" Felicity ran into the Airstream and pulled two banker boxes from the floor of the tiny closet. One was jammed with medical records. The other held proof of her fifty-two years on the planet. She grabbed the car insurance file and ran outside, then held the papers beside the clipboard.

"See?" The driver was pleased with himself. "Now..." He held out a pen. "Would you please sign this so we can leave?"

They weren't gone five seconds before Felicity jumped behind the wheel and slipped the key into the ignition. The engine purred to life. Creamy as butter. Smooth as silk. Just like the day she drove it off the lot, during a Saturn year-end clearance sale, when she had a job she loved and when she and Rich still hoped for children.

Felicity checked the gas tank. Full.

OK. This shit could not *possibly* be right.

Felicity felt off-kilter the rest of the day. Her brain seized whenever she tried to puzzle out the identity of her Secret Saturn Santa. Who would do something like this? Yes, she had a number of friendly acquaintances who still lived in the area, but no one who would go to such lengths or expense. Tasha might, if she'd won the lottery and suddenly been overcome with guilt about the cats. But Tasha preferred her acts of kindness to be public and referenced often, and besides, she hadn't appeared the least bit guilty that morning.

No one in Felicity's family had done it, that was certain. Her brother and his daughters lived in Boston, and they hadn't spoken in years. Her cousins were scattered all over the West Coast, and they'd barely kept in touch—the Cheshires weren't family reunion types. Both her parents were gone. So, that left... exactly nobody.

She kept peeking out the window above the sink to make sure

the car was really there. Part of her wanted it to be a strange hallucination. The other part just wanted a car that worked. She remembered that line from an old movie where a man says he's worried because his brother thinks he's a chicken. When asked why he doesn't get help for his brother, the man says, *We need the eggs.*

Well, she needed a functioning car. And now she had one. Maybe it was best to leave it at that.

She fed Tom every three hours. He seemed to be doing better. He slept almost all the time and didn't move much, but his IV had stayed in place, his wounds looked good, and his breathing was regular and steady. In Felicity's opinion, his heart was beating a little fast, even for a cat, so that nibbled at her peace of mind. Maybe he was just dreaming of chasing mice through the fields.

Felicity used the last two slices of bread to make herself a tomato and butter lettuce sandwich with mayo, then sliced up an apple to go with. She stretched out on the daybed and tried to read the psychological thriller she'd picked up at the library, but couldn't seem to focus. It was another one of those tales where the heroine must find her own kidnapped child because the police had dropped the ball. On this particular day, the premise left Felicity irritated and, frankly, pissed off. Why do women have to do *everything*—even other people's jobs?

She heard a loud *clunk!* on the front stoop.

"Hello?"

No one answered. Maybe Tasha had returned. She and Jim had been gone all day.

Felicity peeled the purring Gumbo from her chest and went to open the door. A large box sat on the stoop. Strangely, it had no shipping label or return address. She carried it inside—not heavy at all—and used a kitchen knife to cut the packing tape.

"*Whaaa?*"

She ripped open the delicate tissue paper. Beneath was absolutely exquisite fabric—a sumptuous, watercolor mix of greens and blues in what felt like the most impossibly soft cotton she'd ever touched. She pulled it out and pressed it to her chest. The fill was as light and fluffy as goose down. Technically speaking, what she held in her hands was a bed comforter. But that would be like calling a Ferrari basic transportation. Never in her life had she owned anything this luxurious, this decadent.

It was a chore to keep the treasure from touching the floor of the Airstream, which was covered in dirt and dust and cat hair. She did her best, then used her free hand to root around in the box for a card or receipt or *something* that showed who had sent this, and why. There was nothing.

She couldn't accept it, of course. It was clearly a shipping error. But when she tried to shove it back in the box, she found that Teena Marie, Rick James, and Boudica had already taken up residence inside.

"Outa there, kids. I need to send this back." They didn't budge. It occurred to her that without a shipping label or receipt, there *was* no "back." Would she throw it away? That would be a waste. Given the circumstances, maybe she should keep it. Would that be so wrong?

The satin-like material kissed her fingertips. The fabric smelled like fluffy sunshine. So soothing, so... well, *comforting*. Exactly what she needed.

She spoke to the cats in the box. "If I'm losing my mind, I might as well lose it in luxury, know what I'm saying?"

That night, Felicity woke with a start, yanked from a restless dream sea, where clean cars and comfy comforters appeared out of nowhere and the trees had eyes. She reached out to silence the alarm, only to find it hadn't chimed. It was two-twelve a.m.

She turned her head, slowly, a familiar tingle racing up her spine. Two mismatched eyes bored through the darkness.

"Tom?"

He blinked.

"Are you all right?"

Mrow.

"Are you hungry?"

Mraooooow.

"Is something wrong?"

Mrrp.

She fed him ahead of schedule and fell back into a muddled and anxious dream-sleep. A few hours later, Felicity shot up in bed, gasping for breath. The Airstream rocked beneath her. A series of loud bangs echoed in her skull. The junkyard Rottweiler barked his brains out.

"Coming! Coming!" She threw on her robe and ran to the front door, deciding that the world better be coming to an end, because otherwise, this level of drama at seven a.m. was completely uncalled for.

"Felicity!"

"I said I'm *coming!*"

She threw open the door, blinked hard, and shielded her eyes from the morning sun. Tasha and Jim stood on the stoop, dressed in their Hillsboro Hops minor-league finery. "What's up? Going into the city for the game?"

"What..." Tasha gestured down the steps to the yard. "...*the fuck is this?*"

Dozens and dozens of cats mewled and paced in a semicircle around the Airstream. They were of every size, color, and breed imaginable. Some were sleek and shiny and wearing collars. Others were ragged and bony and feral. Every one of them either carried a gift

58

in its mouth or had already dropped it to the ground in offering. She saw birds, squirrels, lizards, mice, chipmunks…

"I don't understand." Felicity wiped the sleep from her eyes.

Jim laughed, tugging on his baseball cap. "We understand just fine, you crazy old broad. This is a giant fuck-you to Tasha, isn't it? The woman who's letting you stay here out of the goodness of her heart!"

"Huh?"

"You went out and rounded up fifty fuckin' feral cats and brought them back here just to spite us, didn't you?"

"How would I even do that, Jim? Order from the feral cat store at the strip mall?"

"You're damn pitiful."

"And you're a cretinous jackass."

"Stop it!" Tasha's cheeks were beet red and her lips trembled. "Jim, why don't you get in the car. I'll be there in a minute."

"I think I should stay with you, babe. She's not normal."

"Get in the car, Jim." Tasha spoke through clenched teeth.

"She's unstable."

"The car, Jim." Once he'd complied, Tasha pushed her way into the trailer—and why shouldn't she? It was hers. She glanced at the empty cat food tins on the counter, the pile of eyedroppers in the sink, and the used bandages tossed into the garbage pail. She glanced toward the bedroom.

Tom was perched on the end of the bed, hooked to his IV, staring right at her.

"Oh, Felicity." Tasha collapsed into the booth, immediately sweeping cat hair off her jeans. "I'm worried our friendship won't recover from this. The lies. The bullshit. I feel like I don't even know you anymore."

"I didn't bring all those cats here."

"Then where'd they come from?"

"I have no idea."

"Oh, my God." Tasha let her face fall into her hands. "I'm truly concerned for your well-being." She looked up, her eyes pleading. "You need counseling or an intervention, Lissie. You're a hoarder. Of cats. It's not healthy. Jim's right; it's not *normal*. And it's not respectful of my space."

Felicity scooted onto the opposite booth bench and reached for Tasha's hands. "I didn't bring those cats here. I don't know why they're here or where they're from. But I gotta tell you, something totally weird is going on, and it's bigger than just the cats. Honestly, I feel like I'm losing my mind."

"Maybe you are." She pursed her bright-red lips. "I see you managed to get your car back and it looks... well, brand new." She tipped her chin to the bedroom. "Nice new comforter, too. Same cat, though. So did Rich sell the house?"

"What? No."

"Then how did you pay to fix up the Saturn?"

Felicity decided against answering, since it would only lend credence to the need for an intervention. *The car appeared as if by magic. The comforter was a gift from the gods. The cats were beamed down from outer space...*

"I just don't know what to say anymore." Tasha got up, shook her head, and reached for the door handle. "We'll be back tonight."

She slammed the door. Felicity moved to the sink to watch her best friend march through the swarm of feline invaders, yelling obscenities.

By late afternoon, their numbers reached at least two hundred. Felicity placed several large buckets of water outside for the visitors, but didn't have enough food for them. One cat, in particular, concerned her. The scruffy calico was obviously feral, and very pregnant, with golden eyes that seemed to track Felicity's every move. The wild mama cat walked with a limp. God only knew what she'd been through, and it broke Felicity's heart that there was nothing she could do for her.

But she brought out a bowl of kibble for the little mama-to-be and blockaded the small metal stoop so she could eat in peace. When the cat returned to the crowd, her eyes held Felicity's for a long moment. She was asking for help.

"Oh, honey, no. I can handle a lot, but I'm too squeamish for birth. You'll need to have your babies somewhere else."

Not long after, Felicity sat on the front metal steps to have a chat with the mewling multitude. They pressed closer.

"Please go. I'd love to take care of you—every single one of you—but I can't, and your presence is causing a lot of problems for me. Go home or go back to wherever you're living and take your gifts with you. I'd appreciate it."

As suddenly as the cats had arrived, they left, taking their critters with them. She watched the ones with collars and tags exit through the front gate. Others disappeared into the tree line, the mama cat glancing back one last time before she was gone. Their visit made no sense to Felicity, none at all, but very little in the last few days had.

Felicity was tidying up after a scrambled egg dinner just before sunset when a delivery truck drove through the gate. The driver got out, threw open the back hatch, and used a dolly to unload boxes in front of the Airstream. Some were small and some were larger, and all were emblazoned with the blue logo for Kitty-Korner.com.

Felicity dried her hands on a towel and raced down the stairs. "What's all this?"

61

The driver checked his electronic tablet. "Cheshire? Felicity Cheshire?"

"Yes, but I didn't order anything."

"OK. Can you just sign here?"

"But these aren't for me."

The guy in brown shorts scowled. He pointed to the printed label on the nearest box. "Can you verify this information for me, ma'am?"

Felicity stepped closer and peered at the label. It was her name and her address, all right. "Who bought these?"

The guy seemed stumped. "You?"

"Nope."

"Somebody else?"

"Who?"

"I would have no way of knowing."

"Can't you check for a name or a credit card number or something?"

"I don't have access to that, ma'am. But if you go online and check your account…"

"I don't *have* an account! Or a credit card that wouldn't be confiscated if I tried to use it! I don't even have a *computer!*"

He was about to say something but thought better of it.

"What's in the boxes?"

He shook his head. "I have no idea."

Out of curiosity, Felicity approached one of the smaller cardboard containers. "Do you have a penknife or something?"

"I got a box cutter."

"That'll work."

"You have to sign first."

"Fine!" She threw up her arms in exasperation. "I'll sign!" The driver handed her the box cutter, and Felicity promptly swiped it down the center seam of the packing tape. Inside were two cases of the specialty canned food Boudica needed because of her bad teeth. Felicity leaned closer, the box cutter hanging limp in her hand. "What the hell *is* this?"

The driver peered inside the cardboard and said, helpfully, "Cat food?"

"Yeah, but I didn't order it."

"OK."

Felicity looked up at the sky, a blue-gray field streaked with oranges and pinks. She laughed out loud, aware that she must sound like an escaped lunatic.

Tasha was right. She needed help. She'd had some kind of psychotic break, and she could no longer tell what was real and what wasn't, which made her laugh even louder.

The only other possibility was that she really *did* have a benefactor, someone thoughtful enough to replace her comforter, fix her car, and deliver veterinary-grade cat food. But who could that be? Who even knew she needed these things?

"I should probably head out, ma'am. Can I have that back if you're done with it?"

Felicity glanced at the driver. She'd forgotten he was there. She handed him the box cutter, and he drove off.

She ran inside for a kitchen knife, then proceeded to slice open every box because, really, if she'd gone completely nutso, then none of this was happening anyway. And if she had a benefactor, then *hell yes*, she would gladly keep it all! She ripped them open, one by one, laughing and gasping with each delightful discovery.

There were cat trees, hammocks, scratching posts, and pop-up play tunnels. There was litter, cat beds of several sizes, designs, and shapes, and dry and canned foods. There was medicine for roundworm and feline rheumatoid arthritis. And, yes, there were toys: balls, feather teasers, things that dangled and things that arched, things that squeaked and things that crinkled, things in the shape of mice and birds and bunnies.

This was a goddamn Disneyland for cats, a cat heaven on earth, and it must have cost more than Felicity would see in her lifetime.

As Felicity sliced open the last box, another car came through the gate. What now? Flowers? A fruit basket?

No. It was Rich.

Really? Her auditory/visual hallucinations had to include her ex-husband?

He popped out of his BMW, waving a single sheet of paper over his head, his face as red as a stoplight. His eyes bulged. Rich's loosened necktie swung with every angry step as he marched toward her, his glare locked and loaded.

"You really think harassment is going to solve your problems? Well I have some news for you, old gal! It's *on!*"

He tripped over an open box of cat litter, hitting the dirt with an "*ooooomph.*"

She shut her eyes for a moment. Maybe, if she were really lucky, he'd be gone when she opened them.

Nope.

Rich stumbled to his feet, his hands flailing as he tried to brush mud from his suit. "How did you get the money for all this shit?"

It was then that Felicity noticed Rich's face was dotted with a few large, angry-looking cysts. "What's wrong with your skin?"

"It's just a coupla zits, for fuck's sake! Why all the drama? Can't a man have a zit every once in a while? It's not like I have leprosy!" He slapped the sheet of paper against her chest. "You've got some nerve,

Felicity."

The paper felt heavy in her fingers, a luxurious linen stationery in bright white. The only adornment was raised gold foil lettering, centered along the top:

ALEXANDER HELIOS RIGIAT, ESQUIRE
ATTORNEY AT LAW

The correspondence was all of two paragraphs. Apparently, this Mr. Rigiat, Esquire, whoever *that* was, claimed he'd been retained to represent Ms. Felicity R. Cheshire in a contempt of court filing against Mr. Richard T. Hume for violating the property settlement terms of their divorce.

Huh?

At the bottom of the page was a bold signature in pitch-black ink.

She flipped the stationery over, but saw no phone number, website, or mailing address. "Where's his contact information? Who is this guy?"

Rich laughed. "A blank envelope was shoved under my door, as if you didn't know."

"But I..."

He snatched the paper from her fingers, folded it, and slipped it into the inner pocket of his suit coat. "This is about the baby, isn't it?"

"What?"

"You're absolutely crazed with jealousy that Bethany and I are having a baby."

"That's not true. I..."

"You're pathetic, Felicity. I actually feel sorry for you." He scanned the array of open boxes, raised a single eyebrow in accusation, and nodded. "See you in court."

He turned with a flourish—and promptly fell over another box.

She snorted. She couldn't help it.

Rich ranted and raved his way back to his car, wiping himself off as he went. In his rush to leave, loose gravel shot from his tires.

Felicity remained where she stood for several long moments, untangling it all. If Rich tripped over the boxes—twice—that meant they actually existed. *If* Rich had been real. But Rich had handed her the lawyer's stationery, and that was real. The hideous boils on Rich's face were real because he had acknowledged them, calling them zits, which was a word she hadn't heard since her years as a middle school teacher. The bed comforter was real. She'd snuggled beneath it last night. Her car was real because there it sat, shining in the sunset.

Rather abruptly, her thoughts turned to wine. She was sure there was a bottle of merlot in the Airstream, if she could remember where she'd stashed it.

She discovered it under the sink, behind a box of scouring pads, grabbed the corkscrew and a cracked coffee mug, and retreated to the stoop. She propped her feet on the metal railing and stretched out in the folding chair. Stars began to pop, one by one, like pinholes of light on blue-black velvet. The moon rose, a sharp-edged, icy blue crescent. She drank her wine and tried to relax enough to understand…

Was she so detached from reality that she was creating elaborate make-believe encounters complete with conversations, package deliveries, and paperwork?

Or did she really have a benefactor?

Or, was she so far gone that she'd created an imaginary world complete with a cast of supporting characters and props and a fairy godmother who happened to know exactly what she needed and when she needed it?

Oooh. She liked that last option the best. She took another swig of wine and raised her mug to the moon.

"I'll take crazy cat ladies for six hundred, Alex!" She giggled at her own joke, in a way only a truly crazy cat lady would, and felt curiously peaceful about it all.

Because insanity didn't scare her. She'd beat breast cancer. She'd taught English to eighth graders. She'd survived a divorce, joblessness, bankruptcy, and homelessness. And really, it would be strange if she *weren't* a little looney after all that.

Tasha and Jim rolled in about eleven. The car slowed to a crawl as they passed the Airstream. Jim stared at the boxes and shook his head in disgust. Tasha turned away, as if opened cartons in the grass was a sight too gruesome to contemplate.

"Hey, guys! How was the game?" Felicity lifted her mug in a toast. "Help yourself to some kibble if you want! It's top-shelf!"

They ignored her. Tasha slammed the car door before stomping up her porch steps. Jim flipped Felicity the finger before disappearing inside.

"Suit yourself."

When the mosquitos got unbearable, Felicity staggered back into the Airstream. She fed Tom, who seemed more listless than earlier in the day, then fell into bed, still in her clothes. She drifted off with a smile on her lips, enjoying the feel of the ethereal comforter so deliciously cool against her wine-warmed cheek.

Clearly, psychotic breaks were underrated.

Mrrow.

"Yo, Tom." She reached out and gave him a clumsy pat, her eyelids too heavy to pry apart. "You good, bro?" Then she fell asleep.

The alarm woke her. She was disoriented and her head hurt

like hell. What was she doing still in her clothes? And what…?

Felicity stiffened. She stopped breathing. Couldn't think. Her eyes scanned back and forth, up and down, until she grasped the situation.

She was spooning with a naked man.

The front of *her* body was pressed to the back of *his* body, which was large, warm, and completely bare, from his short black hair to the smooth soles of his feet.

Nude.

A man.

In her bed.

She gasped.

In one swift movement, the man had twisted around, flipped Felicity on her back, and lay atop her, pinning her body to the mattress. He pressed a hand over her mouth.

"Shhhh."

The hand trembled. His weight flattened her. She could feel the heat of his skin through her clothes. He was burning hot, feverish even, and he leaned in until his eyes were just an inch from her own. They were otherworldly eyes, searing, and wise.

One turquoise blue.

One gold.

What the ever-loving fuck?

A bead of sweat dripped from the man's chin and plopped onto the tip of her nose.

Felicity shoved against him with all her strength, then tried to raise her knees to push him away. He yelped in pain but quickly put an end to her flailing. He gripped both her wrists and imprisoned her arms at her sides, pressing his thighs against her knees and jamming her deeper into the mattress.

Stitches. When she'd touched the man's body, she'd felt the rough ridge of sutures in his skin.

Felicity steeled herself, risking a glance at the man's neck. The ornate gold and jeweled necklace glinted against his olive skin, sized for a man and not a cat, an engraved bell dangling above his breastbone.

It tinkled as he breathed.

"*Tom?*"

He nodded. That barest movement made him wince.

Felicity laughed. Out loud. Because the pet cat she'd found on the side of the road had miraculously transformed into a Chippendale dancer! And in her mind, she heard the *bing! bing! bing!* of her final answer: she was certifiably bonkers.

But—and this was the tricky part—her hallucination was two hundred pounds of hard muscle, dripping sweat and squeezing the air from her lungs. She could smell him too. He smelled of baked earth, incense, and musk.

The man who may have once been a cat shifted his weight onto one arm and used his free hand to reach behind his neck. She heard a clasp release. Her vision swirled with white light and flashes of gold, and before Felicity could exhale, the necklace had gone from his throat to hers. The transfer had taken a fraction of a second, yet she'd watched it unfold in slow motion.

How was that possible?

A definitive *click* echoed in her ears. Then the necklace moved. It conformed to the exact contours of her neck and chest, like a living thing. Like magic.

"Felicity." The cat-man whispered her name in a deep and scratchy voice. His muscled arms shook from the exertion of holding his weight, and the tendons in his neck strained. "You'll have to help me. You must fight along with me. Do you understand?"

She tugged at the necklace, terror scrambling her brains. No buckle. No give. An unbroken circle. *Fight along with me.* Why did those words sound familiar?

The man rolled away from her. He went limp, collapsing chest down on the bed, his face turned to her. His broad back was beaded with perspiration, and she could see him struggle to breathe, fight to keep his eyes open. Only then did she notice that in addition to his fresh sutures, he was covered with older scars. They seemed to form a pattern. A pattern similar to the markings of Tom's fur.

Oh, *hell no.*

Felicity yanked at the necklace. Too heavy. Too tight. Too large. *No!* She began to hyperventilate.

He spoke again. Felicity stopped freaking out long enough to lean closer. The substantial weight of the collar—and her hangover—made her feel off-kilter.

"What did you say?"

His hand clawed desperately at the hem of her T-shirt. *"Her body,"* he hissed, *"we must... retrieve... her body."*

Then he passed out.

CHAPTER FOUR

He runs in the night. The stench of the city recedes. Dense brush scrapes his legs. Only when he slips on wet leaves does he notice that his sneakers are saturated with blood—blood of the Acolyte, the Opponent, and his own, pouring from his open wounds.

Was the Acolyte dead? Had her life force drained as she lay in his lap? Had she died in his arms?

He hears a faraway voice pierce the thick fog. The barest whisper. Desperate. Worried. Female.

"*Tom?*"

He's back in the tunnels! His hands tap along the slick stone walls as he shouts the Acolyte's name...

"*Wake up. Please.*"

Ah! He is in the dreamworld. He is in a dream within a dream. But real. A memory. A recounting of events—horrible, unprecedented events.

The Acolyte charged into the tunnel—into battle—without him. Not the plan. Not her training. But she's always been the easily

distracted sort, begging to *get on with it,* as if her sacred calling is part
of a to-do list.

She's always seemed younger than the others, less mature. She's
obsessed with her looks and drunk on the hubris of invincibility. But
if she doesn't grasp the enormity of her duty, whose fault is that?

His. Only his.

"Can you hear me?"

Cool water soothes his feverish forehead. He wants to respond,
to open his eyes, but he's plunged back into the terror.

He sails over the last few crooked steps and is swallowed by
darkness. He races on through the sloping, twisting tunnel at full speed
until he loses traction on the damp stone floor and slams into a wall.
That's when he sees her.

She struggles. Her weapon glances off the Opponent, inflicting
no damage. Her strong arms—arms he's trained, muscles he's honed—
hang weakly from shoulder joints. She is injured and in pain.

The Opponent counters easily, even though the Acolyte's
moves are wild and unpredictable, nothing in order, nothing according
to the texts.

He must step in, now, or the mission will fail. And many will
die.

"Don't die on me, Tom."

Who's talking to him? Who's Tom? Another touch of cool
water on his skin. Is he dead? No. He remembers. Her name is Felicity.
She calls him Tom. There's so much he needs to tell her.

He's back in the tunnel, drawing a small dagger from the
holster beneath his shirt, heavy in his hand and warm from his own
flesh. He's never raised a weapon to the Opponent. It has never come
to this.

The Acolyte rallies. In one smooth motion, she whips the chain from her waist and lassoes the Opponent's ankles. With a steadier hand than he thought her capable of, she attacks with her lance, hitting her mark.

But the Opponent pivots, strikes, and yanks the Acolyte's long hair, twisting her until her throat is exposed. The eyes of prey and predator lock for an instant before the slice, lightning quick and lethal. The Opponent staggers into the shadows before the Acolyte crumples to the floor.

He drops to his knees to cradle her head. Her eyes are wide and blank, her throat, blossoming open, ruby red.

She is gone.

He taps his dagger to the *usekh*, waiting for the heavy gold to fall to his open palm, as designed.

It doesn't.

An ugly laugh leaches from the darkness.

He needs to focus. Precious seconds slip past. If he steadies his hand and slows his breath, the necklace will release. It has to…

A heavy footstep.

He slips the dagger point between the Acolyte's bloody throat and the gold. With one last tug, the loop pops free and he wills it to conform to his own neck—just as the first blow cracks the back of his head.

The world flashes white-hot, blinding.

On his feet. The next blow slices his left flank. He spins. Then his right flank. He can't fight. Too weak. Must run. Must save the *usekh*, if nothing else.

He kicks out. The Opponent staggers enough for him to break free, gain a head start. He lurches through the tunnels, through the pain, to the stairs, out the steel door, then into the rainy city streets. The Opponent is hobbled and badly wounded but stays at his heels.

Run… run… run…

Alleyways. Parking lots. Neighborhoods of tidy homes and tended gardens. Shifting now, hopping into a truck bed at a stop sign. Farms. Rivers. Forest.

Then, the smell of the sea.

Felicity peered at her delirious man-patient. She was sure that after she'd downed some bad instant coffee, she'd discover that it had all been a nightmare. She was certain that she'd walk in here and find the convalescing creature in her bed was just a cat, as he'd always been. Because anything else made no sense. Cats don't turn into people. Never once in all the years she'd had cats had one *ever* become human, even after she'd polished off a bottle of bad merlot.

But there he was. A man. And when she caught the reflection of the necklace in the dingy trailer window, she knew that was real too. Like her car, the comforter, and her delivery-palooza. All too real. All very weird.

"*Noooo,*" croaked the man-who-once-was-a-cat. "*No!*"

She knew if she couldn't figure out a way to lower his raging fever, he'd die. She'd decided against giving him anything like aspirin or ibuprofen because if the stuff could be toxic to cats, what would it do to a cat-man?

She'd already turned to the contents of her mini freezer—a bag of baby peas, a cauliflower crust personal pan pizza, and a Lean Cuisine chicken panini—which she'd tucked around his body. But Tom's temperature hadn't budged from 103.5 degrees, which was brain dead territory if she remembered correctly from *House* episodes.

Whatever she did, it had to be done here, in the Airstream. In private. Because…

The scene played out in her mind. She'd drag Tom to her car.

She'd pull up in front of the Tillamook Medical Center emergency room, open the passenger door, and roll Tom's naked and comatose body to the sidewalk while she peeled out of the parking lot. Security cameras would get her license plate number, and sheriff's deputies would catch her in no time. They'd pepper Felicity with questions that she'd have no answers for: Who is he? How do we contact his next of kin? How did he receive these injuries, and who stitched them up?

Then they'd say, *You have a right to remain silent.*

Felicity gave Tom's foot a gentle pat. "Be back in a jiff."

She threw on a clean sweatshirt and jeans and retrieved what was left of Rich's raincoat cash. It took just a few minutes to reach the Constant Cupboard convenience store at Second and Pollock, where she snagged five bags of block ice from the freezer out front, tossed them into the passenger seat, and went inside to pay. She placed a twenty on the counter.

"These are on sale for a buck ninety-nine each," the cashier said.

"Great!" She took it as a sign that she'd made the right call.

"That'll be…" The cashier looked up and froze. His eyes bugged and his bottom lip hung loose.

"Is there a problem?"

He gestured at her neck. "Pretty fancy for the Constant Cupboard, ain't it?"

"Huh?" Then it dawned on her.

The necklace! Shit! Shit! Shit!

Felicity headed for the door.

"Yo, Cleopatra! Want your change?"

Shit again! Of course, she wanted her change!

Felicity turned back with as much dignity as she could muster, said "Thank you," and then ran to the car and burned rubber on her way out of the parking lot. She pulled over to the edge of a farm lane and adjusted the rearview mirror. She needed to see just how much of the necklace had been visible above her sweatshirt.

Only all of it.

"This thing's coming off. Don't care what I have to do."

Back home, Felicity lugged the ice inside, borrowed a tarp from Tasha's shed, and rocked Tom's feverish body back and forth until she got the waterproof cloth beneath him. She then arranged the ice blocks around him, one against each side, one under his bent knees, and one on either side of his head.

Now she'd wait.

Felicity observed the tight sheet rise and fall with his shallow breath. As soon as she'd realized that Tom had passed out, several hours ago now, she'd turned him on his back, put a pillow under his head, and carefully tucked the white cotton beneath his shoulders, at his hips, and again at his heels. The position made him look a bit like a mummy ready for the sarcophagus, but leaving the poor guy uncovered wasn't an option. First off, jerking and thrashing his way through his nightmare would lead to ripped-out stitches. Also, as the only other person around, she was the guardian of his dignity.

Menopause sucked. No question about it. But the Shriveling Times hadn't left her *dead*, so of course she'd noticed what a spectacular specimen he was, in every way. Tom had flawless, golden-olive skin. His short hair was a shiny, obsidian black, with a bare patch on his scalp where Ronnie had cut away matted fur. His body was muscled but elegant, not bulky. His hands were large and graceful, and his cheekbones were chiseled. His lashes were long and thick, like his...

She cleared her throat.

Yes, it had been a while since Felicity had seen a naked man. Four years, to be precise. It had been even longer since she'd seen a

76

man as exceptional as Tom because that had been exactly *never in her damned life.*

That said, Felicity's instinct was to comfort and protect Tom, not lust after him. She was old enough to be his mother. And even before the Great Shriveling, she'd had only one rule about the male species: *never mess with a man who is prettier than you.*

She caressed his cheek with tender care, the way she would with Gumbo, Circe, Alphonse, or any of her beloved cats. A smile curled her lips. Well, *of course* she'd feel protective of Tom! He was as much cat as he was human.

Theoretically, anyway.

She rested the back of her hand on his forehead. All morning she'd listened to him rave in at least two languages, possibly more, catching only the words *blood, tunnel,* and *no.* A terrifying fever dream, obviously, yet all she could do was drip water between his dry lips, drape a cool washcloth across his forehead, and plop a frozen panini on his chest.

"This ice had better work," she whispered, stroking his shoulder. "I'll be back in a minute to check your temperature."

She stepped through the doorway to find her cats, yet again, sitting ramrod straight on the daybed like a feline security detail. Their eyes were riveted on the man packed in ice.

That's when it dawned on her—her cats had suspected something strange was afoot from the start! Of course, they had! Their fondness for lining up like Beyoncé's background dancers hadn't started until she brought Tom home. It was common knowledge that cats possessed heightened perception and highly evolved senses, so it made sense they'd see that Tom was no ordinary cat—that, in fact, he was a man.

Theoretically.

Felicity wandered to the mirrored closet door, unzipped her hoodie, and studied the perfectly normal lady looking back at her. She was middle-aged, with messy hair, in a ratty Oregon State T-shirt. The reflection sported gray-green eyes framed in crow's feet, freckles sprinkled across an everyday nose, and mostly straight teeth. She had nothing-special lips and a roundish face. The woman in the mirror was so unremarkable, in fact, that she'd blend into the woodwork if it weren't for one detail…

The giant, honking, solid gold necklace resting against her breastbone. The one she couldn't take off! Panic surged from her chest into her throat, but she took a deep breath to calm herself.

Felicity brushed her fingertips across the cool metal. It was delicately meshed, thin and supple but heavy. She swore that over the last few hours it had fitted itself to the base of her neck and over her clavicle like it was adapting to its new home. She knew inanimate objects didn't do those sorts of things, but considering the present context, would it be out of the realm of possibility? No, it would not.

One thing was certain. The necklace was the real deal in every way, probably 24 carats. Those weren't cut glass fakes, either. They were precious stones, gems of every cut and color that framed the striking center stone, a brilliant cobalt blue that shimmered with each breath. Was that a sapphire? And from that center stone dangled a golden bell.

Talk about a statement necklace.

Felicity's fingertip flicked at the bell. A high and clear tone reverberated through the trailer.

The cats advanced toward her as if summoned. They gathered at Felicity's feet, staring up at her expectantly, whiskers trembling in anticipation.

"OK. Super weird."

She peered closer into the mirror, turning this way and that, tugging and rubbing and twisting the collar. The effort did nothing but leave a red welt around her neck.

Though there no was no buckle, lobster clasp, or spring ring, no toggle or twist-together, no magnet or hook, and no give or stretch, she knew the necklace *could* be removed. She'd watched Tom take it from his own neck and place it on hers. So what was the secret?

Felicity glanced to the ice-packed man-cat, wondering whether the collar was some kind of high-tech gadget. Did it unlock with a fingerprint? A retinal scan?

She rushed to the bedside, fishing one of Tom's limp arms from its icy confines. She pressed each floppy fingertip to the centerpiece of the necklace, then all around the circumference. Nothing. She tried his other hand, with no results. She hovered over Tom's face, positioning the center stone directly in his line of sight. She peeled back an eyelid. Didn't work. She peeled back the other eyelid. Nope.

"Crap!"

Her gaze wandered to the junkyard next door, where machinery smashed metal and moved debris, where she'd seen backhoes and bulldozers and saws. Surely, the guy who owned the place would have *something* in his tool chest that could slice through solid gold without cutting her carotid artery. As soon as Tom was out of the woods, she'd walk over there and find out.

Felicity continued to monitor his temperature. She was relieved to see it drop to 101.5 degrees but was concerned that he'd not yet regained consciousness. She ate the personal pan pizza for dinner. It tasted pretty darn good considering it had gone from frozen, to thawed, back to frozen, and then to oven. She used a coffee cup to bail melted ice from the tarp and toss it into the sink. She rearranged the ice tighter against Tom's body, fed him eyedroppers of water, felt his forehead, rechecked his temperature, and worried. A lot.

That night she dozed fitfully on the daybed, getting up often to check on Tom, scooping out the ice melt and checking that he was breathing. At two a.m., his fever was down to 101. At four-thirty a.m., it was 100. At sunrise it hovered just over 99.

Felicity was exhausted. She fed the cats breakfast and made herself her instant coffee, leaning against the counter like a zombie as she sipped, waiting for the brain fog to lift.

Mm-rr-ur-ur-ur-ur! A forlorn P. Diddy Kitty stared under the daybed.

"Not now, Dids. I've got a lot going on."

Rrrr-ur-ur-ur-ur-ur.

With a groan, she set her coffee on the banquette table, plunked down to her knees, and reached under the daybed for the squeaky mouse. She found it, popped to a stand, and tossed it down the center aisle of the trailer. Diddy and Melrose scampered after it.

Just then, she noticed Boudica out of the corner of her eye, perched on the table, one paw extended, in the process of smacking the coffee cup to the floor.

The next thing Felicity knew, she'd snatched the cup in midair and placed it in the sink.

Boudica stared, her single eye widened in surprise. *Mmmrrrooooow!* she said.

Alphonse raised a bushy brow. *P-p-p-prrrrowpt?*

"What the...?"

How had she moved like that? Lightning-quick reflexes had never been her thing. Especially with her bum...

Wait.

Felicity patted her knee. No pain. She smacked it, hard, but

80

still no pain. Which didn't make sense. She'd fallen on it the day she'd found Tom, and it'd been throbbing ever since. But now it didn't hurt. It didn't throb. Which was impossible because she'd just retrieved the squeaky mouse, and her knee *always* hurt after she retrieved the squeaky mouse!

Felicity experimented with a deep knee bend. Still no discomfort, even after a night on the daybed that should've left her as stiff as one of Rich's starched dress shirts. She bent at the waist and touched her toes, something she'd not been able to do since the first season of *Downton Abbey*.

She straightened. Her cats gathered close, some at her feet, some in the booth, and some on the table. They perked their ears and cocked their heads.

"Hold on just a damn minute," she said to them. "Do you guys know what's going on here? If you do, want to clue me in?"

Rrrrp, Mojo said, his head tipping to the mirror.

She looked, saw the gold collar, and laughed. "It's the necklace, isn't it? It's got *powers* of some kind, doesn't it?"

Meeew-mew! said Scratch and Sniff.

Rrrrrrooooooow. Rick James stood on his hind legs and kneaded her jeans.

Felicity stared into the mirror again, Rick James now hanging from her pantleg. "The woo-woo started the morning I went into town and came home with Tom, who wore this as his cat collar." She caressed the gold at her throat.

"The cashier at the Constant Cupboard called me Cleopatra, and I think he was on to something. This looks very... *Egyptian,* doesn't it?"

Rraaorr! Valkyrie's tail twitched.

"But..." Felicity frowned at her reflection, then at the cats. She widened her stance and rested her fists on her hips. "This better not be some curse-of-the-mummy bullshit, because I've been cursed enough for several lifetimes."

Eeeeyerrrrr, Gumbo agreed.

"Let's think this through, step by step." She began pacing the center aisle, Rick James still swinging from her jeans. "The first bizarre thing was my car showing up, all new and shiny. Then the comforter. And the deliveries." She stopped at the daybed and turned. "Wait, that's not right. I'm forgetting something." Felicity nibbled on the inside of her cheek, racking her brain. "The frogs! The black storm! The scorpions! All of it happened just before I found Tom! Is it connected?"

With Rick James still attached, Felicity slid into the booth, brushed aside the crossword book and her current corner of the sand mandala puzzle—plus several cats—and then ripped open a few of the envelopes from bill collectors. At least they would be of some use. She used the first aid kit scissors to cut the envelopes into two-inch-wide squares, then grabbed her crossword pen.

On the first slip she wrote: *Raining Frogs.* On the next: *Alien Mothership Rainstorm.* Melrose chose that moment to hop onto the table, spread out lengthwise, and roll around, purring with such gusto that Felicity couldn't hear herself think.

"Not now, Mel. How about you sit on my lap instead?" Melrose morphed into a boneless blob when Felicity picked him up. "You're such a lump." Once in his new purring spot, the orange fluff ball seemed happy enough.

"OK. Where was I?" She grabbed a few more squares. On the next slip, she wrote: *Scorpion Parade.* Then, *Rich's Boils.* "That really was disgusting," she told Teena Marie, who had curled up next to her hip. "I mean, he's a jerk, but I don't wish him disfigured, and those bumps weren't anything normal. He said he didn't have leprosy, but considering how bizarre everything is, would that be out of the question?" She decided to amend the boil notation with: (*Leprosy?*)

The next few were produced in rapid succession: *Comforter, Car, Swarm of Feral Cats, Kitty-Korner.com, Mystery Lawyer.*

Felicity paused, pen hovering. She'd almost scribbled that the ice had been on sale, but glanced up to find Mojo seated on the opposite booth bench, his frosty green gaze barely clearing the table edge. He seemed doubtful. "No? The ice was a normal coincidence? No deeper meaning? Fair enough."

Rrrrrrp.

"Well, now, hold on, Mo. I'm just laying out all the pieces to see what I'm working with, right?" She gestured at the tabletop. "Shouldn't I focus on collecting as many bits of information as possible for the time being? I can always cull later, right?"

Rrrp.

She nodded in agreement and wrote: *Block Ice on Sale.*

Next, she jotted, *Knee Doesn't Hurt, Quick Reflexes, Cats Line Up,* and *Can Touch My Toes!* After that, she moved on to the big-ticket items: *Cat Survives Mortal Wounds* and *Cat Becomes Man.* The last set of clues were more complicated, so she used the first aid tape to secure three squares together. She wrote, *Man Removes Necklace with No Clasp.* She repeated the taping process for another long clue: *Man Puts Necklace on Me; Won't Release.*

When she was done, she taped each piece to the cabinet doors above the sink, returned to the booth, and examined her work.

"None of this makes the slightest bit of sense. Storms and frogs and boils and magic jewelry…. The only thing I know for sure is that this isn't just about me. I'm a part of it, somehow, but it's bigger. And I need answers."

Mrrp, Gumbo said.

"Right! We're right back at the necklace! How old is this thing, anyway? Was it snatched in a museum heist? A home invasion? Is the FBI tracking it down, right now, as we speak?"

Rrraaaooooow. Circe sashayed toward the booth, her blue point tail slicing the air behind her.

"I'm not being the least bit melodramatic, Circe. In case you missed it, a cat just turned into a human, right here in the Airstream! These are unusual times."

Felicity tapped the pen against the tabletop. Mojo assumed it was an invitation to play and reached out to bat it with a paw. She rescued the pen, feeling her heart pound and her underarms spritz. She'd gone and worked herself into a full-on tizzy.

"What's going on? Who's the cat-man? Who sent me all that stuff and fixed my car? How did a little cat collar become a huge necklace, and why'd he put it on my neck? Does it really have powers? Does it even belong to him, and, if not, to whom does this necklace belong?"

Alphonse's whiskers twitched. *Rrrow.*

"I'm an English teacher, Al. *Whom* is proper syntax, and I won't apologize for using it. So I'll ask again: *to whom does this necklace belong?*"

"Bastet."

Felicity spun around at the sound of the deep voice, shocked to see Tom standing in the bedroom doorway.

"The necklace belongs to the Goddess Bastet."

CHAPTER FIVE

Felicity shot to her feet. "You should be in bed!"

Tom swayed in the doorway, the bedsheet tied low on his bare hips. His left hand was propped against the paneled wall, and Felicity's keys dangled from his right.

"Can't." He spoke in a sandpaper whisper. "Got to collect her body and perform the ritual. I'll be back soon."

"What body? Ritual? Bast*who*?"

He staggered toward the door, but Felicity blocked him. "Don't even think about it, bub. You're weak and wounded. You're naked. You don't have a license. You're a damned *cat*!"

He glanced down at himself and nearly lost his balance. "I'm human. I'm covered. And I'm licensed to drive in the State of Oregon."

She grabbed him before he collapsed, cupped his elbow, and guided him into the booth.

"Sit. Stay."

She filled a tall glass at the kitchen sink, questions flooding her brain. *Is this really happening? Did he kill someone? And wow, they'll give a license to anyone these days, won't they?* "Here. You're dehydrated." She placed the glass in his hands and retreated, uneasy and worried that she might have to make a run for it.

He emptied the water in three gulps and then raised the glass. "More. Please."

She refilled it, and while he drank, she ventured close enough that she could reach out and rest her hand on his damp forehead. "The fever broke."

He nodded, wiping his mouth with his forearm. "How long have I been here?"

"As a cat or…?"

"Both."

"Let's see. I found you last Wednesday morning and now it's midmorning Monday."

He stiffened, eyes widening in alarm. "What? That can't be right. The battle was Tuesday night, which would mean I've been here almost a week."

"I'm not aware of any recent battles around here, but you've been…" she gestured at his torso "you know, a naked person since yesterday morning."

He pushed himself to a stand, and Felicity pressed him down again. She snagged the car keys from his grip and shoved them in her jeans pocket.

"You're in no shape to go anywhere."

"But I failed her. I have to perform the ritual. I have to get back to Portland."

Oh. He was from Portland. That explained at least some of the weirdness.

Felicity leaned against the sink and crossed her arms over her chest. "Look, Tom, I'm on the verge of a complete freak-out right now

86

because you used to be a cat and now you're a man, rambling on about dead bodies and rituals and goddesses, and I'm starting to think you must be part of some shapeshifting murder cult. You can see why I might go there, right?"

"You don't understand."

"No, *you* don't understand." Felicity pointed at him. "I rescued an injured cat by the side of the road. That's all I signed up for, and even *that* was a stretch in my current circumstances. I want no part of whatever *this* shit is."

"A little late now," he mumbled.

"What did you say?"

He shook his head, his breathing still ragged. He looked at her with mismatched eyes filled with torment. "I have no choice, Felicity. It's my sworn duty to get her body and perform the ritual!"

No matter who he was or how implausible any of this seemed, his despair was heartfelt. Maybe yelling at him wasn't the right way to get the answers she needed. "Look, I hear your concern, but if your friend died a week ago, she's still dead, so there's no big rush."

He turned away to stare out the window.

"Let's make a deal, Tom. You'll eat something and tell me what the hell's bells is going on and then I'll drive you where you need to go. Agreed?"

"Fine." He dropped his head into his hands and massaged his temples.

It was hard to take her eyes off him. He was in the middle of a crisis, but, obviously, this guy had survived his share of trouble. He was honed and strong, and his body was so beat up that Ronnie's stitches at his waist looked like paper cuts in comparison. On his right side alone, she saw what looked like old bullet holes, slashes, punctures, and burns. He was a real-life fighting tomcat. Or a soldier. And though he looked no more than thirty, the haunted expression she'd seen in his eyes belonged to a weary old man.

"I'll make you some eggs." She turned to the single-burner stove, fairly certain he posed no physical danger to her, because if that had been his intent, he could have strangled her in her sleep. "It's all I've got so I really hope you like them." She spun around, suddenly aware she might have committed a faux pas. "Unless you'd prefer kibble or a can of…"

"Eggs are fine."

"All right." She grabbed a bowl, cracked the shells, and whisked three eggs with a dash of milk, all while wondering how to start the kind of conversation required under these circumstances. "Let's start simple. I'm Felicity."

"Yes, I know. Felicity Rennie Cheshire."

She poured the mixture into a pan. "It's pronounced Ren-*ay*, actually."

"Apologies."

Felicity saw Mojo break formation and hop down from the daybed. He skulked toward the booth, the hair along his spine bristling. *Rrrrraowp,* he said.

"Someone has a thick accent."

Mojo retreated, then slunk his way back to the daybed.

"I have an accent? Really?" She used a spatula to flip the omelet. "I've never lived anywhere but boring old Pine Beach."

"Why do you call me Tom?"

Felicity looked over her shoulder, the spatula in her hand. "Because that's what you are. Were, when I found you, anyway. A tomcat."

He gave a stiff nod, carefully pushed himself to a stand and bent at the waist. "I am Tubastet-af-Ankh, *hem-netjer-tepi* of the Ever-

Living Goddess Bastet, temple guard of Per-Bast, warrior and trainer of the Acolytes." He winced with pain when he straightened and slid into the booth again.

Felicity's mouth had dropped open. "That's... Tuba*whatnow?* Can I just stick with Tom?" She could have sworn he almost smiled.

"Sure."

Felicity flipped the omelet one more time and turned off the flame. She was determined to sound casual even though the thoughts tumbled inside her head like sneakers in a Laundromat dryer. "So, Tom. You're a cat?"

"Not currently."

"Right. But sometimes."

"Sometimes."

"Um, how does that work, exactly?" She plopped the eggs onto her only unchipped plate and set it in front of him along with a fork, a section of paper towel, and salt and pepper. She refilled his water.

"I've already told you that I'm Tubastet-af-Ankh, *hem-netjer-tepi...*"

"I have no idea what any of that means."

Tom stuck his fork in the eggs and brought a large bite to his mouth, closing his eyes with pleasure. "This is very good. Thank you." He'd gobbled half the omelet before he answered. "It means I'm the High Priest of the Ever-Living Goddess Bastet."

"The one who owns the necklace."

"Yes."

"OK." A mishmash of random trivia began to coalesce in her mind. The kid at the Constant Cupboard had been right. "Ancient Egypt, correct?"

"Exactly." Tom polished off the eggs. Even half-starved, he had impeccable table manners—for a sometimes cat.

"And Bastet is the goddess of cats?"

"Among other things."

Felicity took a big slug of her barely lukewarm coffee, wishing it were Jose Cuervo. What was she *doing*, trying to piece together something rational and normal from what was a completely ridiculous scenario? But did she have a choice? Tom had just snarfed down a plate of eggs. He was real. He was human. And she needed to keep sharp because some ancient goddess's gold necklace was stuck on her neck, and she had a feeling that strings could be attached.

She cleared her throat. "So Bastet, a goddess, gave you some kind of magical ability to be a cat whenever it strikes your fancy?"

He pushed the empty plate aside and took a gulp of water. "It's a power granted to me when my service is required."

"Your service? The sworn duty you mentioned?"

"Yes. I train the chosen human Acolyte who, every sixty-three years, must defeat Apep, the cast-out god of chaos. He is Bastet's nemesis. She defeated him originally, long, long ago, while protecting her father, Ra. Apep was banished from the God Realm and sentenced to exile here, in the mortal world, in a perpetual cycle of reanimation. This means a human must defeat him each time. Do you have any tea?"

She'd lost all feeling in her limbs. She blinked. "*Huh?*"

"Earl Grey, oolong, whatever you have on hand would be fine."

Felicity went through the motions of putting the kettle on and rummaging through the cupboards for an uncracked teacup, all while her mind scrabbled for solid ground. She glanced at the notes taped to the cupboard above her, remembering how she'd convinced herself she wasn't crazy. But now, she questioned that self-diagnosis.

"You know, I don't mean to be dense." She spoke in her most pleasant voice, her back still to Tom. "I'm really trying my best to follow along. And I used to teach middle school English, so I've seen and heard pretty much everything, but..." She found one stray, crunchy tea bag behind a tin of sardines, then placed the teacup with the tea bag on the table before him. "Anyway, how long have you had the warrior priest job?"

Tom seemed to consider her question with care. "I began the year Octavian annexed Egypt as part of the Roman Empire. Do you have any sugar?"

Felicity turned away again, her hands shaking as she found the sugar bowl. "That's..." her voice caught. "That's almost two thousand years ago." She took three deep breaths before she faced him again. "So you're telling me you're some kind of god too?"

He laughed for the first time. "No. I'm fully human. Well, except for when I'm a cat."

"But you're immortal?"

"Obviously not, since I'd be dead if you hadn't saved me."

"Then I'm confused. You're not immortal, but you don't age like a normal person? Or normal cat? Or cat-person?"

"Correct."

When the tea kettle whistled, Felicity nearly jumped out of her own skin. She poured from the kettle, hoping he wouldn't notice how she trembled. She slid into the booth opposite Tom. "You look young for your age."

One corner of his mouth hitched. "You're funny, Felicity. Thanks for the tea." He dumped half the contents of the sugar bowl into his cup.

Funny? Not hardly. She was confused, worried, slack-jawed, and mind-boggled but not anywhere near a joking mood. She leaned across the banquette table to look Tom straight in the eye, making sure he gave her his full attention. "Now, I want to talk about this heavy gold thing stuck to my neck."

Tom let his gaze wander out the window to the garden again and took a sip of tea. "It's a long story. I promise I'll tell you all about it in the car."

Felicity winced. "Yeah, OK, but you can't go to Portland dressed like that. You know that, right?"

He looked down at himself. "I have nothing else to wear. I had to ditch my clothes and shoes near some kid's backyard trampoline."

"Happens to the best of us." Felicity got up and headed to the closet to root around for a pair of sweatpants, an extra-large T-shirt, and some flip-flops. It was her only option, seeing that she was fresh out of menswear. She turned to find Tom already on his feet and untying the bedsheet.

"Wait!" She straight-armed the clothes in his direction and averted her eyes.

"Thank you."

She gave him a moment to dress, turned, and gasped. He couldn't be seen in public like that! It was worse than naked! The sweatpants fit like ballet tights. The shirt exposed his belly button. His long toes flopped over the flip.

"Let's go."

He was already out the door and flip-flopping down the metal stairs. Felicity grabbed an old, crocheted scarf from her closet, then her purse, and ran to catch up.

"We need large, plastic garbage bags. Do you have any?"

"In the shed. But… trash bags are part of your friend's ritual?"

"No, and she's Bastet's Acolyte, not my friend. Her name is… *was*… Misty." Tom marched to Tasha's garden shed near the fence, where she kept the mower, tools, and forty years' worth of broken pots and moldy bird seed. "I take it you've never seen a body that's been dead a week?"

Felicity tasted bile on the back of her tongue and swallowed hard. "I've never seen any kind of dead body."

"I have. Trust me. We need plastic bags." He swung open the door to the shed, grabbed a handful of bags and checked the shelves. "Excellent. These disinfecting wipes will help with the ritual too."

It was a miracle she didn't yarf all over his flip-flops, and though she had a thousand questions about what he planned to do once he got the dead body into the bags, she couldn't bring herself to ask. In fact, she'd rather not know.

Within minutes they were speeding the eighty-plus miles into Portland. "Where to, exactly?"

"Chinatown."

Felicity whipped her head around to stare at him. Cat-man was just full of plot twists. Too bad she hadn't yet been given the title of the story.

"OK, Tom. We're in the car. Tell me about the necklace."

He sat up straight in the passenger seat, his face blank. He was stalling. And Felicity's shock and confusion was morphing into a creeping dread.

"Tom?"

"I haven't thanked you for saving me, Felicity. I'm forever in your debt."

She laughed. "So the necklace is a hostess gift?"

"Not exactly."

"Then what, *exactly*, is it?"

"Also, I want to thank you for helping me perform the funerary rites. Once we're done, her soul can rest."

"And the necklace?"

He didn't respond. He looked out the window at the blur of

tall pines, then glanced down at his scarred hands. He was avoiding her, and it pissed her off. "Cat got your tongue, Tom?"

The car drifted toward the center rumble strip.

"Stay in your lane. The last thing we need is to be in an accident."

"You're telling me how to drive now?"

No response.

Finally, he spoke again, in that deep, rough voice. "Have I mentioned that I've never performed the funerary rites before? I've never had to. The Acolyte has never lost the battle until now."

The dread was no longer creeping. It had lodged itself in the back of Felicity's throat and sunk in its sharp claws. "Take the necklace off me."

"I can't."

"Won't."

"No, I physically can't remove it. The *usekh* will only release at the appropriate time." He leaned back against the headrest.

"Which is…?"

"Sometime after the funerary rites."

"Uh-huh." Felicity's classroom years had made her downright psychic when it came to predicting those dog-ate-my-homework moments, and what was unacceptable from a twelve-year-old was insulting from a grown man. "Well, listen up, ye olde trainer of Acolytes. I need you to tell me everything. The truth. Now."

She turned to see that Tom's eyelids had drooped, and her hackles smoothed a bit. "You look like death warmed over. No offense."

"None taken. Moving from cat to human takes a huge amount of energy."

"Then why'd you do it?"

He shrugged. "I became a cat to escape Apep. It's easier to heal as a cat, too. But I had to be human... in order... to..." His eyes shut. His thick, black lashes lay against the rise of his cheekbone. His mouth went slack.

Great. Felicity tugged at the heavy necklace around her neck, worried she was choking. It was psychosomatic, surely. Probably. But then she found it difficult to breathe. She needed to calm herself. "Damn it, I need this thing off me."

Tom mumbled something that sounded a lot like *least of your worries,* but before she could get clarification, he was snoring.

The guy sure knew how to nod off at the most inconvenient times.

Tom slept most of the way to the city. Felicity appreciated the quiet; it gave her some time to think, to wrap her head around the truly *incredible* turn of events.

She failed.

So instead, she played a vocabulary game with herself to think of as many synonyms for that word as she could.

Impossible. Remarkable. Implausible. Hard to believe. Spectacular. Extraordinary. Inexplicable. Abnormal. Uncanny. Eerie. Supernatural. Psychedelic. Nightmarish.

Eventually Tom woke up, stretched, and took a few deep breaths before he straightened in the seat. "Sorry. I didn't mean to pass out for so long."

"Guess you needed it."

"You doing all right?"

She glared at him.

"I mean, with the driving?"

She snort laughed.

"I know you want answers."

Felicity waited. Until she'd had enough waiting. "That's it? Isn't this where a normal person would start filling me in on what's going on? The last I heard, your student, the Acolyte, died fighting the chaos dude."

"Apep."

"Who killed her and attacked you."

"Yes."

"While you were human?"

"Yes."

For some reason that comforted Felicity, knowing someone wasn't so evil that they'd go around trying to murder innocent cats. On purpose, anyway. But wait.

"Did—what's the guy's name again?"

"Apep. In the Hellenic tradition he is called Apophis."

"So when Apep attacked you, did he know… you know… that you're also a cat?"

"Of course."

"Oh." Well. *Asshole.*

Tom's breathing deepened again, but Felicity wasn't letting him off the hook. "After we find your friend's body and do your fancy Egyptian funeral thing, the necklace will fall off, right?"

"No."

"I have to do something else?"

"Yes."

"Something easy?"

More silence, and it pissed her off.

"Tom!"

He wouldn't look at her, just closed his eyes again. The jerk.

"What else do I have to do to put this insanity behind me? The funeral stuff and then what? Burn incense for your goddess lady friend? Mumble an incantation? Walk like an Egyptian? All I know is that if this requires any amount of cash, you've put your fancy collar on the wrong woman. Joke's on you, bub!"

Finally, he opened his eyes, one turquoise and one gold, and looked at her. Felicity had to focus on the road but felt the heat of his gaze nonetheless. The necklace warmed her throat, too, and a tingle raced across her flesh.

"The *usekh* you bear belongs to Bastet."

"You said that."

"I mean, it's personally *hers*. She used to wear it. So long ago that it's incomprehensible to humans."

"An actual ancient goddess wore this?"

"Yes. It still carries her essence. It's a great honor, you know, to wear it. Apart from me, only the Acolyte gets that privilege."

It took a minute for Felicity to register the words. Then they began to sink in. "This necklace can only be worn by the Acolyte? As in the *dead* Acolyte? The one we're about to scoop into plastic trash bags?"

"Yes."

"Are you telling me that *I'm* now the Acolyte?"

He shot her a dazzling smile. On any other occasion, she might have allowed herself to be dazzled, but at that moment, all she wanted to do was slap him.

"Congratulations, Felicity," he said.

Blood throbbed in her ears. She scanned road signs for the next available exit, and though her mouth suddenly felt as if it were filled with sand, she managed to ask one more question.

"How does the Acolyte get out of the fucking necklace, Tom?"

His smile fell. His expression turned stone-cold serious. "You have to save the world, Felicity Renee Cheshire, or die trying. Only then will the necklace release."

CHAPTER SIX

Felicity paced up and down the length of the gas station parking lot, fighting a full-on panic attack. It seemed like a lifetime ago that her biggest concern was that she might be crazy. Crazy would have been way easier than this. Crazy got you a nice room where they spoon-fed you soup and let you watch home renovation shows on an endless loop.

But no. She'd been chosen to fight an ancient Egyptian god of evil and chaos, who'd been exiled from the immortal realm eons ago, when the cat Goddess Bastet vanquished him while protecting her father, Ra, who, Felicity had just learned, was none other than the creator god of Egypt. The Big Kahuna.

Sure. Why not?

Felicity pivoted and marched back to where Tom leaned against the car in a patch of sunshine. At that instant, she hated him for his ability to be so calm, so freakishly still, the way he'd been as a cat.

"Why me?"

"I told you."

"Right. Every sixty-three years, you trap some clueless fifteen-year-old…"

"It's a great honor…"

"…in this necklace and train her for three years, make her fight to save humanity against the god of chaos, who, as you mentioned as an aside, sometimes takes the form of a snake! Are you joking? A *snake*?"

"It's a bit more complicated…"

"Why *me*? I'm not a teenager, in case you hadn't noticed!" She stormed off again, lapped the windshield squeegee, only to head back his way. This time, he intercepted her and steadied her by holding on to her upper arms.

"Listen carefully, Felicity. Humanity is in danger. Right now."

She tried to squirm from his grip. "Humans are always in danger—fires, floods, disease, war, hurricanes, asteroids…"

"Danger from Apep."

She stopped squirming. "How much danger?"

"End-of-the-world danger. Unimaginable cruelty. The more suffering he can inflict, the better. An asteroid would be merciful in comparison."

"All that from Apep?"

"Yes. And the only one who can stop him is a champion chosen by Bastet. The woman who wears the *usekh*."

She spun away from his grasp.

"I know this is a lot to take in. I'm sorry."

Felicity made another loop through the parking lot, wondering if she was somehow to blame for this. Was it punishment for taking home another wounded cat? Poetic justice for a cat lady with a savior complex? Or had the mortally wounded cat she rescued become human at the first chance he got, just so he could slap the damned necklace on her without her permission? Talk about your basic lack of consent!

Well, fuck it all. She understood now. She stomped right up to Tom again. "You picked me because you were in a bind and you had no other choice."

"Yes."

"Because I was *there*."

"Yes."

"How flattering." Her head swam with too much oxygen. She attempted to slow her breathing, but couldn't. When she stared off into to the trees and saw that the world had begun to spin, she released a panicked laugh. "Why sixty-three years, Tom? That's oddly specific. Can't you just ask for an extension and find someone better?"

"That's not how it works, but I will answer your question."

"Can't wait."

"Certain numbers are divine, and three is the sacred foundation of plurality. Once Bastet's Acolyte destroys Apep, he requires time to regenerate from the piece of himself he's left behind, hidden somewhere on the earthly plane. And three times three is nine; seven is the number of the gods; and nine times seven is…"

"*Math?*" Felicity stalked toward him. "Are you *kidding* me? Saving the world involves *math*? I was an English major!" She began to hyperventilate in earnest. "We are so fucked."

"You're in shock, Felicity."

"Ya *think?*" She yelled so loudly that people looked up from their gas pumps.

"Lean forward. Place your palms on your knees."

"My knees!" She spun in a circle, the gas pumps and mini-mart blurring in her vision. "Why don't my knees hurt anymore, Tom? Huh? Is there something going on with the necklace and my body?"

"Yes and no."

"I just wanted to help an injured cat."

"I understand. Breathe deeply." He pressed on her upper back until she was bent at the waist, hands to knees.

She turned her head and glanced up at him. "You said you spend three years training fifteen-year-old maidens."

"I do."

"Using an old book."

"The Priestly Texts describe the Six Steps of Defeating Apep."

"That's all very Buffy-fabulous, but…"

"Her name was Misty, Misty McAlpine of Clackamas, Oregon."

"But fifteen is *decades* in my rearview mirror! I haven't been a virgin since the summer Tasha and I… never mind." She straightened, fighting off the dizziness.

"I'll be right beside you the whole time, I promise."

"Yeah, but you trained Buffy…"

"Misty."

"To beat the snake…"

"Not always a snake."

"Not always a snake, not always a cat; was the necklace girl always a girl or did she presto-change-o into…"

"The Acolyte."

"The point is, you trained Buffy for three whole years and she *still* lost. She's dead!"

"Not quite the full three years, and Misty hadn't mastered everything. On top of that, she was undisciplined and impatient, immature for her age. She went after Apep before she was ready, without me."

Felicity saw guilt flash in his eyes. Pain. And though she felt bad for him, she had bigger concerns. "You didn't get the whole three years with Buffy, but *I* get the full three, right?" He didn't answer. "*Right, Tom?*"

He guided her to the edge of the parking lot. Whatever he was about to share was for her ears only, apparently.

"You aren't grasping what I'm telling you, Felicity. Apep is already here. *Now.* Once he recovers from his battle injuries, he'll carry out his plan. Unfortunately, I don't know what that plan is."

"Excuse me?"

"The attack—whatever form it takes—could begin at any time, if it hasn't already. We don't have three years."

Felicity swallowed, trying to stay calm, which was impossible because she was starting to get the big picture: she was being thrown to the wolves. Or, more accurately, a single demon snake.

"I don't get the full three years?"

"I'm afraid not."

"Fine. I can do an accelerated program. I'm a fast learner. I used to teach English. Did I tell you that?" Her words came too fast. Hysteria slithered up her throat. "Six steps from some old magic scrolls. Totally manageable. I mean, the electric slide has over twenty steps, and I learned most of them in one night, half snockered. I can lock down six steps in...so how long do we have?"

"Two weeks."

"Two weeks." Felicity's lips went numb.

"Maybe a few more days." Tom tried to sound reassuring. He failed.

She rubbed her hands over her face, as if she could scour away the panic, then looked up at him. "You expect me to shove three years of training into two weeks and then defeat a powerful ancient Egyptian homicidal maniac? Or disaster befalls all of humankind? Do I have that about right?"

Tom nodded solemnly. "Yes."

Felicity looked him right in his beautiful, mismatched eyes. "That's a hard *no*."

She turned around and headed into the mini-mart.

After two thousand years in this job, he should be better at it. He'd been in charge of Bastet's Acolyte since the Romans defeated Egypt and took over the temples, preventing him and fellow priests from performing the ritual to defeat Apep.

Damn the Romans, the arrogant bastards, with their roads and aqueducts and infuriating numerals.

This was all their fault.

He found a sunny spot on the hood of the car, stretched out, and watched Felicity inside the mini-mart.

She was the thirty-second Acolyte of Bastet. The only one, though, who had not been called by the Goddess herself. *He'd* called Felicity, and that made him very nervous.

Bastet always called wisely. The chosen Acolyte was young and agile, usually descended from one of the old families, prepared from birth for her sacred obligation. The chosen one began instruction once she was on the verge of womanhood and imbued with the optimism and nobility of purpose required to transcend her fears. Her unwavering faith propelled her through grueling training and into victory over darkness. And for many, many centuries, all had gone according to plan.

Until the thirty-first Acolyte. For the first time in his service to Bastet, he had failed. His Acolyte faltered, and he did not usher her to victory in battle.

He stretched, careful not to tug at the itchy sutures at his sides.

He scratched his scalp where his hair had started to grow back.

Had he gotten lazy? Complacent? Had he somehow started to underestimate Apep, forgotten all the Opponent was capable of?

He'd had his share of close calls. He remembered how number twenty-five's *khopesh* repeatedly became tangled in her farthingale, but she was too modest to change her style of clothes as he'd instructed. She'd persevered, however, and was victorious in the end.

Number seventeen accidentally beheaded her nursemaid during training, and she'd been temporarily hobbled with fear for the eternal damnation of her soul. Yeah, things got pretty dicey in that go-around, but even she managed to bounce back in time to defeat Apep.

This time, the Acolyte was dead, the replacement was untrained, and the end was right around the corner. The cracks in the world were already apparent. The god of chaos and destruction was preparing to strike.

He looked into the mini-mart to see Felicity Cheshire perusing the market's snack food aisle.

She was a spirited woman, he'd give her that, but one so beaten down by life that she struggled to maintain faith—in herself, in anything. Felicity had other important traits, though. She was humble. She was courageous. She had retained a sense of humor, a sharp mind, and a strong body.

Yeah, that last part was a stretch.

Felicity's body was flawed and scarred, with its share of wrinkly bits. But he was scarred too. They had that in common; both were survivors. Felicity had persevered through disease, divorce, despair, and deprivation. That gave him some comfort.

As a bonus, Felicity possessed extraordinary empathy for her fellow living creatures. Her actions reflected a sincere generosity of spirit. And she enjoyed the company of cats.

Lots and lots of cats.

Considering all this—and the fact that he had been forced to make a desperate choice when time was short and the stakes were dire—he supposed he could have done worse than Felicity Cheshire.

He watched her through the glass doors—apparently torn between a chocolate bar and a bag of tortilla chips—and asked himself the only question that mattered: could Felicity carry out the mission? If Misty had faltered despite her youth and devotion to training, how could Felicity succeed?

Two weeks? They'd be lucky to get even that. And if they didn't move aggressively and soon, the bastard would gain the upper hand and choose the time and place. Almost a week had passed since Misty's death. It was a miracle that Apep hadn't already struck. Misty must have wounded him badly in those tunnels.

Thank you for that, Misty McAlpine of Clackamas, Oregon.

It looked like Felicity had chosen a candy bar and a can of something. She exited the store and slumped against the outside wall, near the front doors, talking to herself.

There she was, Bastet's thirty-second Acolyte.

Likely the last.

He climbed back into the car and slithered down into the passenger seat. Yeah, Felicity was right.

They were so fucked.

The double-chocolate crunch bar helped.

So did the cold Diet Coke that Felicity sipped as she leaned against the outside wall of the mini-mart, watching Tom lounge in the car. It was so damn unfair. What had she ever done to deserve this shit-show of a life?

Well, Tuba-what-the-fuck could just find someone else to do

his dirty work. Someone younger and spryer. Someone who could still manage a good cry every few years.

She took another swig of her soda, then laughed so hard it almost shot out of her nose. "It's always the same ole same ole, isn't it?" She spoke aloud, but to no one in particular. "It's always been, *Hey, Felicity'll do it. She always says yes. She always tries so hard. It's not like Felicity Cheshire has anything else going on. Ha!*"

She glanced around, embarrassed that she'd been ranting to herself in public. But no one had noticed. No one paid any attention to the middle-aged woman in a winter scarf, sucking down a Coke, snarfing a candy bar, and talking to nobody.

This, also, was the same ole same ole.

She shoved the rest of the candy into her mouth, thinking about the novel she'd been reading when she found Tom. Life imitating art again because here she was, expected to clean up a man's mess, and oh, by the way, would she mind doing it immediately and while wearing a magic gold necklace?

Was this supposed to be OK? What was next? Maybe get him a beer while he's watching the game or make him a sandwich or put her own dreams on hold so she can support him through law school, and then what? She gets tossed aside for a younger model!

Felicity tossed the wrapper in the trash and sighed.

True, Tom wasn't Richard Hume, but he was male and he was asking her to do something she didn't want to do, and it pissed her off, *damn it.*

"Cool necklace." The young hipster's eyes widened in interest as he strode up. "Where'd you get it?"

Felicity snorted, thinking how it would sound if she spoke the truth. "Oh, just some little shop in Cannon Beach. Sorry, don't remember the name."

He walked away with a disappointed shrug.

Yeah, well, he'd better get used to disappointment since there'd be a lot of it when the world ended.

The world…

was about…

to end.

Everyone was going to die.

As she threw her can into the recycling bin, she saw through the glass storefront to a smiling young mother who helped each of her kids pick out a candy treat. She noticed two teenage boys trying to buy beer with a fake ID and an old man scratching off a lottery ticket, hope springing eternal.

A warm tingle settled across her breastbone, beneath the necklace's blue center stone. She felt the heat spread into her limbs.

The necklace. Around *her* neck, not the hipster's neck. Not the neck of a fifteen-year-old maiden with plenty of cartilage in her joints. The necklace was, for whatever unknowable reason, *hers*. And it wouldn't come off unless she was dead or kicked Apep's ass.

All right. *Fine.* Maybe just one last time, but this was it.

If she survived this, which was a big if, she'd never again drop everything and do what no one else could or would. Never again would she rescue a damn cat or speak to a damn man.

Because look what it got her!

Felicity tossed the scarf around her throat, making sure the necklace was covered, then made her way to the car. Without a word, she started the engine. The two of them nursed their respective affronts in silence as she continued on to Portland.

About ten minutes from their exit, Felicity realized her back didn't hurt. Maybe it was another effect of the necklace. Or maybe it was because she hadn't been holding herself rigid to fight the Saturn's shimmy to the left when the speedometer went over thirty.

She cleared her throat. "Thank you for fixing my car, by the way. I'm still not on board with this whole thing, but I know you fixed the car and got me the comforter and the stuff from Kitty-Korner and the fake lawyer, too. I appreciate it all."

"He's real."

"Who?"

"Alexander. The lawyer. He arranged for everything."

"How'd he know, though? Those were things I'd wished for privately."

"I told him."

"You *told* him? You talked with him when you were a cat?"

"That's when connecting with Alexander's easiest. Otherwise, I have to use a phone like everyone else."

"But not when you're a cat?"

He frowned. "Cats don't use phones. Some use toilets, I've heard, but not phones."

Felicity rolled her eyes. "What I'm asking is *how* did you contact him when you were a cat?"

"We have a strong connection; you might call it telepathy. Like what you have with your cats."

She huffed. "I don't do psychic shit with my cats."

"Of course you do."

"Nope. I don't."

"You have the strongest connection to the one you call Boudica. It's not her real name, by the way, but she doesn't mind."

"Not her real...?"

"Take a left here."

Felicity made the turn and followed his directions through Chinatown because he had a certain place he wanted to park, apparently.

"Your cats are devoted to you, Felicity," he continued. "They're all quite perceptive... well, except for the one you call Gumbo. He's an idiot. But still, devoted. When I was deciding whether to bell you, I..."

"*Bell* me? I'm pretty sure I'd remember if someone *belled* me."

"When the *usekh* is given to the new Acolyte, she's belled. Because of the bell on the..."

"Got it."

"Anyway, I took into consideration your loving connection between you and your cats before choosing you."

"Remind me to thank them."

They found a parking spot in an underground garage, but even after she'd turned off the engine, Felicity hesitated to get out. She turned in the seat to face Tom. "You did a mind meld with the lawyer. Fine. Not the weirdest thing that's happened today. But how did *you* know what I needed?"

He blinked, thick lashes shadowing his mismatched irises. "I just listened. I don't think you realize how much you talk to your cats."

Was he *laughing* at her? "Well, that's totally normal. Everybody does."

"OK, but you have lengthy conversations with them."

She stiffened. "I live alone. What's your point?"

"You asked how I knew what you needed, and that's the answer. Though Boudica was the one to suggest the new comforter, and since I'd bled all over it, I figured it would be a nice gesture. Aren't we getting out?"

Felicity turned to stare at the gray concrete wall of the parking garage. She felt uneasy, spied upon, like someone had invaded her privacy. But he was right—she did talk to her cats. She'd talked to Tom when he was in cat form, too. She heard herself mumble, "*You must fight along with me. Do you understand?*"

"Exactly."

They remained quiet for a moment. Then, in a gentle voice, Tom asked, "Are you all right?"

"We're headed to the underground Shanghai tunnels, aren't we? That's where Apep killed Buffy."

"Misty. But yeah."

"I took a guided tour of the tunnels once. Must have been fifteen years ago. That place is creepy as hell."

"It is."

"There's supposed to be all those secret passages down there. The legend is that people were kidnapped from taverns and hotels and dragged through the tunnels to the waterfront, where they were sold for blood money."

"Are you afraid?"

She whipped her head around to look at him. "Apep won't still be here, right? He doesn't live here, does he?"

"No. Apep's living large in a penthouse somewhere. He likes the finer things in life. I think he picked the tunnels because they were a good place to trap her, hidden and underground, where her ever-present cell phone wouldn't get a signal."

"How'd you know where to find her?"

He shook his head, clearly not looking forward to the explanation. "Misty left a note that she'd gone to face Apep, and where. She thought she was ready for battle, that I was holding her back with all my attention to detail. She was actually mad at me, if you can believe it." His laugh was dark. "So I raced to stop her. I was too late."

Exhaustion and grief shadowed his face. As unwelcome as this whole situation was for Felicity, it was probably worse for Tom. She was afraid she'd fail. He had to live with the knowledge that he'd already failed and probably would again.

"I just wish I knew what Apep is up to."

"So why don't you?"

"He changes it every cycle, adjusting for time and place."

Felicity laughed. "So he's got a plan specifically for modern-day Portland? What's he going to do, poison the craft beer supply?"

Tom looked alarmed. He didn't get the joke. Typical cat.

"I've usually figured it out by this point, but Misty wasn't interested in analysis. She just wanted to *get to the fighting part*. It was impossible for her to focus." He sighed.

"What'd he do the last time?"

"He orchestrated a misunderstanding between nuclear superpowers that brought the world to the edge of annihilation."

"Oh. Yikes. And before that?"

"He attempted to enslave humanity to industrialization and greed."

"Not sure you won that round, Tom."

He shrugged. "We will never know how much worse it would have been if we'd failed to stop him. His initial plan is only half the overall equation."

"Huh?"

Tom held her gaze, measuring his words. "It's a chain reaction, Felicity. First, he launches a plan to make humanity weak, vulnerable, and divided. He thrives on chaos."

"OK."

"And once the balance of the universe is thrown off—with war or mass casualty or catastrophe—he feeds on the suffering and grows stronger until he's powerful enough to destroy the world. Only one thing stands in his way."

"The Acolyte."

"Specifically, the Acolyte's *usekh*. Apep can't come into his full power until he kills the Acolyte and destroys the *usekh*."

Felicity raised a palm. "Back up." She squeezed her eyes shut, giving herself a moment before she spoke. "Are you sitting there telling me *he's still hunting for the necklace?*"

"Yeah. The instant Misty's life passed from her body, the necklace released, and I escaped with it before Apep could destroy it. He senses it's still on the earthly plane, and its very presence blocks him. He can cause mayhem, but he won't have the power to destroy the world unless he's crushed the *usekh*."

An icy-cold shock raced up her spine. Of all the news she'd had to digest since that morning—*had it only been that morning?*—this was the most alarming. She stared down at her hands, twisting in her lap, then looked up. She spoke through gritted teeth. "HE'S HUNTING THE FUCKING NECKLACE AROUND MY NECK?"

"Well..."

"You dragged me here as bait?"

"*What?* I would never...no, Felicity!" Tom ran a hand through his short hair and took a deep breath. "It's not like GPS. He can't track you in real time on a street map."

She couldn't remember the last time she was this furious.

"Apep feels the necklace's collected energy, and that's on the coast, where I've been since Tuesday night. He assumes *I'm* wearing it. He definitely doesn't know a new Acolyte has been chosen."

"I don't want to hear any more." She reached across Tom and opened the glove box, grabbing an old flashlight, then snatched the trash bags from the back seat. She got out and slammed the driver's side door.

Tom jumped out. "This way."

Felicity followed him across the parking garage, through a fire door, up two flights of stairs, and then into an alley.

"You should have told me I had a target on my back, Tom."

"Down here."

"That should have been the first thing out of your mouth this morning."

"I had to first explain the nature of the target. Over here."

Tom held up the corner of a trashed metal fence and waited for Felicity to duck under, then followed. They turned a corner and squeezed between two old buildings, where they reached the open loading dock of a restaurant. "We can get in here. Nowhere near the tourists." He helped Felicity climb up onto the small cement platform.

"I guess there's one benefit to being the Acolyte."

"What's that?"

Felicity tugged on his hand and made him face her. "Since Apep's gonna kill me first, I won't have to watch the apocalypse."

He stilled. "That's not funny."

Felicity gave his cheek a gentle pat. "No, cat, it isn't."

Once they weaseled their way into the prohibited sections of the tunnel system, progress was slow. There were no electric lights, and the dirt and plank floors were strewn with debris. Felicity's small emergency flashlight didn't provide much illumination, so she was glad Tom knew where he was headed.

"Stay vigilant," he said over his shoulder. "Watch your step right there."

But Felicity had already cleared the pile of bricks, even before his warning. How had she seen them? With her lousy night vision, she fully expected to be lost and disoriented down here. But she wasn't. It was almost as if her eyes had adjusted to the inky blackness, allowing her to see in the pitch dark.

"It's the necklace, isn't it?"

"What?"

"My optometrist told me I shouldn't drive at night because my rods and cones are shot to shit. But right now, I can see everything just fine. And my reflexes are quick. I actually have a sense of direction for once. My knees and back don't hurt. It's all from the necklace."

"Probably."

Felicity let herself get a bit excited. "I'm getting superpowers, aren't I? I mean, I'm still furious that you didn't ask me before you slapped it on me and made me the target of a psycho snake demon who needs to kill me to survive, but, you know, superpowers might make up for some of that. I could get into being a superhero."

"They're not exactly superpowers. Sorry."

She followed him as the tunnel sloped further downward and made a sharp turn to the right. "Regular powers, then?"

"The *usekh* amplifies the abilities the Acolyte already has, such as strength, stealth, vision, reflexes, hearing…you know, foundational attributes."

"Gotcha. That must really be something applied to a teenager in peak condition, huh? So what's it going to do for a middle-aged woman who's gone through three rounds of chemo?"

"I have absolutely no idea."

"How reassuring." Felicity let her right hand slide along the damp tunnel wall, keeping her steady as the tunnel twisted.

Tom slowed suddenly, and Felicity bumped into him. "Sorry."

"This way." They turned into a narrower tunnel to their left.

"Hey, Tom? Why do they have to battle over and over again? Why can't someone just win the Superbowl and be done with it?"

Tom turned, his face serious. "Because evil itself is never

obliterated. Evil is a cancer: if the smallest speck remains, it can, and does, regrow. Each time Apep regenerates and is vanquished, he hides a tiny bit of his flesh somewhere on the earthly plane. From that, he regenerates, and it starts again."

"An endless cycle. Depressing."

Tom came to a halt. "This is the place."

They had entered a chamber. The dank air made Felicity shiver. She inhaled a tangy whiff of what smelled like a mix of copper and mold. Not pleasant.

Tom rushed forward and scanned the floor, his horror palpable. "She's gone."

"Are you sure this is the right...?"

"Absolutely. Her body is gone."

Felicity looked around too, seeing what appeared to be dark slashes on the floor and splatters on the tunnel wall. It was blood. She shuddered, unsure whether it was her imagination or she could actually feel death in this place, heavy against her, reverberating through the small room like a shockwave of sorrow.

Her last trip to these tunnels had been creepy, but *this* nastiness? It was like no living thing should dare enter here. She struggled to keep the anxiety from her voice.

"You know, a lot of homeless folks stay down here. Someone probably found her and called the police. Maybe we can make some phone calls and find out where they took..."

"I can't do the funerary rites." Tom wiped at his mouth and chin, flustered, turning one way and then another like a panther in a cage. "I'll fail again."

"This isn't your fault."

Tom reared back and punched his fist into the tunnel wall. She heard something crunch. Stone or bone, she couldn't be sure. He barely reacted to any pain, but instead stood there, stoic, waging some silent war with himself.

"Her throat was slit." Tom swallowed hard, as if he felt the cut.

Felicity cringed. Nope. She refused to let that image take hold in her brain.

"And if the police have her, it's now a murder investigation, and if I try to claim her body… what would I even say? I'd end up in jail."

"My God! What about her parents? Do they know?"

Tom nodded. "Alexander's told them. He's taking care of them."

"They won't demand justice?" It was unthinkable to Felicity that they'd just accept that their daughter was slaughtered and move on.

"There are higher forms of justice, Felicity. The old families know what is expected of them and consider it an honor. They'll grieve. Of course, they will. But Apep can't be tried by a judge and jury. He's dealt with in only one way—by being defeated in battle according to the ancient texts."

Tom looked so dejected she couldn't help herself—she stepped close, wrapped him in her arms, and squeezed. He stiffened, like Mojo sometimes did. Tom was just another big, tough tomcat who liked to strut and holler but shied away from a good cuddle. She released him and walked away to give him some privacy. That's when she saw it.

The object was in the far corner, cloaked in shadow and partially hidden beneath chunks of fallen rock. In her pre-necklace days, she would have missed it entirely. Today, she saw a clear outline of something metallic and shiny.

She rushed to the corner, reached down, and grabbed a cell phone. Its screen was shattered, but otherwise it looked brand-new, encased in pink aluminum dotted with bright, stick-on rhinestones. It hadn't been in the corner long.

"Is this Buffy's?" She held it out to Tom.

"Damn straight it is!" He snatched it from Felicity and toggled the power switch, to no effect. Suddenly, he spun to her, energized, his face lit up. "This has to be how Apep contacted her and lured her down here! We need to get this phone working and get into her messages. This phone can lead us to Apep."

"I don't know the first thing about electronics, Tom. Sorry." Then it hit her. Felicity smiled. "But I know someone who does."

CHAPTER SEVEN

Portland rush hour traffic was a hellscape. By the time they made it out of the city center, past the suburbs, and back to Pine Beach, the veterinary clinic was scheduled to close. But luck, or the Goddess, must have been with them, because just as they pulled into the clinic parking lot, Ronnie Davis exited the glass double doors, yanked them closed, and raised a jangle of keys to the locks.

Felicity was out of the car in an instant, Tom at her side. "Ronnie!"

She didn't turn around. Her voice was unfazed. "Hey there, Felicity. Everything OK?"

"Yeah. Sure. Sort of."

Ronnie kept her back to them.

"That strange stray cat any better?"

"Strange?" Tom looked offended.

"Much better. So, Ronnie, I need your help."

Ronnie turned toward them then, clipping the key ring to the belt of her cargo pants as she studied Tom. "Who're you?"

"Oh, sorry. This is my… nephew, Tom. He just popped in for an unexpected visit."

Neither Tom nor Ronnie offered a hand in greeting. Ronnie studied him, wary and watchful, and Tom picked up on her suspicion.

"Nice outfit." Ronnie headed for her Jeep. "Must have been quite unexpected if he had to borrow your clothes."

Tom started to respond, but Felicity held up a hand to shut him up and pursued Ronnie. "He had a bit of a… motorcycle accident on the way here. Lost his duffle bag. I had to loan him something until we get some new stuff."

"Uh-huh." Ronnie clicked her key fob and pulled open the driver door.

"I need a big favor."

Ronnie turned, arms crossed. "Another cat, I assume?"

"Not this time, believe it or not. You said you're really good with computers and phones and stuff, right?"

"Riiiight." Ronnie shifted her stance, frowning.

"I have this cell phone… my teenage niece's… Tom's little sister's. She's…"

Tom handed the sparkly, pink phone to Felicity.

"We need to get into it," Felicity said.

"Into it?"

"You know, to see her calls and stuff."

"Why?"

"We need to see who she's been talking to."

Felicity had to pause and catch her breath. She was impressed with herself. Turned out she was a very good liar. Far better than she'd anticipated.

In silence, Ronnie continued to assess Tom. He really did look ridiculous, yet he didn't seem to care in the slightest.

"Do I know you from somewhere?" Ronnie cocked her head. "There's something familiar about…"

"No! It's his first time visiting Pine Beach. You've never met him. Ever. Not."

Ronnie raised an eyebrow. "OK."

"Can you help with the phone?"

Ronnie dragged her gaze away from Tom and produced a slight nod in Felicity's direction. "Maybe. Follow me."

As soon as they were back in the Saturn, Tom grabbed Felicity's arm. "That's the woman who stitched me up."

"Yeah. She's into electronics and stuff too."

"She might recognize me."

"How? You were a *cat* before. Now you're…" Felicity let her eyes wander over his muscular body, from thighs to shoulders "…not."

"We have to be vigilant. We can't jeopardize our mission in any way. This could be dangerous, Felicity."

"You're overreacting. We need her help, right?" She pulled out of the parking lot behind the Jeep. "Maybe you should nibble some 'nip when we get home. Just to take the edge off."

Ronnie's tiny studio apartment was enclosed in floor-to-ceiling shelves along the perimeter, packed with computer monitors and electronic parts and books and keyboards and all kinds of doodads Felicity didn't know the names for. It was claustrophobic.

"This is some impressive setup, Ronnie."

"Sorry it's such a mess. I'm taking college classes at night, and I don't have time to clean up." She removed stacks of papers and textbooks from an ottoman and tossed them to the floor. "Here. Pop a squat."

Felicity sat while Ronnie collapsed into a black leather swivel chair at a crowded U-shaped computer desk. She pushed a few papers out of the way and clicked a button on a tower near her feet. One of the four large screens came to life.

Tom remained standing close to Felicity's side.

Ronnie spun in the chair. "I like you, Felicity. I respect the hell out of how you care for your strays. That's why I'll try to get into this phone for you."

"I know breaking into someone's phone isn't a polite thing to do."

"Or legal."

"It's *illegal?*" Felicity blinked in surprise, her thoughts wandering to the day she'd pilfered Rich's raincoat. Was she really about to commit two illegal acts in the same week? That was unheard of! She always followed the rules. Well, except for the unpaid bills. But really, why bother anymore? Anyone could see that a lifetime spent as a compulsive rule-follower had gotten her exactly bupkus.

She shot a glance at Tom, who appeared unconcerned.

Illegal. Possibly a felony! A little electrical charge skittered up Felicity's spine. "You're sure it's against the law?"

"Ooh, yeah." Ronnie held out her hand. Felicity dropped the pink case into her palm and watched her spin to connect the phone to a power cord attached to the tower. Ronnie rested her combat boots on the chair's roller legs, then settled in. "It's taking a charge, so it's intact."

Felicity noticed how Tom stood perfectly still, watching Ronnie. It was awkward. *He* was awkward. If she didn't know he was a cat, Felicity would consider his behavior downright rude. Which was probably how Ronnie saw the situation.

"So!" Felicity's exclamation came out chipper, but nervously so. She tried again. "So, computer science-y stuff. That's what you want to do?"

"Yeah."

"You were a medic and now you're a great vet tech. I mean, I figured if anything you'd be studying medicine."

Ronnie gave a half-hearted shrug. "I'm ready to work with things that don't die."

Nobody breathed. And in the silence, Felicity's heart broke for Ronnie Davis. Who knew what invisible burdens the young woman carried?

Ronnie's fingers clacked on the keyboard, ending the quiet. "I'm in!" she chimed.

"That's wonderful!"

Ronnie sat back and laughed. "Not really. I just always wanted to say that, like in the movies."

Felicity realized she'd never even seen Ronnie smile, let alone laugh. Her whole face lit up and the shadows retreated from her sparkling eyes. Beneath all the eyeliner and the hacked-up bangs, Ronnie was a beautiful, young, vibrant woman.

The kind that should be wearing the necklace.

Ronnie's laughter wound down to a sigh. "Forgive me. Hacker humor."

"Can we focus?" Tom pressed behind Ronnie, agitated. He leaned over her to peer at the computer screen, tapping his fingers on the monitor.

"Back the fuck up, dude." Ronnie placed her open palm in his face. "You don't touch shit that doesn't belong to you. You wait for an invitation. And do not *ever* loom over me. You won't like the consequences."

Tom stepped away, but his eyes didn't leave the screen. "My apologies, but we need to see the text messages and calls."

"Yeah, I got that." She gestured for him to take another step back and waited until he did. "I can try to bypass the biometric lock, but it'd be easier if I had her cloud password. Don't suppose you know it?"

Tom closed his eyes and swiped his hand downward, as if touching an imaginary phone screen. He frowned. "I watched her do it a million times for her accounts. I think she used the same password for everything."

Ronnie sniffed in disgust. "Teenage girls."

His eyes opened. "Try BastetsBitch." Tom spelled it out slowly, noting the uppercase letters. "No spaces."

"You're kidding." Felicity decided she didn't like Buffy, and then immediately felt guilty. She may have been an entitled, spoiled brat, but she'd paid the ultimate price.

Ronnie made a few keystrokes and gave her head a single shake. "Not it. What else you got?"

Tom massaged his jaw. "Try BastetsBitch18, again, no spaces. She may have put her age at the end. She'd recently celebrated a birthday."

Felicity felt even sadder for the kid. She'd just celebrated a milestone. Her life was just beginning. And now she was gone.

"We've got a winner!" With a few more keystrokes, Ronnie's monitor filled with a long text message exchange. "Wow. Hope your sister's on an unlimited data plan."

"What's this very last text?" Tom stepped forward again, pointing at the screen.

Ronnie zoomed the text and gestured for Tom to use the computer mouse. "Go ahead. You know what you're looking for. Have at it."

Tom swooped in as Ronnie rolled her chair away from the

desk. By now, it was obvious that Ronnie didn't want to be anywhere near Tom. Not that Felicity blamed her; Tom looked like an escaped mental patient. And he'd been wary the whole time they'd been there. Felicity knew why, but still…

He settled in at the monitor, at ease with the mouse and keyboard. This gave Felicity pause. Tom had somehow managed to familiarize himself with computer technology this time around. How bizarre it must be to come and go and have to catch up with the world's changes for each visit. Tom had seen civilizations rise and collapse, weapons evolve from bows and arrows to nuclear bombs, and societies advance from horseback to Hubble telescope.

"What *is* this?" Tom stopped scrolling. His shoulders tensed.

"Did you find something?" She tried to see the screen, but his body blocked her view.

"He was taunting her. He lured her to the tunnels by appealing to her vanity. She went right to him."

"Oh, my God." Felicity felt sick.

"Pestilence?" Tom raised his voice. "He actually typed the word *pestilence* in a text, so that's where he's going? *Again?*"

"As in a disease?"

"What other kind of pestilence is there, Felicity?"

"OK, but how did he know to contact *her*, that she was, you know…" Felicity shot a glance to Ronnie, stopping herself from saying the word *Acolyte*.

"I have no idea."

Ronnie left her chair and wandered to lean against the sliding glass doors to the apartment balcony, arms crossed over her chest. "Look, I realize I'm not privy to the details of your family drama, but it sounds like your girl is in some kinda trouble. I assume you've already called the police?"

"Not an option." Tom clicked the mouse, eyes glued to the monitor.

"But she's safe, right? She's not in any physical danger?"

"It's a long story, Ronnie." Felicity produced a reassuring smile that must have failed to reassure because Ronnie wasn't having it.

"Then just give me the punchline."

"The danger has passed, but it's really important that we figure out exactly who she was communicating with a few days ago."

"Then I suggest you start with her social media accounts—TikTok, Twitter, Instagram…"

"Instagram." Tom rapped his fingers hard against the computer screen, impatient. "Open her Instagram."

Ronnie pushed away from the sliding doors. "You know what, dude? You are in desperate need of some manners. Move aside."

Tom stepped back as Ronnie reclaimed her chair and mouse, then readjusted the angle of the monitor without bothering to hide her irritation. After a few rapid-fire clicks on the keyboard, she sat back.

"Whoa. Misty McAlpine—your *sister*—is quite the teen influencer. Over a hundred thousand followers on Insta." Ronnie gave Tom some serious side-eye. "Looks nothing like you, though. All blonde and blue-eyed and cutesy. Must be from the opposite end of the McAlpine gene pool, huh?"

Ronnie scrolled through Misty's many, many posts.

"Stop!" Tom surged forward to point accusingly at one image. "How could she have *done* this?"

Ronnie enlarged the selfie of Misty, then leaned away from the screen. Felicity immediately saw what Tom had seen: the necklace. Bastet's sacred necklace. The very one now around Felicity's throat, hidden under a scarf.

Misty McAlpine had worn the necklace on her profile picture.

On Instagram. Where she had over a hundred thousand followers. What had that girl been thinking?

"Search this." Tom looked to Ronnie while pointing at the monitor. "I need to see how often this shows up."

"Her face?"

"The necklace."

"All right."

Ronnie clicked on the necklace, cropped it, copied it, and entered it into the search engine. A screen full of images appeared. Felicity's mouth fell open in disbelief.

Bastet's necklace was on display for anyone to see, all across the Interwebs, thanks to Misty's desire to document the minutiae of her life. The gold and jewels went to the beach, a school dance, and several restaurants. The necklace peeked out of a sundress here and a winter coat there and a hoodie over there. It was visible when Misty went for coffee with friends or passed her driving test or volunteered at a carwash fundraiser. It was on display throughout Misty's makeup tutorial video where she matched her eyeshadow color to the *usekh*'s center stone.

Tom mumbled under his breath. He'd gone pale. He looked to Felicity. "These texts. We have to know whose number this is."

"The number is blocked," Ronnie said.

His eyes never left Felicity. "She's got to find it."

"Hey!" Ronnie was done with Tom, and rightly so. "*She*'s over here, and *she* has a name. It's Veronica Davis—Ronnie to my friends. Which means *you* will need to ask me, nicely, in these exact words: 'Hey, *Veronica*? Would you *please* try to find the number? I'd appreciate it. *Thank you.*' Got it?"

Tom shook his head, clearly distraught. "This is not a joke, not a game!"

Felicity jumped up and placed a hand on his arm. He flicked her away and spoke to Ronnie. "Please understand. If I don't figure out whose number this is, a lot of innocent people will die. Including you."

"Is that a threat?" Ronnie jumped up and got right in his face.

Felicity pushed between them. "No! Not a threat. It's just a really... we're in a horrible situation and we need your help, Ronnie."

She dropped back into her chair, scowling. "Come on now, Felicity. People could die? Seriously? What's next? You're gonna tell me you're a spy?"

"Tom is right. People could die."

Ronnie folded her hands in her lap. "Then go ask the FBI to help you."

"We can't." Felicity couldn't afford to lose Ronnie's aid, but she had to be careful how much she revealed. "Please. We need you."

Ronnie was quiet for a moment, weighing her options. "Fine. I'll do it for *you*, Felicity, and your cats." Exhaustion settled on Ronnie's shoulders. She nodded toward Tom. "Since you're already up there, looming again like an asshole with no manners, hand me that black box from the top shelf."

When Tom turned and reached, the way-too-small T-shirt rode up his torso, exposing his scarred back and sides. Felicity marveled again at his physique, but in a detached and clinical way, without the smallest bit of sexual tingle. Which was bittersweet, truth be told. Or maybe just bitter.

Tom handed the box to Ronnie. She balanced it on her lap, her expression unchanged, but Felicity noticed how she now clenched her jaw. She'd gone stiff. After a moment, Ronnie lifted the box lid to dig through the contents. She pulled out a purple flash drive.

Then she just sat there, fidgeting, rubbing the data stick between her thumb and forefinger, over and over and over.

"You know that I served." Ronnie spoke only to Felicity. "Lance Corporal, 11th Marine Expeditionary Unit out of Pendleton. Oo-rah. Tried to save the world one IED wound at a time. Failed."

Ronnie looked up at Tom, studying him impassively, still playing with the flash drive.

Tom didn't shift under her stare. He just glared right back, his mismatched eyes unblinking. Felicity was about to intervene—*again*—when Ronnie turned her way.

"I wanted to earn a medal. Earned myself some nice PTSD instead. What I'm trying to say, Felicity, is that I've seen some shit. Shocking shit. Horrifying, strange, *unexplainable* shit." She trailed off, lost in her own thoughts.

"You've been through more than I can ever imagine." Felicity leaned forward to pat Ronnie's knee.

Ronnie stopped fidgeting and turned a blistering glare on Felicity. "But right now, I'm looking at a man with the sutures I gave a dying *cat*."

For an instant, there was only shocked silence. Tom shot Felicity an *I told you so* look, shook his head, and stared out the balcony doors, whispering, "*Fuck*."

Felicity let loose with a high, fake laugh. "What? Remember, Tom was in a little motorcycle accident on his way up to see me and..."

"I'm left-handed, Felicity. I tie my knots backward. It's very distinctive."

"Maybe the emergency room doctor was left-handed, too..."

"And the bald spot on his head where I cut away the fur?"

"It's..."

Ronnie reached out, moving so quickly that Felicity was taken completely unaware. She ripped the scarf from Felicity's neck.

"You're wearing the gold collar that was on your stray cat, the same collar that's in all these selfies."

"It's not..."

"There's blood spatter on the damn phone case." Ronnie jerked her thumb toward the still-charging phone.

"Misty probably cut her hand on the..."

"Stop." Tom slowly approached Ronnie, then came to a standstill before her. He gave a low, formal bow, his impressive form bent in deference. It was a courtly gesture, something deserving of a cutaway and cravat instead of the rejects from Felicity's closet.

"I'm Tubastet-af-ankh, *hem-netjer-tepi* of the Ever-Living Goddess Bastet, temple guard of Per-Bast, and trainer of Acolytes." He grimaced when he straightened, obviously still in pain, but managed a polite smile. "The world needs you, Lance Corporal Veronica Davis of Pendleton. You saved my life and I am truly grateful, and now, if you're tough enough to hear the truth and brave enough to help us, I'll be forever in your debt."

Ronnie took it better than might be expected, all things considered. She listened patiently to Tom's explanations and Felicity's interjections. She chose her questions with care, sticking mostly to the bottom-line issues.

"Are you sure Felicity is our only hope?"

"Yes," Tom said.

Ronnie nodded. "I need a beer." She went to the tiny kitchenette and opened a mini fridge not much bigger than the one in the Airstream. "Anybody else?"

"Not for me." Felicity was driving and, well, saving the world.

"I'll take one." Tom noticed Felicity's surprise. "What? Ancient Egyptians invented the stuff."

Ronnie brought two frosty bottles of beer and handed one to

Tom, who was perched on the edge of her futon. "If you're Egyptian, why don't you have an accent?"

"Maybe because I haven't been in ancient Egypt for two thousand years." He took a long pull from the bottle.

"Where have you been, then?"

He gave a dismissive shrug. "Around."

Tom was being downright antisocial, which seemed counterproductive. "He spends most of his time in the Realm of the Gods, isn't that right, Tom?"

No response. Felicity wanted to kick him. One minute he seemed to enjoy the conversation and the next he just tuned everyone out like…

A cat.

Oh.

"So you've been *around* for two millennia. How many languages to do you speak?" Ronnie sipped her beer.

"Fluently?"

She tipped her chin in challenge. "Yeah. Fluently."

"Fourteen." He took another drink.

"*Alearabia?*"

"*Bi ta'keed.*" Tom answered Ronnie without hesitation.

"*Beh Farsa?*"

"*Chashm.*"

"*Hablas Espanol?*"

"*Ahora estas siendo ridicula.*"

Ronnie released a short laugh, acknowledging her defeat. "Well, that's all I've got."

Tom didn't say anything more, just studied Ronnie, curious.

"I'm gonna have to call bullshit, though."

Tom raised an eyebrow.

"Because, fourteen? Really? All with no accent?"

"Ah, you caught me, Veronica. I'm told I do have a slight accent when I'm a cat." He finished his beer and examined the label. "This was pretty good."

"It's a local microbrew."

"Not quite as good as what I used to brew way back in the day. My secret was toasted pistachios." Tom got up and tossed his bottle into Ronnie's recycling and returned to his spot on the futon.

The silence returned, thicker this time. Tom watched Ronnie. Ronnie watched Tom.

"Oookay, so I think that's everything!" Felicity slapped her hands to her knees. "You'll help us then, Ronnie?"

She finished her beer and gave a slight nod in response, still observing Tom.

"Thank you! What's next?"

"I run some software, scrape up the blocked number, and then try to track it back to an owner. It'll take some time, though. Maybe a couple days. I can't guarantee anything."

"Thank you." Tom stood, ready to go.

"Sit down," she said. "I got a few more questions."

Tom sat.

"Do you really plan to go after Apep with—whaddya call them?"

"Priestly texts," Tom supplied.

"Have you considered a nice shoulder-fired missile? I love me an FIM-92 Stinger. Or an anti-tank Javelin? Because either of those would light his ass *up*."

"As tempting as that sounds, the attack has to come from the Six Steps of Overthrowing Apep."

"Why?"

"Because that's the way it's done."

"Always?"

"Always."

"But… hear me out." Ronnie leaned forward, elbows on her knees. "The best battle strategy is a flexible one, right? You've got to be able to switch it up if there's a change in your own level of preparedness, or weapon technology, or battlefield conditions, or the capabilities of your opponent."

"I'm aware of that."

"But your Acolyte here is your principal weapon, right? And this time she's a middle-aged lady."

Felicity squirmed. "I told you, he didn't have a choice. It was an emergency!"

"I got that."

"He was dying. There wasn't anyone else around!" Felicity couldn't stand it another second. She jumped to her feet. "I'm sorry, OK?"

Both Tom and Ronnie seemed confused.

"For what, Felicity?" Tom's voice was gentle.

"For being completely inadequate. It's absurd, and we all know it. In a matter of hours, my entire understanding of space and time and the nature of reality has changed, and now the future of humanity rests in my hands, and everybody knows I can't do the job!"

Tom began to speak, but Ronnie cut in. "Not necessarily true," she said.

That stopped Felicity cold. "What?"

"You said everybody knows you can't do the job, and all I'm saying is that might not be the case."

"Really?" Felicity stood straighter.

"Really."

Felicity wanted to believe Ronnie, but just couldn't. "I'm just so… nothing. Life has beaten me to a pulp. I'm nobody's idea of a superhero. I'm invisible, bankrupt, practically homeless…"

"Stop." Tom's voice was firm.

"For once I agree with him." Ronnie gestured to Tom without taking her eyes off Felicity. "I get it. I do. You're scared. Everyone's counting on you, and you worry you'll fuck it up. And you wish there was somebody else to do it–*anybody* else—but, news flash, there's not."

"Um." Felicity's left eye began to twitch. "Is this supposed to be a pep talk? Because…?"

"Your little pity party needs to end."

"My…?"

"And you need some words of wisdom, courtesy of the US Marine Corps."

Felicity dropped back to the ottoman.

Ronnie leaned forward, inching her chair quite close to Felicity. "*Embrace the suck.*"

There was a beat of silence, then Tom started laughing—really laughing—a scratchy, rusty, deep belly laugh that reminded Felicity of a cat's loud purr. It was strangely calming.

Even Ronnie smiled. "I believe in you. Hey, you've been saving strays your whole life, hopeless cases nobody else would touch. How much harder can one mangy planet be?"

Felicity was speechless.

"Besides, you've got me and Tom on your side now." Ronnie looked sincere.

"I… thank you."

Tom stood again. "We really should go."

"Wait. I've got stuff." Ronnie opened a desk drawer and pulled out a cell phone. "Not the newest but it works. I put it on a prepaid card."

"But Ronnie…"

"Just pay me back by, you know, saving the world and shit."
She handed the phone to Felicity, then leaned across to the futon and
grabbed an oversized sweatshirt from a pile of clothes. "Take this." She
put it in Felicity's other hand.

"What for?"

"Your cat popped a couple stitches. You should get him home
before he bleeds on my carpet."

With that, Ronnie spun around in her chair and went to work.

Tom was fading fast on the drive back to the Airstream, and
Felicity noticed that specks of blood had seeped through the borrowed
sweatshirt he wore.

"You OK, Tom?"

"Worn-out. But we should start training."

"Absolutely not. You need fresh bandages. And we both need
to eat and sleep."

He nodded.

She liked this new Tom, the one too tired to argue.

When Felicity pulled through the gate, her headlights bounced
over the Kitty-Korner boxes strewn across the yard. "We've got to clean
this up first thing in the morning or Tasha's going to kill me." She
parked and turned off the engine. "There's not much food in the
house, but that panini's probably still good."

"Yeah, no thanks." Tom got out and headed for the steps.

She closed the driver's side door and spoke over the car roof.
"You don't have to worry about ptomaine. I've eaten stuff after it's
thawed out."

Tom laughed. "I appreciate the reassurance, but I just don't like Italian food."

"Really? That would make you the first person I've ever met who doesn't like Italian food." She reached the bottom of the stairs. "Even chicken parmesan? Are you sure?"

He paused, hand on the door latch. "Have you ever met a Roman, Felicity? In the flesh?"

What a strange question. "No."

"I have."

When Tom opened the door, Felicity heard him mumble something that sounded a lot like *Roman bag of dicks,* but that couldn't be right. Then she heard something along the lines of *Idioto stronzi.*

"Spanish?"

"Italian." He went inside.

Just as she reached the landing, Tom came barreling outside with the bundled tarp, then dumped the collected water and deflated plastic bags over the railing.

"I think your bed is mostly dry." He shook it out and drops rained onto the ground.

She sighed deeply. "I bailed the best I could."

Tom's lips quivered in a smile as he spread the tarp over the railing, then turned back to her. "Actually, you didn't *bail* at all, Felicity. You saved a dying stray cat in a rainstorm. Most people would have just kept driving, but you saved my life. And you're going to save everyone. You got this."

"OK, but I gotta feed the cats first."

Moments later, Tom sat at the booth and quietly observed Felicity's routine of cans, bowls, and crunchies. He chuckled to himself.

"What's so funny?"

"These two." He gestured to Circe and Diddy, spaced five feet apart down the center aisle. Their munching had been interspersed with the usual growling, hissing, and side-eye, and at one point, when Diddy crossed the DMZ and invaded Circe's space, all hell broke loose.

"Hey!" Felicity shooed them apart.

"She's very high-strung, even for a blue point Siamese." Tom stretched an arm over the back of the booth. "Diddy will do whatever it takes to get her riled up and Circe never disappoints."

"I can't figure out why they don't get along."

Tom looked up, blinking in surprise. "Don't you *know?*"

"What?"

"They're a couple."

"Say what?"

"Diddy worships Circe, and she feels the same about him, though she'll never admit it. You know how that goes; the one who loves the least wields the power. In withholding affection, she retains control."

Felicity let go with a heavy sigh. "Why do relationships have to be so damn complicated?"

Once the cats were done eating, she set the table for dinner. It wasn't a gourmet feast, but it was all she could scrape together. Tom accepted his cup of chicken noodle soup, saltines, and peanut butter with appreciation, and Felicity slid into the opposite bench and began to slurp. She was starving. It occurred to her that she could really go for a nice salmon filet. Or maybe some sushi. Which was weird because despite the fact that she lived in a fresh seafood paradise, she'd never much cared for it.

Hunh. She touched the necklace, wondering.

"You know, Circe is still really grateful for what you did for her," Tom said, spreading peanut butter on a cracker. "She was on death's door when you found her under that discount store loading dock, all covered in fleas and ticks. You pulled her from the brink, and she loves you for it."

Felicity was taken aback. "She told you all that?"

"Oh yeah." Tom popped the whole saltine in his mouth, and it took him a moment to swallow it down. "And man, does she ever despise your husband."

"Ex-husband."

"Right. *Der arschloch*. I got an earful from your cats last night when he came by with Alexander's letter; they aren't big fans."

"Nobody is."

"Alexander will deal with him from now on."

It was hard to believe that there was someone willing to help her with Rich. "Thank you for that, Tom. You know, I look back now, and I can barely fathom how I ever…" Felicity shook her head and stopped, deciding there was no point in beating a dead marriage. "Rich loved the least. I'll just leave it at that."

"But you survived." Tom smiled. "You're stronger than you give yourself credit for, and starting tomorrow, I'll prove it to you."

"That'd be nice."

Felicity finished her soup, stuffing the cup with saltines because speaking of Rich had left a bad taste in her mouth. She noticed how the cats had relaxed around them, some on the booth, some on the floor at their feet, some on the daybed.

"I'm glad they're finally chilling out," she said. "The toy soldier routine was wearing thin."

"My surprise visit freaked them out a little, I'm afraid. They thought I'd come to call them to serve Bastet."

"Huh?"

"Cats serve Bastet. They recognized me and waited for my instructions."

Felicity cocked her head. "You're serious."

"Absolutely."

"What exactly do they *do* once they're called?"

"Whatever the Goddess needs to have done."

"Is that why all those cats showed up here?"

"Yep. They wanted to pay their respects, bring gifts to the Goddess."

"Then why did they leave?"

"I told them you had enough to deal with right now."

Felicity shook her head. "Just when I think I've heard it all."

She sliced up her last apple and set the plate in the center of the table so they could share. She watched as Tom studied her collection of envelope scraps taped to the cabinet fronts, and felt slightly embarrassed.

"You're sharp, Felicity. Observant. That's nothing to be ashamed of." He gestured to the squares of paper with an apple slice. "You see patterns where most see random chaos."

She laughed. "Ha. Well, I've been a chaos magnet the last few years."

"You have been a warrior the last few years."

She felt her cheeks burn. "I guess I have, haven't I?"

Tom helped tidy up. They agreed that Felicity would keep her bed and Tom would sleep on the daybed, which Alphonse, Mojo, and Melrose wouldn't appreciate since that was their preferred spot.

Felicity handed him a folded blanket. "Wish it were fancier, but it's all I have."

"It's perfect."

"I'll get you some clothes tomorrow before we start training."

"Clothes would be good."

"There's a thrift shop in town, and Tuesday is senior discount day and I can lie and…"

"Felicity?"

"Huh?"

"You're an extraordinary person."

"Not really."

"You don't have much, but you're generous with what you do have, which makes you extraordinary."

She laughed. "That's a nice thing to say, but I'm down to my last few extraordinary dollars, and if Rich doesn't sell the house soon, I don't know…"

"All will be well. You'll see."

Tom's feline stillness was back, and his mismatched eyes were kind.

"I hope you're right."

Despite her exhaustion, Felicity couldn't fall asleep. Maybe it was the strangeness of another person spending the night in the trailer. Maybe it was the weight of everything she'd learned that day, every impossible, abnormal, and nightmarish new reality.

But Boudica was there, curled up into the crook of her arm, purring. In the darkness, the cat's single eye shone like a miner's headlamp.

"Should we check on everybody?"

Mmroaw.

"I hope the boys aren't giving Tom a hard time out there."

Mrrp.

Felicity took that as a yes, put on her chenille robe, and poked her head out the tiny bedroom, just to be sure all was well.

Tom was soundly asleep under the extra blanket, his borrowed clothes folded with military precision on the windowsill above the daybed. Every remaining cat, friend and foe alike, had found a place to curl up against him, on him, or near him, tails tucked and resting peacefully.

Felicity returned to her own bed and gave Boudica's chin a scratch. "They're all asleep, *together*."

Mmmrrrow.

"I know. I didn't expect it either, but maybe they see it as a privilege." Felicity gently swiped her palm along the length of Boudica's back and all the way to the tip of her tail. The purring returned, falling into its familiar rhythm and singing its sweet lullaby. Felicity had always been amused that even though Boudica was head bitch in charge at Chez Cheshire, her purr was as soft as a caress, as steady as waves on a beach, and as soothing as a heartbeat.

She remembered what Tom had said about her telepathic connection with Boudica. Ridiculous, right? Felicity lay her head on her pillow and gazed into Boudica's one yellow eye.

Let's see if this works. If you hear me, Boudica, put your left paw on my cheek.

Nothing happened, of course. She might as well have asked Gumbo to explain the principles of quantum mechanics.

But then, Boudica raised her left paw and delivered a soft pat somewhere between Felicity's chin and cheek. The cat closed her eye and drifted off.

It'd been a coincidence, of course, but now Felicity had something pleasant to think about. It wasn't long before she followed Boudica into sleep.

CHAPTER EIGHT

It really ticked Felicity off that the clerk at Debbie's Secondhand Treasures automatically gave her the discount. True, she was about to ask for it, but why did everyone assume that she was older than she was? Maybe someday, when she had money from the sale of the house, she'd buy a good moisturizer and get her hair professionally colored and highlighted and learn how to apply eyeshadow to match her jewelry.

Then she remembered Tasha's slavish fight to stay attractive and reconsidered. Perhaps it was too late for Felicity. Perhaps that was for the best.

Well, crap. That kind of negative thinking wasn't going to help defend the world from evil, now was it? Besides, *attractive* didn't equate with *valuable*. The concept of attractiveness was a trap. It begged the question: what were women supposed to be attracting? For every straight female who had ever walked the earth, the answer was *a man*. Or men in general. And for what, really?

Sex?

She was living proof that celibacy wasn't fatal.

Companionship?

That's why God made cats.

Security?

No such thing.

Children?

A roll of the fertility dice.

What if the goal wasn't getting something, but instead was an attempt to *avoid* something, as if staying attractive could fend off decay and death? Worse yet, what if a woman's devotion to staying attractive wasn't about the woman at all, but the man who needed an attractive woman on his arm to keep his own mortality at bay?

Women had been fed such a crock of...

"Is there something else you need, lady?"

"Huh? Oh!" Felicity saw she was holding up the thrift store line. "No. Sorry."

She clutched the plastic bag of recycled treasures to her chest and headed for her parked car. She felt a sense of accomplishment for what was folded inside that bag. She'd found a pair of jeans and a pair of cargo shorts, two T-shirts—one short-sleeved and one long-sleeved—and a button-down dress shirt. She'd found a nice cardigan, a pair of slightly used leather loafers that looked like they'd fit, two pairs of socks, a belt, and a three-pack of men's briefs.

Fortunately, the briefs were new and still in the original packaging. But now she doubted the purchase. She'd not asked Tom if he wanted underwear. She wasn't even sure ancient Egyptians *wore* underwear. Maybe they were like Highlanders, preferring to let it all hang out under their skirts. Egyptian men wore skirts, right? No? A trip to the public library was now at the top of her to-do list.

"Felicity!"

She turned, startled by the vision of Saint Bethany, Our Lady of Perpetual New Car Smell, exiting the barbershop and stepping into a halo of morning sunshine.

"I thought that was you!" Bethany flashed a sparkly smile and marched down the sidewalk, stopping close to Felicity, uncomfortably close.

She wore leggings, athletic shoes, and a fitted workout shirt. She carried a shiny new reusable water bottle in a frosty shade of lavender, which, Felicity couldn't help but notice, was an exact color match to the scrunchie she wore in her hair. Since when had scrunchies come back in fashion? Did everyone coordinate their water bottles with their hair accessories nowadays?

"Hi, Bethany. I'd love to chat, but I'm in sort of a hurry." *A naked man is waiting for me in the Airstream.*

"No problem! I completely understand. Doing some shopping? I just love thrift stores! You can find the cutest stuff *ever* if you're willing to sort through all the cheap junk, you know?"

Bethany tried to peer inside the bag, proof that perpetually perky pregnant people with perfect purple ponytails don't necessarily know how to *take a freakin' hint.*

"What did you get?"

Felicity whipped the bag behind her back, not exactly eager to explain why she was in the market for men's briefs.

"Placemats."

"Ooh! Super cute!" Bethany took a sip from her designer water bottle. "Rich said he accidentally ran into you a couple nights ago."

Felicity nodded, fascinated that Rich believed driving all the way out to her place to threaten her was an *accident*, but, sure, whatever.

"Did you see his disgusting boils?"

"Impossible not to."

"I know, right? But here's the weird thing." Bethany pressed her lips to Felicity's ear, as if she was about to reveal state secrets. She was so close that Felicity got a whiff of a citrusy-floral perfume. It was actually nice. A hellava lot better than the septic tank spritz Jim had given to Tasha.

Bethany whispered, "There are a couple guys in the barbershop with Rich right now, and they have them too! Like, all down their necks and all over their faces. It's super gross. Do you think it's something contagious in the barbershop? Should we call the health department?"

The necklace beneath Felicity's scarf rested heavy on her breastbone. Barbershop customers were erupting in boils? That might deserve its own slip of paper. In fact, the whole situation had overtones of a biblical plague. An *Egyptian* biblical plague.

A *pestilence*, even.

The necklace warmed against her skin.

"Hey, Beth, do you remember when the boils started?"

"Beth*any*." She smiled sweetly while correcting Felicity, then took another drink from her bottle and retreated to a more polite distance. "It was last Wednesday, when you were at the office, right after his weekly trim. You know how he likes to look good. *Appearances matter*, he's always saying, ha, ha." Bethany's smile had slipped at the end.

"The day of the frogs, right?" *And the scorpions. And finding Tom.*

Bethany's eyes widened, and Felicity couldn't deny that they were, in fact, lovely, baby-blue eyes. She was a lovely girl. Woman. Girl-woman.

"You know, I think you're right! I hadn't even connected them!

Rich said the frogs were just one of those crazy Oregon weather things. We sure don't have that kinda stuff back in Pennsylvania, and, you know, I haven't lived out here very long, so he set my mind at ease. But you are absolutely right! Two creepy things in one day!"

"Super creepy," Felicity agreed. Hadn't Tom said Apep had already started his attack? Were frogs and scorpions and boils part of it?

"Oh!" Bethany touched Felicity's arm. "Rich is waving at me. Gotta go. Good to see you!"

Felicity watched Bethany sweep through the barbershop's glass door and pitter-pat down the center aisle, her perky butt drawing appreciative glances from the pimply male clientele.

As Felicity thought about her own post-pert posterior, she felt something scuttle across the top of her shoe. She nearly jumped into the gutter. It was a big, black beetle. And it wasn't alone.

There were dozens, shooting out the narrow alley along the side of the barbershop. They marched in a line, around the corner, and west toward the waterfront.

She peered into the alley, empty but for an old, wooden ladder leaning against the brick wall. She was about to turn away when two more bugs scurried out. Where had they come from? Cracks in the pavement? Between the bricks? She entered the narrow space and squatted, hoping to catch them in the act. Another black beetle skittered out from beneath the ladder. Then another. But she hadn't seen the origin of either; it was as if they'd manifested from thin air.

Just to be sure, she examined the other side of the ladder, but saw no holes, no cracks, and no beetles. In fact, it looked as if someone had recently swept. Felicity backed away just as another beetle materialized.

With impressive speed, she bent, snagged the bug, dropped it into the thrift shop plastic bag, and hurried to her car.

The bug was a puzzle piece. She was sure of it.

He liked to be naked. Maybe it was the cat in him, which never completely disappeared, but clothes irritated him. They felt restrictive and rough against his skin. And while he generally preferred human form, which was, after all, how he was born, he did find himself missing his soft fur every now and then.

He was naked as he paced the length of the Airstream talking to Alexander on Felicity's new cell phone. They spoke in Egyptian so Gumbo wouldn't eavesdrop. That guy was a blabbermouth who enjoyed spreading gossip among the cats so he could sit back and watch the fur fly.

He had arrangements to make that he didn't want Felicity to know about just yet, and she intuited things from her cats, even if she didn't realize it. They had trained her well, which was a hopeful sign. Maybe he could train her too.

Once the call was done, he lay down on Felicity's bed. The comforter beneath him was soft and of very fine quality. Alexander had impeccable taste, as had all generations of his family. The Rigiat clan had been serving the Goddess and her *hem-netjer-tepi* for centuries, but he found it interesting that this trip had been the first time he'd become true friends with the Rigiat representative. Alexander was brilliant, with a dry wit, and had patiently guided him through the labyrinth of modern American society.

There was a problem with friendship, however. He didn't relish the idea of saying goodbye to Alexander when his work was done and it was time to leave the mortal realm. They'd likely never meet again. Alexander would have to survive to the age of 110 for that to happen.

The thought gave him pause. Would there even be a next time? He touched his fingertips to the sutures at his left flank, reminders of his failure, and hissed with pain. The wounds were healing but stung if he moved suddenly, and the itching was driving him insane. She'd done a good job, though, Lance Corporal Veronica Davis. She was something of an enigma, from parts unknown, and she had secrets. He knew the only way to handle a woman with secrets was not to handle her at all.

He heard footsteps on the metal stairs, then a light knock at the door. He bolted upright. Felicity wouldn't knock, so who could it be? He heard the click of the latch. *No, the bedroom door was open!* He had only seconds to return to cat form or be discovered.

"Lissie?"

It was Tasha.

He pressed his palms together at his solar plexus, raised them to his forehead, and began to softly chant the transformation incantation. Nothing—no surge of energy. His last transformation had drained him, and he was too weak to spark the process.

Too late now. He went completely still.

Tasha nosed around the trailer. She stared at Felicity's little scraps of paper taped to the cabinets and groaned with disapproval. She looked through her friend's mail. The whole time, he sensed the cats' distress and distrust. Circe hissed a warning.

"Mind your manners, cat," she snapped.

He tried again to transform. Failed. Just then, Tasha's back stiffened and she slowly turned to look into the bedroom doorway.

She shrieked, her hand pressing to her chest. "Who the *hell* are *you*? Where's Felicity? What have you done with her?"

Her horrified gaze zeroed in on his lap. She staggered back and grabbed the sink for stability. "Holy *shit!*"

Tom moved to the edge of the bed, noting how Tasha's eyeballs bulged. He draped the comforter across his loins and mumbled to himself, "*Hùnzhàng!*"

"What?"

"Sorry, Tasha." He forced a smile. "Didn't mean to scare you. I'm Felicity's nephew, Tom."

It took her a second to respond, but when she did, it was a loud accusation. "Really? Because she doesn't have a fuckin' nephew, let alone a *naked* fuckin' nephew who speaks Japanese!"

He spread his arms and shrugged. "Mandarin. And yet, here I am."

Tasha's expression went from terror to disgust. "She found you on Craigslist, didn't she?"

"Uh…"

"Did she promise to pay you? If so, you're in for a rude awakening, buddy, let me tell you."

As she spoke, Tasha's gaze slid from his bare feet to his abdomen, chest, and shoulders. Eventually she looked at his face, which he appreciated.

"So older women are your fetish? Is that it, you perv?"

"Felicity is not old." At least not compared to him.

"I *knew* it. I knew she was cracking and something like this would happen. I just didn't think…" Tasha stopped. "Wait. How do you know my name?"

Tasha was a prickly sort, more difficult to reason with than anticipated. "Felicity talks about you all the time. You're her best friend."

"So where is she, huh? Have you hurt her? *Killed* her? Did you stalk her along the side of the highway? What have you done with her body?"

"I believe her body is in town running an errand."

"OK, that's it, asshole." She pointed to the door. "Get outta here!"

"I can't. I have to wait for her to come back."

"You should be ashamed of yourself, taking advantage of a disturbed, vulnerable woman, a sad little cat lady! And with your…" Tasha gestured wildly at his lap and lost her train of thought. "Oh, lord. Anyway, I'm calling the police!" She headed for the door.

Tom grabbed a bedsheet and quickly wrapped it around his waist like a *shendyt*. He rushed to catch up with her, standing on the metal stoop as she marched across the yard, arms swinging.

"Wait, Tasha. Please."

She spun around, lips tight and eyes narrowed with suspicion.

The knot of his *shendyt* began to slip and he grabbed it just in time. "OK, you're right, I'm not a blood relation, but I'm *like* a nephew to her. That's all there is to the story."

She picked at a fingernail while trying to keep her gaze from any part of his body.

Oh, man. If he'd learned anything on this trip to the earthly plane, it was that modern Americans were a confused blend of prude and profligate, bouncing from one extreme to the other and not finding joy in either place.

"There's no need to call the police."

She glanced nervously around the property.

"I'm not here to hurt anyone. I'm not armed. I mean, there'd be nowhere I could conceal carry even if I wanted to, right?"

Tasha crossed her arms and gave him a quick once-over.

"I even helped Felicity clean up the yard first thing this morning! See? We broke down the boxes for recycling and what didn't fit in the trailer is stored in the shed. Would I do that if I didn't have good intentions?"

"Hmph," she said.

He made his way down the stairs, the sheet fisted in his hand just to be safe. "How about we sit on the porch and wait for Felicity? She's probably on her way back right now."

Uh-oh.

Felicity steered the Saturn through the gate to find Tom and Tasha sitting on the front steps of Tasha's porch. Tom was dressed like a one-man toga party. Tasha flashed an accusatory glare in her direction, and Felicity acknowledged it with a nod. She cut the engine and took a deep breath.

This was going to be some fun.

The good news: the police had not been called and Hair Gel Jim was nowhere to be seen. The bad news: everything else.

Felicity wondered what Tom had told Tasha. Had he gone with the nephew cover story—which Tasha would know was utter garbage—or had he blurted out that he was the immortal emissary of an ancient Egyptian cat goddess and Felicity had been chosen to save the planet?

Either way, the situation would require diplomacy, because her friendship with Tasha was on shaky ground. They had always been straightforward with each other, truly caring about each other's well-being and safety. They'd never hidden stuff from one another or dodged earnest questions, even of the most personal kind.

Until recently, anyway, when Tasha had become cagey about Hair Gel Jim and Felicity had been in full cover-up mode. It didn't feel good. The new distance between them wasn't right.

She approached the porch, noting that Tom looked relatively tranquil. Tasha, on the other hand, was wide-eyed, sitting ramrod straight at a safe distance from the mostly naked Egyptian.

"I see you've met Tom." Felicity waited cheerfully for a hint about which direction this conversation was about to take.

"Tasha came to the trailer while I was napping, and I explained that I was *like a nephew* to you."

Tasha said nothing.

"We were just chatting about how I'd be staying for a while, recovering from my motorcycle accident injuries."

"Ah. Right. Good." Felicity glanced at Tasha, who had not dropped her guard in the slightest.

"And I mentioned that I might be working with you to improve your physical condition, that she might see us outside doing exercises and drills."

"*Drills?*" Tasha and Felicity said it at the same time.

Felicity felt something crawling along her forearm and gasped. The alleyway beetle was making a break for it! She caught it and held it out to Tom. "I saw a whole bunch of these suckers marching through town. I thought maybe it was important."

Tom opened his palm to receive the bug. Alarm flashed in his eyes. He nodded curtly. "Yeah. Important." He rose, adjusting his bedsheet. Felicity handed him the bag of clothes, and he excused himself. "Enjoy your visit, ladies. Thank you again, Tasha." He walked to the trailer.

Felicity plopped on the steps next to Tasha and braced for impact.

"*What...*"

It appeared that Tasha would be going full drama.

"*the actual...*"

Felicity was ready.

"*FUCKING DAMN HELL IS GOING ON WITH YOU,*

FELICITY?"

Unsure whether Tasha had finished her inquiry, she decided not to rush to answer.

"Where did you find him?"

"It's a really long story."

"OkCupid? Hinge? Tinder?"

"I don't know what those are, Tash, and I'm guessing that's a good thing."

"Exercises? *Drills?* Oh, *come on*, Felicity! Have you gotten involved in some kind of sex cult? Is he some kind of Internet guru?"

"No."

"Because let's be completely real here." Tasha's voice had risen an entire octave. "I have *never* seen a man built like that in all my life and neither have you and neither has anyone we know, so finding *that* naked specimen in your bed was a little unexpected if you get what I'm saying!"

"Unexpected is a good word."

She pointed. "What's with the scarf? It's eighty-five in the shade."

Felicity pressed her hand to her collarbones, feeling the outline of the necklace. "I'm experimenting with accessories."

"Are you having sex with him?"

"Absolutely not."

"Well, why the hell *not?*"

"Because that's not the way it is with us."

"What is it, then? And don't tell me he's your personal trainer because I was in gym class with you from kindergarten to senior year and I *know* that's not right."

"Not in the traditional sense, no. More of a teacher."

"Like a *life* coach?"

"Sort of."

"A smokin-hot, naked life coach? Really? Where do I find me one of those?"

Felicity shrugged.

"You've gone completely off the rails."

"I know."

They sat on the steps, not speaking, while the junkyard clanged and smashed and the Rottweiler-in-residence decided to chime in. When the discord subsided, Felicity dared look over at Tasha. A tear had tracked down her face, a long black streak of mascara connecting her lower lashes to her jawline.

Felicity reached out and touched her shoulder. "I've upset you. I'm sorry."

Tasha sniffled.

"I promise to explain everything soon. All I ask is that you give me some time to sort this out for myself. Besides, I'm not sure you'd believe me if I *did* tell you. Can you do that? Can you just give me a few days?"

She nodded. "If you promise me that you're safe. That he's not a danger to you."

"Not at all." *Apep was another matter, however.*

"How did he get those deep cuts? At least tell me the truth about that."

Felicity took a deep breath and let it out. "He got the shit beat out of him trying to protect someone in trouble."

Tasha swiped at the tear and looked off into the distance. "How did we get here, Lissie? I mean, how did we get so goddamn *old?*" She gave her a sideways glance. "Do you remember the Beastie Boys concert our junior year?"

"*What?*" Felicity let go with a startled laugh. It took a moment to recover from the conversational whiplash. "Of course. It was the first time our parents let us drive to the city on our own. We felt so grown up. I remember you wore that cute crop top and the flower barrettes."

Tasha turned to face her. "And you wore that houndstooth miniskirt with the black leather vest over a little white T-shirt. You always could rock the layered look."

Felicity giggled. "The same could be said for you and your knee socks."

"I miss those days."

"We're not dead yet. What's stopping us from taking in a concert some night and going for a drink after? You could wear your knee socks."

"But not my crop top," Tasha said.

"Why not?"

"Fine. I'll wear the crop top if you wear the mini skirt."

"Deal."

"Deal."

"Bethany's pregnant."

Tasha jolted. "Fuck!"

Felicity felt a rush of relief. She hadn't shared the news with anyone, and it felt good to let it out. The development had stung at first, but so much had happened since that it felt like an event from the distant past, from someone else's life. In fact, Bethany's mother-to-be status had barely crossed Felicity's mind in the last few days. But maybe it had bothered her more than she cared to admit.

"I'm sorry, Felicity."

"The world just seems so unbalanced. Bethany's baby was clearly an accident. Whoops, preggers! And me?" Felicity shook her head, sadness choking her. "I tried so damn hard, year after year, shot after shot, procedure after procedure..."

Tasha opened her arms. Felicity fell against her, pressing her cheek to her friend's shoulder. She felt Tasha's arms encircle her and her hands pat her gently.

"When did you find out?"

"At his office last week."

Tasha ended the hug, steadied Felicity at arm's length, and tipped her head with concern. "I'm sorry I've been so tough on you, hon. I can't even imagine how rotten this feels. You do whatever it takes to get through this, OK? Detailing your car? Sure. Online shopping or hiring a gigolo? You go, girl. Dressing like a bag lady? It's all good."

Bag lady? Felicity would have to ditch the old, crocheted scarf and find another way to hide the necklace. Did she even own a turtleneck?

"I need to get something off my chest, too." Tasha rolled her head from side to side, then rested her wrists on her knees, letting her hands dangle. "Something's going on with Jim. I can't quite put a finger on it, but something's wrong."

Felicity bit her tongue. Diplomacy was indeed the vocabulary word of the day. "Tell me what you mean. We'll talk it through."

"It's probably nothing. Maybe I'm just getting forgetful, like Jim says."

"You're not the forgetful type, Tasha."

"Maybe he's right and I'm just getting older."

"Tell me what's happened."

"Money went missing from my wallet the other day. It wasn't a lot—just forty bucks—but when I asked Jim about it, he laughed and reminded me that I'd bought gas with it."

"Did you?"

"That's the thing." She looked at Felicity with one perfectly shaped eyebrow raised. "I always use my credit card for gas because I get cash back on each purchase. I checked my online account and, yep, I did use the card, not the forty bucks."

"He's stealing from you."

"But *why*? Honest to God, Lissie, all he has to do is ask. I've never said no."

Oh, boy. Oh, shit. Felicity had to tread lightly. If she came down too hard on the lying scumbucket, Tasha might freeze her out again. But the situation wasn't good, and it had to be dealt with. "Anything else gone missing?"

"Not that I've noticed."

"Has his behavior changed?"

"Not in any specific way. He's still good to me, bringing me little gifts and doing sweet stuff all the time. But it almost feels like he's faking it. I can't...I just don't know what's going on."

"But you do know," Felicity said. "Trust your instincts."

Tasha's jaw stiffened. "I hear you. I will."

"And now it's my turn to ask. Are you safe? Are you sure he's no danger to you?"

Tasha laughed, then put her arm around Felicity. "Of course, I'm safe! Hey, I've got an idea."

"Yeah?"

"It's not a concert in Portland, but maybe we could hit The Roundabout sometime soon, just you and me, like the old days."

Felicity nearly choked. The 'Bout was the absolute last place on earth she would choose to spend an evening. It was a big, wooden barn packed to the rafters with desperate divorcees and dairy farmers in their finest Western wear, well marinated in Coors Light and bargain-bin body spray. Just the thought of it made her woozy.

But Tasha was smiling. Her eyes sparkled. She was extending

an olive branch.

"OK. I'm in. Let me know what night works for you." Felicity popped to a stand, not the least bit stiff despite the long heart-to-heart on the hard steps. "I'm glad we talked, Tash."

She nodded in agreement. "Me too. Hey, one thing. Tom isn't really his name, right?"

"It isn't, but I can't pronounce his actual name, so we've agreed to stick with Tom."

"Huh. And what's with the bug? That was weird."

"Yeah, I guess you could say that Tom has a wide range of interests." Felicity gave her friend one last squeeze and returned to the trailer.

She found Tom at the booth, watching the beetle crawl from one side of the table to the other. He was fully dressed, having chosen the short-sleeved T-shirt, jeans, and belt.

"Hey, how come you didn't switch back to a cat when Tasha came over? Wouldn't that have made life simpler for everyone involved?"

He didn't look up from his beetle observations. "I tried, but I don't have enough energy yet. It might be a couple of days."

"Well, the cat's out of the bag now, as they say." That's when Felicity noticed the garden bounty piled by the sink: basil, parsley, onion, oregano, garlic, two small-but-ripe zucchini, and more butter lettuce. "When did you do all this, Tom?"

He continued to watch the bug. "Right after you left. Just took a couple of minutes."

Felicity was shocked, but moved. She couldn't remember the last time someone had done something for her without being asked. "Thank you, Tom."

"Sure." He picked up the insect again and let it scuttle across his palm.

Felicity shivered. She didn't much like bugs. "So what do we have here? Do you know?"

"It's a scarab of some kind."

"I've never seen one around here."

"You said there were lots of them?"

"Yep. Is this what Apep meant by pestilence?"

"Doubt it."

"But you're not sure?"

"No."

Felicity grabbed a plastic baggie form the drawer and handed it to Tom. "Put your little friend in the bag. We're going on a road trip."

Tom looked up and frowned. "I agree that I need to see where you found the scarab, but it's equally urgent that we start training."

"I know. But there's something we need more than those things." She ushered him out the door and to the car.

"Felicity…"

"We're going to the library."

"Why?"

Felicity took a deep breath, got behind the wheel, and started the car. "You and I have been thrown together, right? I didn't go looking for you and your sacred calling, and you certainly didn't go looking for me to be the Acolyte."

"This is true."

"You know very little about me."

Tom seemed intrigued. "Go on."

"I know *myself*, though. And I can tell you that I get overwhelmed when I don't have enough information. I become anxious and unpleasant to be around."

SUSAN DONOVAN & VALERIE MAYHEW

"OK."

"But once I have facts and context, I have knowledge, and knowledge settles my nerves and helps me focus. Knowledge is *calm.* Do you get what I'm saying?"

The corner of his mouth curled. "I do now."

"So, whenever I feel like I'm flying blind, I go to the library. I went there to understand Oregon divorce law and to get perspective on my cancer treatment and prognosis. I've researched cat first aid, muffler repair, bankruptcy, you name it. Want to talk about superpowers? Let me tell you something, Tom, the public library is my superpower."

He was speechless.

"And I've never had to fly so blind as I have in these last couple of days. I need more information—about Egypt and Bastet and Apep and even your little buddy Ringo there in the baggie." She turned to him, expecting she'd have to explain the joke.

But he smiled at her. "Very funny, Felicity."

CHAPTER NINE

The North Coast Public Library and Community Center was small but nicely designed and well stocked, with a computer zone, clusters of comfy reading chairs and large desks, lots of natural light, and a view of the Pacific Ocean. There was a children's area, a reference room, and divisions for history, science, arts, and every literature genre imaginable. Felicity set up shop at a worktable in the back corner of the reference room, and once Tom knew where she'd be, he wandered off to the biological sciences section.

A librarian took Felicity to the shelves housing ancient Egyptian mythology, religion, and ritual, government and military history, language and writing, social structure, and Egyptology. Felicity moved through the stacks, filling a rolling cart to capacity. She carried what had to be a seventy-five-pound mountain of hardcover reference texts to her table, not realizing anything was amiss until two elderly gentlemen stared at her, awestruck.

"Good afternoon." Felicity smiled.

As she dumped the armload on her worktable, something

dawned on her. She hadn't made a big deal of carrying the books. She'd just done it. It seemed like the less planning she put into something, the more competent she was. The less she strained for perfection, the easier things became. Who knew? She'd have to keep that in mind.

She devoured the content, soon realizing her biceps weren't the only enhanced thing about her. She was whipping through chapters, pages, charts, and graphics, taking no notes but retaining even the smallest of details. She'd always been an academic plodder, slow and meticulous. Today, she was a genius.

She hadn't expected her cerebral cortex to rejuvenate the way her bum knee had, and the realization was as terrifying as it was exhilarating. What else might be happening to her?

After a quick check to make sure no one looked her way, she cupped her boobs and gave them a little jiggle. It appeared the march of time continued within the confines of her 48-hour bra. A girl couldn't have *everything*, right?

Felicity learned the basics of the grammatical structure of Egyptian hieroglyphs. She learned that ancient Egypt, like most civilizations, had a real problem with female power, and had done their best through the ages to erase female pharaohs from the historical record.

A whisper snatched her away from a paragraph about Apep's dark nature. She looked up but found no one speaking. She went back to reading and swore she heard someone say *scorpions*.

Her eyes followed the sound. The two elderly men she'd greeted earlier sat across from each other at a table, heads bent together, all the way across the reference room. She shouldn't be able to hear their murmured conversation. And yet, she did. Felicity closed her eyes to focus on their exchange.

"I'm telling you what I saw, Frank. I may wear trifocals, but

I'm not blind."

"I've lived in this region fifty-three years and there's no such thing as a herd of scorpions."

"They crossed Pacific Street right in front of me and the missus, last Wednesday when we were down in Rockaway Beach. A million of 'em! Look." Felicity heard the rustling of book pages. "These fellas right here—Pacific Northwest forest scorpions—but bigger."

"Give that to me." The other man chuckled. "Rare and shy, John. Says right here that they're so shy they're rarely seen. No mention of stampedes down Main Street."

"I said a *herd*. Not a stampede. I swear on a stack of Bibles it's true."

"Maybe you should swear off the Bushmill's instead."

Tom found her then. He brought with him an opened reference book, pointed to one of the photos. "As I feared. Our beetle friend is *Scarabaeus sacer*, the Egyptian scarab beetle, otherwise known as a dung beetle, found only in the Mediterranean Basin. See the distinct horn? The ridges of the thorax?"

"It's a symbol of immortality, right?"

"Yeah, they're sacred. It's been a helluva long time since I've seen one in person."

Felicity nodded. "How'd it get to Pine Beach?"

"I don't know. But you need to show me where you found it. Now."

She grabbed her purse and the slim-but-oversized book on hieroglyphs, then rushed to the checkout desk at the front of the library, handing the clerk the book and her library card.

"I'm sorry, ma'am. Reference books can't be checked out."

"Shoot! I completely forgot. Thanks." *Damn it.* She really wanted to keep reading that book.

She was about to return it to the shelf when, on impulse, she shoved the bottom of the tome down the front of her pants and covered the top with her shirt. And just like that, she wobbled past the busy checkout counter and into the sunlight, Tom at her side.

She'd stolen a library book! She'd broken another rule. She'd broken another *law*. If she kept this up, her mug shot would be on display at the post office.

Delight shivered through her.

As soon as they climbed into her car, Felicity pulled the book from her pants. "I stole this! I'm as wild and reckless as a teenager! I'm out of control!"

Tom didn't look impressed. "We both know you plan to return it. Maybe, as a thanks, they'll let you keep your library card."

He was such a buzz-ruiner.

They were on their way to Pine Beach when Felicity said, "Oh, before I completely forget, the beetles aren't the only game in town. Did I tell you about the boils?"

"Boudica said she'd seen them on your ex-husband."

"Turns out it's not just him. All the customers at the barbershop have them, too."

Tom's head whipped around. His stare was intense.

"And the frogs and the scorpions—the notes taped to my cabinet?"

"Yes?"

"At the library just now, I heard two old guys talking about a herd of scorpions crossing the street in Rockaway Beach, south of us. And I saw a line of them in a parking lot. These aren't normal things, are they?"

"What do you think?"

"I think it's all about Apep."

"I think you're right."

Felicity found a parking spot just down the street from the barbershop. She led Tom into the alley and was relieved to see a few straggling scarabs still coming out from under the ladder.

"This is the spot. I have no idea where they're coming from, just under here somewhere." She reached in to wave her hand under the ladder…

"Stop!" Tom grabbed her wrist and yanked her away so hard she hit the building wall.

"What's your problem? Ow!" She rubbed the back of her head where it had hit the bricks.

"You almost entered, Felicity." Tom closed his eyes and tilted his face to the sky. "*Wir sitzen ganz schön in der scheise!*"

"Entered where? What are you talking about? Was that Swedish?"

"German. And this is bad."

"There's a lot of bad right now. Can you be more specific?"

Tom pointed to the open space between the angled ladder, the ground, and the wall. "That's a doorway. It's how the scarabs are arriving."

Felicity looked closer and noticed the air appeared thicker there, almost shimmering, something she hadn't noticed earlier. "A doorway from…?"

"The Realm of the Gods."

"Is that a triangle?"

"Not a triangle. It's a pyramid. Sacred. Don't *ever* enter a space like this."

She watched Tom pace back and forth in the alley, hands on his hips, like a football player shaking off an injury. She was about to tell him he was overreacting when… "Hey. Is that where that stupid superstition comes from? That it's bad luck to walk under ladders?"

"Stupid?" He huffed, insulted.

Since a sullen tomcat was the last thing she needed, Felicity apologized. "Sorry. Let's back up. This is a doorway from the Realm of the Gods?"

"Yes."

"So why's it here?"

Tom thought, then cursed under his breath. "*Pizdets!*"

"Doesn't sound reassuring. *That* was Swedish, right?"

"Russian. Someone's come."

Felicity felt a surge of hope. "Did Bastet send reinforcements to defeat Apep?"

Tom shook his head. "Felicity, you *are* the reinforcements."

"Oh. Right."

"But someone has arrived from the Realm of the Gods, and we need to find out who."

At that moment, two more scarabs darted out and made a beeline to Main Street. Tom took off after them and Felicity followed.

They tailed the beetles across the street, down several blocks, and past the train tracks. They briefly lost sight of them when they scampered under a chain-link fence at the docks, but they found a gate and caught up to the little buggers just before the two insects split up; one went right and one went left.

Tom pointed. "You take that one. I'll follow this one!"

Felicity had to speed walk to keep up with the beetle. It led her down a narrow and rickety finger pier where the only docked craft was an old ferry boat. Weathered lettering along its side read: The Aken. She watched in wonder as her beetle climbed up the gangplank and disappeared onboard like an invited guest.

Felicity wasn't sure what to do. She looked around, didn't see anyone, so took a few cautious steps up the ramp. "Hello?" Did she need permission to come aboard? Was that even a thing? She continued slowly until she stepped onto the deck. "Hello? Anyone here?" She saw no sign of life, not even the scarab beetle.

"*Get off!*"

She spun around to see a huge man lumber her way, the boat rocking with each stomp. He had to be close to seven feet tall, roughened by water and wind, with shaggy hair. He wore faded waders clipped to frayed suspenders and a very pissed off expression.

"I'm sorry, I…"

He slapped his meaty hands on her shoulders and hauled her toward the gangplank.

"No. Please! I didn't mean…" Felicity stumbled over a cleat, but the giant only tugged harder. When he spun her around to shove her onto the pier, her shirt ripped and her scarf fell loose. She braced herself to go flying through the air, but instead, he stilled behind her, his grip tightening. She dared peek over her shoulder and found two endlessly dark, angry eyes.

Felicity tried to tug free. "Let me go. I'm sorry. I was just following… forget it."

Still, the huge man didn't ease his grip or speak. He squinted as if trying to focus.

"You're dead."

"I said I was sor…"

Oh. The ogre's gaze was fixed on the now-visible necklace.

"Clearly, she's not dead." Tom had arrived without either noticing. "Let her go, Mahaf."

The huge man frowned but released his hold on Felicity, lifting his chin in a sign of greeting. "Tubastet-af-ankh. I was told your mistress's champion had finally failed."

"Unfortunately, she did. But another was chosen."

He raised a bushy eyebrow. "I had not heard." Mahaf looked Felicity up and down, then shrugged. "She is neither a youth nor a maiden."

"Hey! You don't know that. The maiden part, I mean."

She felt Tom's hand on her arm. "He knows, Felicity. Come down before you hurt yourself." Tom assisted her onto the pier.

From this angle, the man Tom called Mahaf looked both larger and scarier. Felicity shrunk back a bit as Mahaf continued to examine her. Suddenly, he cocked his head to one side as if listening to something.

"No one makes an accusation against her."

Felicity snorted. "Except my ex and a couple of collection agencies."

Tom tightened his fingers against her flesh as a warning to stay quiet.

The man listened for another moment and turned to Tom. "Indeed, she is righteous. But it may be pointless. I have, after all, already been summoned."

All the while, Tom had been slowly walking them back from the boat, moving Felicity out of the man's reach. "I admit I'm surprised you're here, Mahaf. I hope you were awoken in peace."

"The peace is broken, Tubastet-af-ankh."

Felicity really couldn't control herself. "Who is this guy?"

The giant of a man straightened and held his shoulders back. "I am Mahaf, the ferryman."

Tom shifted until he stood between Felicity and Mahaf. She could tell Tom wasn't afraid of him, but he was definitely wary. She peeked out from behind Tom's back. "What do you ferry?"

"He ferries the dead, Felicity."

"Uh... oh." Not good.

"Why here?" Tom asked. "Why were you drawn to this small town?"

Mahaf pointed at the necklace. "The peace is broken and the Goddess's *usekh* is here. This is where it will begin."

"What will begin?"

"The death."

Tom stiffened to his full height. "Not if we can help it."

Mahaf nodded slowly. "Perhaps you will triumph."

"Do you have a sense, oh Wise Mahaf, of when Apep will strike again?"

"I only sense the time is not yet nigh. Your previous Acolyte battled well before her defeat, and you can hold your head high. Apep is not strong enough to destroy you and the necklace at present. But soon."

"How long?"

"I do not know, but surely you can see with your own eyes how the universal forces are no longer in balance."

And the Oregon coast has become ground zero for raining frogs and boils and scarabs and stampedes of scorpions.

"When the god of chaos begins his reign, I will have many, many dead to carry. Soon. Unless the foretold path is altered." Mahaf turned away, the conversation clearly over.

As they walked along the pier and back through town, Tom seemed lost in thought.

"You found me just in time. He's scary." She was still trying to process what had just happened. "So where did the other scarab go?"

Tom shrugged. "A dead end. My dung beetle found a fresh pile of, well, dog dung."

"Just making sure there isn't another supernatural being lurking nearby."

"There may be."

Tom didn't elaborate, and Felicity didn't ask. One gargoyle per day was her limit.

When they reached the alley, Tom rushed to the ladder, said a few mumbled phrases in what Felicity assumed was Egyptian, and lifted it away from the wall. He laid the ladder flat on the dirty cement.

"What'd you do?"

"Closed the door."

"Probably a good idea."

Tom leveled his stare at her. She saw the tension in his neck and jaw. "Time to go, Felicity." He took her by the arm and guided her to the car. "Training starts now."

She was going to strangle him. Seriously.

"*Three* sit-ups?" Tom's expression was a mix of disappointment and horror. "You can't be done. You've only done three barely sufficient sit-ups."

Felicity crumpled to the patch of grass between the garden and junkyard fence, the most private spot they could find for training. She flopped an arm over her eyes. "I haven't attempted a sit-up since my sadistic gym teacher, Mrs. Frankel, threatened me in eighth grade."

"Oh, c'mon."

"I'm serious. She told me if I couldn't do ten sit-ups in a row, she'd make sure I never made it to high school."

"What happened?"

"I cried. Mrs. Frankel gave me a C. Life went on."

"Without the ten sit-ups?"

"Not then. Not ever."

Tom took several slow deep breaths. "Bastet's powers course through your veins. You need to trust in that and push yourself beyond your self-imposed limits."

Felicity just stared up at him. "Where do you think the three barely sufficient sit-ups *came* from, Tom? That *was* Bastet's powers, as applied to me, Felicity Cheshire, a cranky fifty-two-year-old lady." She struggled to stand. Tom reached out his hand to assist her, and she smacked it away. Eventually, grunting loudly, Felicity reached an upright position. It took a lot of work.

Tom was appalled.

"What?"

"I... I had no idea..."

"Well, now you do. So fuck you, and fuck your sit-ups!" She headed toward the trailer stairs, but Tom snagged her arm.

"How about push-ups? Can you do those?"

"Yes, but only the girl push-ups where I'm allowed to let my knees touch the ground."

"All right." Tom let his gaze travel over the property, his attention landing on Mrs. Romero's T-shaped laundry pole in the side yard. It seemed like yesterday when Tasha's mother, dressed in a jumpsuit with jumbo shoulder pads, had hung sheets on the clothesline while a Virginia Slims menthol hung from her lips.

"Pull-ups?"

"Of course not."

"Would you at least try?"

She sighed. "I'll try, and then I'm calling it a day."

Tom popped up from the step and clapped his hands. "Race you to the pole!"

"Race? As in run?" The last time Felicity had run, for any reason, was the day she ran from Richard Hume's house after she was served with surprise divorce papers. And that was only because she'd been in shock and was having an out-of-body experience.

Tom grabbed her arm and pulled her along. No matter how hard she pumped her legs, it was a struggle to keep up. They made it to the laundry pole, but instead of slowing, Tom made a U-turn and headed back toward the trailer, pulling her with him.

"That's not fair!" Felicity gasped for oxygen.

"Apep's not fair. Keep running."

Only then did she see Felonious Jim on the front porch, his pie hole gaping open in stupefaction.

When they reached the laundry pole again, Tom tested the steel, ensuring that it was cemented in place. "Up you go."

Felicity raised her arms. She couldn't reach.

"Jump."

"I jump like I run."

Tom grabbed her around the waist and lifted. She slapped her palms to the cool metal and gripped her fingers tight.

"Lift your knees. Keep your elbows pointed to the ground. Make sure your chin clears the bar."

Felicity could do none of those things, and her arms already quivered. She looked down to see her feet pedaling through the air.

"Let me give you a boost."

Just then, Felicity saw that Tasha had joined Jim on the porch. They both stared, slack-jawed.

She strained. She pulled. But even with Tom supporting her weight, she could not get her chin anywhere near the T-bar.

"You're not even trying." Tom gritted his teeth and added, "*Lasciami in pace pezzo di merda.*"

"Oh, yeah? Well, fuck off!" Felicity kicked at him until he released his grip. She immediately hit the ground and collapsed.

"Let me help."

"Back away!" She scrambled to her feet and walked briskly—but did not run—toward the trailer. "I'm done. That's it."

He was right behind her. "That was just the warm-up. We haven't even begun Step One."

"If Step One doesn't involve my foot in your ass, then it's not on the agenda."

"Step One involves..."

Felicity ignored him, retreated into the trailer into her little bedroom, shut the accordion door, swallowed two aspirin, and fell on top of the comforter.

Once everything was chopped and the sauce set to simmer, he checked on Felicity. She was out cold, which meant he'd have time to perform the protection ritual. He'd decided on mustard, since he'd found a nearly full squirt bottle of the stuff shoved in the back of Felicity's little refrigerator. It had expired two years earlier, but Tom wasn't interested in eating it. He planned to use it as paint.

He knew he should have done this sooner, but a fair amount of energy and focus was required to thoroughly shield a space from dark energy, and he hadn't felt up to it until now.

He pulled on his jeans but skipped shoes and a shirt. It was easier to connect with the earth's sacred energy that way, bare soles to the ground and skin exposed to the sun and wind. He hoped neither Tasha nor Jim were around because he really didn't feel like explaining. He wasn't sure what words they would comprehend, let alone accept.

He left the trailer, headed down the steps, and scanned the large property. It was sunset, which made it easy to figure out where he needed to begin.

The south.

Interestingly enough, south was in alignment with the front gate to Tasha's property. So he dipped a madrone twig into the opened mustard and drew the Eye of Horus, the sign of the daughter of Ra—a *Wadjet*—upon the mailbox. He drew each of its six parts in a separate unbroken motion, from the eye's left corner to the bold mark extending down from the eye's right corner.

He gave a slight bow of his head, mumbled the incantation in his first tongue, then straightened.

He raised his right index finger and followed the sun's western path. He circumvented the garden, and stopped before a towering alder, where he began the process again, using the stick to paint the *Wadjet* upon the bark of the tree, then repeated the incantation.

He found north. Marked an old concrete cistern lid with the *Wadjet*, and cast the spell of protection. He moved on to the east, which turned him directly toward Tasha's house.

Damn. Jim stood on the porch exhaling cigarette smoke through his nose, like a bull ready to charge, and he was in no mood for a pissing contest.

Jim flicked his cigarette over the railing and into the weeds. "Welp, I've seen it all now, brother. The evil eye of Satan, drawn in mustard!"

"Not exactly." He turned but Jim stepped in his way.

"Wouldn't ketchup work better for demonic shit, since it looks like blood?"

He took a deep breath, accepting there was no way to avoid this little conversation. "It's called a *Wadjet*. It's protective."

Jim laughed. "Until the first rain. Then all you're gonna have is a runny puddle of fuckin' mustard."

"If you say so." Jim was wrong. Once the incantation was in place, the *Wadjet* could only be purposefully wiped away by a human.

It wasn't foolproof, but it wasn't something Apep could manage since he was far from human.

"Besides, *I* already protect this place."

"Good to know." He stepped around Jim, knowing he had to perform the spell at the east point of the property to complete the circle of protection. He made the mark on a fencepost, spoke the sacred words, and was done. When he turned, he found Jim waiting.

"Seriously, I don't care what kind of freaky shit you're doin' with the crazy cat lady, but if you even *think* of laying a finger on my Tasha…" Jim lunged in his face. He could smell the man's tobacco breath and the odor of stale beer that clung to his clothing. "I'm watchin' you. You got that, asshole? You are officially on my shit list, you get me?"

"Yeah, I get you." He wanted to put his fist through the bully's face, but that wouldn't help Felicity.

"And you need to get rid of this stupid shit." Jim reached out and dipped his finger into the bright-yellow *Wadjet* on the fencepost. The instant he touched the symbol, he yelped in pain and jerked his hand away. Jim clutched his wrist and stared as small blisters formed on the pads of his fingers. "What the fuck did you just do to me?"

Interesting.

"Hey! I'm talkin' to you, fuckface! You'd better watch out, you hear me? God! I'm going to need a Band-Aid!"

Jim stormed into the house.

Felicity awoke to the smells of cooking, something aromatic and savory. She peeked through the door to gasp with surprise. Tom was setting the table with two mismatched plates, dingy forks and knives, and cracked plastic tumblers. The table setting may have been mid-century yard sale, but the scent was big-time *Bon Appetit*. She glanced to the stovetop, her stomach rumbling and her mouth watering.

"Ah, perfect timing. Dinner's ready."

Felicity emerged from the door, already regretting how grumpy she'd been with Tom. He'd only been doing his job. And he'd obviously gone out of his way to create a feast. But with *what?*

"I found two opened boxes of noodles in your cupboard, a jar of artichokes, and a small container of tomato paste. Inside your refrigerator was a bag of shredded cheese with only a few moldy clumps, which I removed."

Felicity stared in wonder. The cat *cooked?*

"I sauteed the squash with your herbs, onion, and garlic, and added a dash of the red wine I found under the sink behind the cleaning pads. The lettuce is tossed with oil and vinegar, salt and pepper, and some of the mandarin oranges I found at the back of the cupboard."

Felicity was speechless. And still a bit guilty. "I don't even know what to say, Tom. This is loaves-and-fishes-level shit."

It was also the best thing she'd eaten in ages, and not just because she was as hungry as a high school football team. Between the two of them, they polished off every bit of the pasta and salad.

But she felt compelled to bring something to Tom's attention. "I hate to break it to you, but pasta is an Italian dish."

He smiled, placing his fork along the edge of his plate. "The Chinese invented noodles, and tomatoes are native to the Americas, not Europe. So the Romans stole these the way they have stolen and destroyed everything they touch."

"I stand corrected."

"They did invent the panini, though."

As they cleaned up, Felicity found a deflated squirt jar of

mustard on the counter, and was puzzled. "I didn't taste mustard in the sauce."

"That's because I didn't use it for the sauce."

She frowned. "What did you use it for, then?"

"To protect the property."

Felicity laughed. "So mustard repels monsters or something?"

Tom shook his head, all business. Felicity's stomach dropped. She set the dirty plates into the sink. "What's wrong?"

"Why do you think something's wrong?"

"You're upset about something."

"But how can you tell?"

"Shit, Tom, I live with twelve cats! I can tell when someone's fur is rubbed the wrong way."

He leaned back against the counter. "You're right. I had a run-in with Jim."

"Sorry. Hair Gel Jim is a real assclown."

"Definitely. But there's something you need to know about him. He burned his hand on the *Wadjet*."

"The wah*what*?"

"The *Wadjet*. It is a protective symbol I painted in mustard at the four points of the property."

"OK. And he burned his fingers? Hey, maybe he's just another supernatural monster who's come through the doorway! It sure would explain a lot." Felicity laughed.

"He's fully human. Fully shithead, but human." Tom was taking all this very seriously. "He could approach the *Wadjet* and even touch it, so he's not supernatural in any way." He looked up at her, concern in his eyes. "But there's a deception about him, Felicity. He's lying or hiding something important."

"Yeah, well he's stealing money from Tasha."

"That could be it. Or it could be something else."

Felicity had a bad feeling about all this. She just wanted everything to go back to normal, whatever that was.

Tasha knocked, not waiting for an answer. She pushed the door open, smiling. "It's Ladies Night!"

"It is?" Felicity had no idea what she was talking about.

"At the Roundabout. Ladies get in free and beers are half off. Let's do it, Lissie. Right now. Let's just…go. No thinking. No excuses. Let's just go and be crazy best friends like old times." She stopped. "Oh. Hey, Tom."

"Hey."

Tasha's eyes sparkled. They pleaded. It took all of five seconds for Felicity to give her answer: "Hell, yeah!"

"Meet you in the car." Tasha left as abruptly as she'd arrived.

Felicity turned to Tom, not sure what to expect. Would he be angry and remind her about training? She wasn't about to ask his permission, that she knew.

"Sounds fun," he said, producing a tight smile. "And I know you could use some fun right about now, so go blow off some steam. Just remember that training kicks into high gear in the morning."

"You got it!" Felicity kissed him on the cheek, which seemed to shock him, then rushed into her room to change clothes. Now, if she could only find something with a seriously high neck.

CHAPTER TEN

The place was packed. Ladies' night meant that bottled Rainier was two bucks per vagina, which was supposed to lure women who would, in turn, lure men. Looking around, Felicity thought the Roundabout might have to change their marketing strategy because they were swimming in a sea of maleness.

"The odds are good tonight," Tasha said.

"But the goods are odd."

The two of them laughed, like they used to, and sipped their beers. They sat at a wobbly, pockmarked wood pub table along the far edge of the dance floor. The country music pounded so loud they had to shout at each other.

A moment later, Felicity's eyes began to water. She was hit with an unpleasant, but familiar, odor. "Are you wearing that perfume Jim got you?"

Tasha extended her wrist so Felicity could get a sniff, though the gesture was unnecessary. The stuff could be detected through the steel door of a fallout shelter.

"It's called Passion's Fire. Is it too much? I mean, I like it, but, look, it's not French *parfum* or anything."

Felicity tried to nod convincingly. The concoction smelled like unwashed butt crack, though she couldn't tell Tasha that. "It sure makes a statement."

"Yeah. That's the thing about Jim; what he lacks in sophistication, he makes up in enthusiasm. Oh, and I meant to tell you. You look really cute tonight." Tasha grinned. "There's something different about you."

"Thanks. I took a nap."

"That'll do it." Tasha cleared her throat. "So, we saw you outside today... um... what exactly were you doing?"

"A fitness evaluation."

"What are you being evaluated for?"

"Oh, you know." Felicity smiled. "Tom's into the mind-body-spirit thing, the holistic approach to life coaching. So..." It was time to change the subject. "How does Jim feel about you going out with me tonight?"

"He's fine with it. He trusts me and knows it's healthy to want a night out with my girl."

"Sounds real progressive of him."

Tasha pursed her lips. "And how does *Tom* feel about you being out with *me* tonight?"

Felicity laughed, picturing him cuddled up on the daybed with the cats. "Oh, he's a lifelong feminist, a warrior for women's rights. It's practically his religion, really."

Tasha squinted, suspecting sarcasm.

"Cheers to us!" Felicity tapped her Rainier can to Tasha's. "Just a couple of girls left unsupervised on the North Coast!"

He kneeled, naked, in the center aisle of the trailer. A single candle flickered before him. Offerings of cinnamon, milk, and sunflowers were placed in a semicircle before him. The cats gathered around, silent and still in their service. This was why he'd encouraged Felicity to go out with Tasha for the evening. He desired privacy for this. He needed it. Because he did not want her to witness another of his failures.

It was long ago that he'd last tried to reach the Goddess from the earthly plane. And it had been during a time when magic was employed and creator gods were remembered, and yet, even then, the connection had been weak. Her voice had been a faint whisper, her warm touch cooled by distance. And so now, in a time when magic had been shoved into the shadows and few even knew the gods' names? What did he expect? How could he hope?

It was not that he doubted her. *Never.* He knew she heard, saw, and loved from afar. Yet the speaking, the connecting, might be impossible.

He had to try.

He rested his palms upon the floor and bent at the waist, head lowered in supplication.

"O, Ever-Living Bastet, great protectoress, daughter of light, she who is dual Goddess of moon and sun, at once most gentle and loving nurturer and the fiercest of warriors. I come to you as your humble priest and servant, to ask for guidance and strength."

Mew-mew.

Hsssss. Boudica shushed whichever kitten couldn't stay quiet.

"Great Goddess, I have failed. I ask for your forgiveness. The Acolyte was defeated, and I chose anew when you could not. I ask that you grant your new Acolyte the strength of body and purpose, heart and soul, necessary to defeat Apep."

The junkyard dog barked.

He let his forehead touch the floor, closed his eyes, and readied to speak the ancient invocation he'd learned as a small boy: "With your graceful stealth, anticipate the moves of all who perpetrate cruelties and stay their hands against the children of light!"

The trees outside rustled in the wind.

"And ever watch over us in the lonely places into which we must walk."

He straightened, resting his hands on his knees while he waited. He heard crickets in the forest. An owl in a faraway tree. But he did not detect the voice of his mistress. Disappointment washed over him.

Just then, Boudica slipped her head beneath his arm and rubbed against him, purring.

It was enough. It would have to be.

They hit the dance floor and enjoyed themselves immensely, laughing and kicking up their heels. It wasn't long before Felicity found herself spinning, twirling, and adding an occasional flourish to the standard line dances, which was new for her. She was nowhere near as good as the other dancers, but it certainly was fun.

"Since when are you so good at this?" Tasha shouted.

"My knee hasn't been hurting me as much!"

"That's wonderful!"

It really was. Felicity had forgotten how much she loved to dance. It was something she did just for the joy of it, and Tom had been right—she really did need to blow off some steam.

The music blasted, and like all classic country lyrics, they heard tales of trustworthy two-ton pickups and suspicious women, one-night stands and summer nights. She and Tasha were inundated with offers to two-step swing or partner-up for a country waltz, and for the first time in forever, Felicity said "yes" a few times. But she had to be careful, since Tasha had dated most of these men at some point in the past, and unlike her inevitable battle with Apep, that was one bit of trouble Felicity could avoid.

After a particularly exuberant turn on the floor, she took a seat by herself at a table while Tasha twirled with a newcomer. She felt perfectly content, great even. It was a strange sensation.

She was happy for all the younger women there, too. They strutted in their Daisy Dukes, midriff-tied flannel shirts, and cowboy hats, flirting and flaunting their way through the songs. Good for them. They should enjoy it while they could.

Felicity suddenly felt someone's eyes on her. With a slow scan of the room, she saw a man looking her way. He was for sure a dairy farmer, sitting between two of his buddies. He had sandy brown hair cut short, handsome in a wind-worn way, maybe in his late forties, trim and clean. No hat. She noted the sharp crease in his Wranglers and the high polish of his cowboy boots. She decided to smile back, which caused him to immediately break eye contact and blush.

He *blushed?*

Before she could stop herself—before she even realized what she was doing—Felicity grabbed her beer and walked right on over to his table, sitting down across from him and his buddies. The two men sputtered their excuses and took off.

"Hi," Felicity said.

"Hi, yourself."

So he wasn't an orator. What did she expect? And he *was* cute, maybe even cuter up close than across the room, which wasn't how it usually worked. Felicity began to feel light-headed. What was happening? She swore she felt her nipples tingle.

Hello?!

Then a bolt of heat spread low in her belly. This was either a bladder leak or her lady parts were emerging from suspended animation, thawing after light years in cryogenic storage.

"I noticed you," the wordsmith said. "You're an amazing dancer. Are you a professional?"

"Dancer?"

"Yeah."

"No. I'm a former eighth-grade English teacher."

He grinned at her. Another *zing!* went directly to her nipples. This was no longer debatable. Something sexual was happening. Something unexpected and thrilling and, she'd assumed, impossible for her.

"If I promise to keep my participles from dangling, will you dance with me?"

Felicity nearly spat out her beer. *Grammar humor? At the 'Bout?* Her shock must have been plain because he laughed.

"I read a lot. Even dabble with a bit of my own writing. I'm kind of a nerd. My name is Cass. And you are…?"

"Felicity."

He held out his hand for a shake and when she obliged, he yanked her to a stand. "Let's cut a rug, Felicity."

More like they burned the rug and the floorboards beneath it. After a rigorous triple-step with a twirl and a dip, Cass bought them refreshing shots of tequila, and Felicity got up the courage to ask him a few questions. She decided to get the big stuff out of the way first. "Who ironed your jeans? Your wife?"

"Never had one of those."

"Girlfriend?"

"Haven't had one of those since last year."

"Mother? Grandmother?"

"Gone and long gone. I ironed them myself. See, I actually enjoy ironing. It's meditative. It gives me a real sense of accomplishment because I can iron something on Monday and it's still hanging in the closet on Friday, all nice and tidy and ready to wear."

He said all that with a glint in his eye, and if she were not mistaken, a dollop of self-deprecating humor. Felicity liked that in a person. They got back out on the dance floor to join a watermelon crawl that had the whole place rockin'. They followed that up with a Texas two-step, a waltz, and another shot of tequila. Tasha came over to their table to say hello, flushed from dancing and wearing an overly protective squint.

"This is…" Felicity hadn't asked for his last name! Cass rescued her by standing up and shaking Tasha's hand. "Cassius Schwindorf. Pleasure to meet you."

"Hey! Are you Lou Schwindorf's son?"

"I am."

"He was a buddy of my dad, Raffie Romero."

"Sure, I remember him! Hey, I think I met you when I was little."

Felicity sat back and enjoyed Tasha and Cass reminiscing about their fathers. Then they worked out how many years apart they were at school. Turned out Cass was forty, which would put him in diapers on the night of the Beastie Boys concert. And if things were headed where Felicity suspected they might be, that meant she could never again criticize the age gap between Tasha and Hair Gel Jim because she would be just as guilty.

Their conversation wound down and Tasha got asked to dance again. Cass bought them another round of shots before they enjoyed a bit of traveling cowboy cha-cha to the classic "New Moon" by Brooks & Dunn, a sexy and slow glide along the boards, which involved lots of hip rotation, his arms around her waist, and even some butt-to-crotch contact. At one point, Cass dipped Felicity in his arms, down a little too low and held a little too long, his gaze locked on hers.

Right then, Felicity was sure: *I'll be gettin' some tonight.*

Not five minutes later, she rushed toward Tasha, pulled her from her dance partner, and breathlessly explained that she was leaving with Cass. Tasha was dumbstruck. "But it's ten o'clock!"

"I know! I can't believe I'm up this late either!"

Tasha shook her head. "I meant it's early; never mind. If you're going, I'm going. We'll all walk out together."

Once in the parking lot, Tasha pulled her aside and shoved her cell phone into Felicity's purse. Felicity gave it back. "I got a phone, just like you said."

Tasha laughed. "Good for you! Have fun. Be safe." She checked to make sure Cass was out of hearing range. "He seems really nice and I know his dad was good people, but lots of serial killers come from good families. Call me for any reason, any time."

"Thanks. I think."

It was a twenty-minute ride to his place, a charming farmhouse outside Tillamook. Felicity wasn't sure what she expected once they entered the living room. She barely remembered her last random hookup, which had to have been during Clinton's second term, but she vaguely recalled that it had involved awkward chitchat and an offer of a night cap.

The times must have changed because she and Cass two-stepped their way right into the bedroom, ripping at one another's clothes like sex-starved maniacs, throwing boots across the room, tossing underwear on chairs and bureaus, and before Felicity knew it, she was naked, on her back on the bed, and Cass stood over her, looking like he'd just seen a ghost.

Oh, no. She'd totally forgotten.

Felicity sat up, covering herself. "I feel awful. I should have warned you; I had breast cancer. The scarring is from a series of lumpectomies and biopsies. I probably should have had reconstructive surgery, but I couldn't afford it. I completely understand if..."

"*What?* No! Stop! You are beautiful, and I'm damn glad you're alive but it's just..." He pointed.

Felicity looked down. At the necklace.

Shit, shit, shit.

"Oh, this old thing?" Felicity smiled up at him and batted her eyelashes. "It's just an ancient Egyptian amulet that gives me superhuman powers. The lock's broken, and I can't get it off."

"I can fix that for you," he offered.

"Maybe later."

Cass tipped his head playfully. "So tell me about those powers of yours."

"Superhuman *grammatical* powers. So don't even *try* to split your infinitives in my presence."

His laugh was raspy and wicked as he lowered himself on top of her, his warm lips hovering just over hers. "What happens if I misplace my modifier?"

She brushed her lips against his, teasing, light as a whisper, with just a little tongue. "I get the feeling that won't be an issue for you."

And it wasn't. Cass was the most spectacular lover Felicity had ever had. He was generous and patient and had the stamina of a man half his age. If life were fair, she would have found Cass back in college, and the knowledge that men like him existed would have helped her relegate Richard Hume to the reject pile, where he surely belonged.

But life was not fair, and Cass would have been in elementary school while Felicity was in college.

She surprised herself that night. All her parts seemed to work just fine. She remembered what to do, how to do it, and the correct timing for doing it. She allowed herself to wallow in the pleasure of his body on hers, his hot flesh sliding beneath hers, his mouth everywhere a man could put his mouth on a woman. She lost track of how many times she orgasmed, which was probably the way it was supposed to be. She couldn't know for sure, though, because her marriage to Rich had been twenty years of orgasmic computer code—a lot of zeros with an occasional one.

Felicity barely had time to catch her breath or gulp down water before they were at it again. *Goddam*, Cass was fun.

In addition to losing her inhibitions and self-doubt, Felicity had lost track of time. While stretched out on her stomach taking a breather, she noticed a pale streak of daylight peek through the draperies.

"Uh-oh."

"Everything good?"

Cass lay on the floor near the bed, on his side, head propped on his hand as he gazed up at Felicity. She couldn't remember how he got there, but he didn't look injured. He looked satisfied.

She smiled down at him and rested her chin on her crossed forearms. "I should probably get home. I have to feed the cats."

"How many you got?"

Did she ever want to see this man again? Because if she did, giving him an exact number could be a mistake. On the other hand, she was too old to waste time on someone who didn't know the truth of who she was. Besides, the world was about to end, so Cass had no time to waste on someone who wasn't exactly right for him either, whether he knew it or not.

"I have thirteen damn cats."

"Wow." He pushed himself up and sat on the bed next to her. His legs were covered in a blondish fur and he had long, pale feet. He smelled good—like clean laundry and rolling hills—and though it had been a long time since she'd been with a man, Cass had managed to make it all seem so comfortable, like they'd known each other for years. He stroked her back.

"I got a boatload of barn cats myself," he said. "Every good dairy farm needs them. Honestly, I have too many to keep track of, so I have the vet come out a couple times a year just to make sure none of them are sick or injured."

"That's good of you."

"Should I drive you home?"

She nodded. "Yeah. Unfortunately."

He gave her bottom a friendly pat. "I'll make us some coffee while you get dressed." Cass collected her clothes from the floor and laid them on the wrinkled sheet. Then he fetched her boots, one from the hallway and one half-hidden under a dresser. He went out to the kitchen in all his God-given glory and fired up the percolator.

As Felicity watched him, she decided it was nice to be with a man who was comfortable in his own skin but not infatuated with himself. How refreshing. How unusual.

On the fifteen-minute drive to her place, Cass was anything but tongue-tied. He told her all about his 325 head of cattle, mostly Holsteins, Jerseys, and Brown Swiss, and the six hundred acres passed down from his father and grandfather. He told her he'd been working on a historical fiction novel based on the area's most infamous unsolved murder case.

"Interestingly enough, Oregon has more than its share of psycho killers."

Felicity wondered if that was why Apep had chosen Oregon for his latest rampage—because he would blend right in.

Cass pulled up to Tasha's place and cut the engine of his pickup. Both the house and the trailer showed no signs of life.

He leaned in and kissed her gently. "I'd really like to see you again. Can I have your number?"

"I'll call you. Are you in the phone book?"

"I am."

"How do you spell your last name?"

He laughed. "It's a tongue twister, I know. Here." He reached across her lap and wrote down his number and on a pad of paper from the glove compartment. He tore off the top sheet and handed it to her. "Call me. Promise."

"Promise." She began to exit the truck but turned around, cupped his face in her hands and kissed him, hard. "Thank you, Cass. I needed this more than you will ever know."

The cats swarmed when she opened the door. Felicity reached down to scratch as many ears as possible when a low growl echoed through the trailer. She was about to scold whichever cat was responsible when Tom emerged from the corner bathroom. Everybody but Boudica scurried to the daybed and clustered together for safety.

Boudica looked up at Tom and yelled, *Mmmmrrooooww-mrrp!*

"Oh, really?" Tom snapped. "How about *you* grow up!"

"Is everything OK?" Felicity's sleep-deprived brain couldn't figure out what was happening.

"Wouldya look what the cat dragged in." Tom sniffed the air, and, with chin held high, he approached the daybed, sending the cats scattering. He sat down stiffly, then promptly turned his back to her.

That was one pissed-off cat. Felicity dropped her purse on the table, sat beside him, and touched his shoulder. He retreated. "I'm sorry, Tom. I should have asked Tasha to let you know I'd be late."

"That would have been the polite thing to do. But it's not late, Felicity. It's *early*. You've been gone all night."

"Yeah. Sorry."

"The kittens were worried."

"They were?"

"They thought you'd been eaten by the Rottweiler."

"No. I was…"

"I know what you were doing. I can smell him on you." Tom examined the pulled threads on the old blanket.

Raarooo! Mojo hopped up on the other side of Tom.

"You and me both." Tom shook his head. "It feels like eons since I got myself some pu…"

"Don't even. Besides, you're a priest."

"Yeah, a celibacy-optional kind of priest, thank you very much." Tom looked up from the blanket to face Felicity. His lips were drawn tight and his eyes remained aloof.

"I'm sorry you were worried."

"I said *Scratch and Sniff* were worried, not *me*." Tom was a terrible liar.

At the mention of their names, the kittens joined the party on the daybed, happily crawling into Felicity's lap. She rubbed their respective chins and bellies, the way each preferred. "I don't know what came over me, Tom. It was just… bizarre. I initiated flirtation with a man, which I never have the confidence to do, and it was so much fun! I danced the night away, forgetting to feel self-conscious. It was unbelievably freeing."

"I see."

"I went back to his place, and I had no idea sex could be like that! I mean, my whole life, sex was just…"

"No details, please. I get it."

"It was completely unexpected. Absolutely wild. I couldn't get enough. It was…"

"The necklace."

Felicity froze. "What?"

"Bastet is the Goddess of sex."

Well, hell. Now it was her turn to be pissed off. "Ya think maybe you should have mentioned that *before* I went dancing at a country and western pickup joint?"

"It's never been an issue before."

"Right, because you've always chosen a teenage virgin before."

"Yes. You're very different."

"No shit! I'm a grown-ass woman who's been to hell and back. Anything else you need to share with me? Any other cravings or behaviors that might create problems for an old broad such as myself?"

Tom looked a bit sheepish. "Let me think on this. Bastet influences fertility…"

"That ship has sailed."

"And marriage."

"That ship has sunk."

"She is the Goddess of secrets, of the moon, the hearth, and offers protection against contagious diseases and evil spirits. Some think she's connected to jokes, too, and though she has a very dry sense of humor, I've never really asked her."

Felicity stood up. She felt different; well, of course, she did! She'd just spent an entire night dancing, making wild, passionate love, laughing, downing shots of tequila, and rolling off beds. She'd just used parts of her body, mind, and soul that had been in the deep freeze for years.

She headed to the bathroom. Tom was behind her.

"Where are you going?"

"I need a shower."

"We have to train."

"I know. Just let me shower and change. So what's on the agenda today? The first step?"

Silence.

Felicity turned to see Tom holding the note Cass had given her. When Tom glanced up, his expression was one of torment.

"*Cassius?*"

"Huh?"

"Your new lover is a Roman?"

"Oh, my God, Tom. No! He's a Tillamook dairy farmer."

Tom straightened. "Good." She watched him transition from disgruntled feline to badass drill sergeant. "We'll begin at the beginning, from the priestly text *The Book of Overthrowing Apep*, Step One: Spitting upon Apep."

Felicity let out a surprised laugh. "*Spitting?*"

"Spitting."

She'd obviously misunderstood. "Spitting as in hocking a loogie"?

Maybe she'd shower *after* Step One.

Two hours later, her cheeks were killing her. And her jaw. Even her eyebrows hurt. Who knew there were so many muscles in the human face?

"Again." Tom didn't bother to mask his frustration. "We've been over this time and again, Felicity. Your spit must have range because you cannot risk standing near Apep at the start of battle when he is at his peak strength. Once more: fill your mouth with water and expel it quickly and forcefully!"

They were between the garden and junkyard fence again, away from prying eyes. Earlier, Tasha had dropped by to make sure Felicity was home safe, but there hadn't been time to give her the details of her night with Cass. And though Tasha had been warned to expect more training, Felicity would rather not have to come up with an explanation for how spitting was part of life coaching.

"Tell me again why I have to spit on him?"

"Because it is the first step in the ritual."

"But why?"

"Because that is the way the steps are ordered."

"But why?"

"Because that's the way it has always been done, and we believe that if something works for thousands upon thousands of years, there is no need to alter it."

Felicity sighed. "All right, I guess."

"*You guess?*" Tom threw up his hands. "There's no guesswork in smiting Apep! Only when the steps are carried out in the correct order, with the proper incantation, can the god of chaos be burned to ash and vanquished until the next cycle begins! End of story!"

"*Burned?* You never mentioned that part."

"We'll get to that later. Now, can we please continue? Remember, I need a directed spray of fine mist, shot straight at me. Do it!"

Felicity dutifully filled her mouth with water yet again. She returned the tumbler to the flat rock, stood tall and straight, and prepared to spit all the way to where Tom stood. She put all her breath behind it, she really did, and thrust forward from her torso and throat, but her lips were numb at that point and what she produced was more of a sloppy dribble than a directed spray.

"The incantation. Now say the incantation!" Tom was losing

his patience. She was too.

"*Dehpehk AH-hapep —*"

"*Ah-HA-pep.*" His correction was sharp and ill-tempered.

"Can't I just say it in English? I'm lucky to remember where I put my car keys and now you want me to recite ancient Egyptian while drooling on myself?"

"Fine. English. But I don't know if it'll work."

She placed a hand on her hip. "Oh, come on. You mean to tell me that every other Acolyte in history has learned all the incantations perfectly, in ancient Egyptian, no matter their native language?"

"Yes."

"Well, they had three fucking years, didn't they?" Felicity marched around to the other side of the trailer, plopped down on the stairs, and massaged her jaw.

Tom followed and sat beside her. "You're right. I'm sorry. Just memorize the English translation first, and if we have time, we'll learn the original Egyptian. I just hope it works."

"Can't you just ask Bastet if it'll work?"

"I… no."

"Why not?"

"Because I can't communicate with her when I'm here."

Felicity reared back. "Wait. You can't even talk to her in prayer or meditation or dreams or something? Not even a ritual?"

Tom took a deep breath and let it out slowly. "There was a time, long ago, when that worked. I could reach out with my spirit, in humility, and get an answer from the Goddess. Or at least feel an answer. Not anymore."

"What's changed?"

"People have changed. Culture has changed. Her memory has faded, and humans aren't as open to the old ways, or as willing to believe the unbelievable, or see beyond the impossible to the possible."

"You mean magic?"

He picked a blade of grass and fiddled with it. "I just know that the barrier between the realms is thicker now. The distance is too far."

"So Bastet is stuck up there and Apep is stuck down here and that's where you come in?"

"No, Felicity. That's where *you* come in." He stood and offered his hand, then pulled her up.

"Hey, I have a request. Can we move on to Step Two, Tom? I'm sure I'll do better at that. I mean, I can't do any worse, right?"

"All right. Step Two it is: Defiling Apep with the Left Foot."

She crumpled back down to the step.

"What's wrong? The incantation for Step Two is short, and the footwork doesn't take much skill."

"I..."

Tom sat again too. "You know you can tell me anything. Just spill it, and we'll figure it out together."

She worked her jaw again. "Well, it's just that I suffer from performance anxiety, and when I have to do something perfectly, on command, I get my right and left mixed up."

Tom stared at her.

"It's so bad that I had to quit first-grade ballet. At our fall recital, when all the other little girls were moving to third position with their left hand, I went to my right and accidentally broke another dancer's nose—blood all over her tutu."

Tom's mouth hung open.

"Studies show it's more common with women than men, something about how our brains are wired. And it appears to worsen with age."

"But you like to dance."

"It's not a problem when I'm relaxed. Or doing shots. It's just when I'm under stress and nervous about doing something correctly. And knowing I have to save the human race is fairly stressful."

Tom considered this for a moment, nodded, and slapped his hands to his thighs as he stood. "Felicity?"

"Yeah?"

"Does Pine Beach have a liquor store?"

"I probably shouldn't drink while training."

"Oh, I agree. It's for me."

Tom insisted they go to the grocery before the liquor store, but Felicity knew the order didn't matter since their little excursion was doomed from the start. Her next Oregon Trail SNAP deposit didn't hit for several days. And inside her wallet was every dime she had to her name—a whopping sixteen dollars and seventy-three cents—the remaining cash from Rich's raincoat plus the lint-covered change from the bottom of her purse. She'd do the best she could. She couldn't let them starve.

Tom grabbed a grocery cart from the corral and headed to the produce section.

"Tom!" She caught up to him and leaned in close to whisper the awful truth, as if every soul in town didn't already know. "I'm serious; I don't have much money."

"There's nothing in the house to eat."

"I realize that, but…"

"It'll be fine. Don't worry."

Don't worry? Ha! Tell that to security when they're escorting us from the premises!

Tom tossed a bag of apples into the cart and just like that, a third of her resources were gone. Next were fresh strawberries and blueberries and a bundle of broccoli, followed by fresh asparagus. She heard him hum to himself as he headed to the bakery section. She swallowed down a lump of dread. She had to stop him.

"Felicity?"

That voice.

She turned, already knowing what awaited her, and sure enough, it was Lady Bethany, Princess of Pregnant Perfection. Today's ensemble featured black leggings, a blindingly white T-shirt, and a coordinated zebra-stripe scrunchie/water bottle combo. A giraffe-print canvas grocery tote hung from her grip. She looked like a zoo volunteer.

"What'cha up to? How've you been?"

Felicity stared at her, mute. What was this girl's deal, anyway? They weren't enemies, but they sure weren't friends, so why was Beth*any* always so smiley and cheerful?

"Shopping," Felicity said. Her voice had a deadened quality to it, even to her own ears.

"Me too!"

"There's a lot of that going on here, at the Safeway."

Bethany laughed, like that was the most hysterical thing she'd ever heard. "You're so funny, Felicity. I mean, well, to be honest, you're nothing like how Rich describes you."

"I just bet."

Felicity saw the store manager heading her way with some urgency, marching past the display of gluten-free products. He waved at her.

Oh, shit. Maybe she should just make a run for it now, let Tom fend for himself. Being invisible, no one would even notice!

Bethany touched Felicity's forearm. "Well, I just wanted to say hi. Nice seeing you. Take care." She headed for the automatic exit doors.

"Ms. Cheshire!"

Felicity snuck a peek at his nametag to jog her memory. It had been eighteen months since they'd spoken, when the very last personal check she'd ever written was returned from the bank, a big, red NSF stamped across her handwriting. The bank closed her account the next day.

"Hello, Mr. Fischer." Felicity's mouth had gone dry. Her greeting sounded sticky and panicked. Did Mr. Fischer have ESP? Had he foreseen a disturbance at the checkout line?

"How've you been?"

Felicity glanced around to make sure there was no one else he could be addressing. "Uh, fine. Yourself?"

"Excellent! Just wanted to assure you that we received the instructions from your lawyer. Your account is all set up and ready for to use whenever you'd like."

"My account?" *My lawyer? Alexander?*

Tom rounded the corner then, pointing into the basket. "I got us a German chocolate cake. I meant to ask, do you like New York strip or filet? Does Tasha have a grill?"

She nodded, stunned and confused. Tasha did have a grill, but Felicity couldn't even remember what steak of any cut tasted like.

"All you have to do is sign the receipt when you check out, and I'll take care of the rest." Mr. Fischer smiled widely. "And, of course, should you ever need delivery, it will be free of charge."

"Right. Thank you." She watched Mr. Fischer walk away and then searched for Tom. He was in the dairy aisle by the whipping cream, arm resting on the cart handle. He grinned like the mischievous cat he was.

Back at the training spot behind the Airstream, Tom had already drained three beers and achieved an enviable state of relaxation. He'd enjoyed a large piece of the Safeway three-layer German chocolate cake too.

Felicity had not been allowed either. Tom said that the beer and cake would be her reward for mastering Defiling Apep with the Left Foot.

"You lied," Felicity said, panting. "You said this step was easy."

"No, I said it didn't require much skill. I wanted to avoid triggering your performance anxiety. And look at the progress you're making!"

True, her performance had improved dramatically since she'd tied a purple-feathered cat toy around her left ankle to remind her which foot to kick after the turn and squat. But really, what kind of sadist invented a turn-squat-kick?

Fucker.

And now, counting to herself, she turned, squatted, straightened, and then kicked out with her left foot. "Rise thee up, O Ra, and crush thy foes!" As soon as the words were spoken, she doubled over, hands to knees, and gasped for breath.

"Yes! You did it! Good work!"

Felicity didn't straighten.

"Which do you want first—beer or cake?"

Felicity remained folded over.

"You all right?"

"Tom?"

"Yes?"

"I can't move. I think I broke something."

Tom rushed to her side, helped her straighten, and supported her weight as they made their way around to the front of the Airstream.

"You will be fine, Felicity. It's just a muscle spasm. Nothing a hot shower and some rest won't fix. The lance and knife will be here tomorrow, and we'll start Step Three."

"Lance and knife? I could poke an eye out with those things." She gritted her teeth against the pain and climbed the stairs to her front door.

"And a fetter. A fetter is on its way, too."

"Kinky." Her legs hurt so much she could barely walk. "Hey, can I have a beer *with* my cake?"

"Sure. You deserve it."

They got inside the trailer, and Felicity collapsed in the booth. Tom grabbed a bottle from the fridge and brought the grocery store cake to the table, along with a plate and fork. He took a seat across from her.

"We'll start tomorrow with stretches and some *Tahtib*. Then we'll revisit sit-ups."

Felicity glared at him over the cake, stabbing her fork directly into the three layers of chocolate and coconut and shoving a huge bite into her mouth. She washed it down with a swig of beer.

"*Tahtib* is an ancient stick-fighting martial art, something like the Japanese *Bojutsu* tradition."

"Rock on." Felicity hacked away at the cake and shoveled an even bigger bite in her mouth, then another, closing her eyes with ecstasy as the chocolate melted on her tongue.

"*Tahtib* is fun; you'll like it. It's incredibly satisfying to bang shit with a stick."

She woke with a start. Tom lowered her onto the bed. "Whaaa happened?"

"You fell asleep in your cake." Tom yanked off her shoes and pulled the comforter over her. "*Jayidaan, maharib 'anthaa.*"

"Huh?"

"Sleep well, warrior."

And she did, right up until a loud banging penetrated the depths of her dream. It took a moment for Felicity to be sure the noise was real—and select the perfect words to rip Tasha and Jim to shreds for doing this to her again—when the noise stopped. A second later, there was a delicate knock at her bedroom door. She sat up, the hair on the back of her neck bristling. Something was wrong.

"Yes?"

Tom peeked his head inside. "I need you. Now."

CHAPTER ELEVEN

Felicity rushed out in her ratty pajamas to see Ronnie perched gingerly on the edge of the daybed. The room was lit only by moonlight, but Felicity's improved vision gave her a clear picture of the awful sight—Ronnie'd been badly beaten.

"Oh, my God!" Felicity rushed to her side, dropped to her knees, and was overwhelmed by the coppery smell of blood. Not the stale must of the tunnels, but fresh bleeding. Her stomach churned. "Who did this to you?"

When Tom switched on the lights, Ronnie hissed in pain and hid her eyes behind her hand.

"Sorry." Tom arrived with a bowl of water and a clean dishcloth.

"There were two of them; surprised the hell outa me." Ronnie's voice was ragged, her eyes still shielded. "I'd taken my laptop to bed, and I must have fallen asleep without setting the deadbolt. So incredibly stupid! That's how they got in the front door."

Felicity reached for the cloth, but Tom had already settled at

Ronnie's side. He pried Ronnie's hand away and began wiping blood from her forehead, cheekbones, and around her eyes. Ronnie talked as Tom cleaned her up.

"My first thought was that they were just punks after my computers. But..." She stopped to glance at Felicity. "They came for the phone."

"*What?*" This was all her fault; she'd dragged Ronnie into this mess, and now someone had tried to kill her!

"One of them took the phone from the desk while the other grabbed me, demanding to know where I'd gotten it."

Tom tipped up her chin to get a better look. His hands moved quickly, poking and prodding, with confidence and obvious practice. It was clear he'd seen this kind of thing before.

"I told them I found it in an alley in Portland." Ronnie winced as Tom pressed a sensitive spot.

"Fast thinking," he said.

"They didn't believe me. That's when the knives came out."

"*Knives?*"

"Veronica, your nose is bleeding but not broken." Tom turned her head toward the overhead light. "You're going to have a shiner on this eye but no permanent damage." He then tilted her head to one side, pushed her hair out of the way, and exposed several thin, horizontal lacerations across her neck. "Three blade wounds, none deep. You must be fast."

"They put a knife to your *throat?* Oh, God. This is bad. Ronnie, I'm so sorry we put you in this position. It's my fault."

She shook her head. "No. It's *my* fault for powering it up again. I turned it off right after you left, specifically so no one could track it, but then I wanted to double-check something so..." she jerked back in pain when Tom touched her cheekbone.

"Headache? Dizziness? Nausea?" Tom had been holding aside her dark curls but let them go, moving his hands across her shoulders and down her arms.

"I don't have a concussion. They didn't land a hard-enough blow to take me down. I don't think they expected me to fight back."

Felicity took Ronnie's right hand and gave it a reassuring pat.

"I got in a couple of good ones, though, and I know at least one of my kicks connected, hard, a direct hit to the jaw. I still can't believe how stupid I was, though. *Stupid, stupid, stupid.*"

"Stop, Veronica." Tom's voice was steady and soothing. "You endured a surprise, two-against-one attack and walked away. There is nothing stupid in that." He lifted her left arm and ripped open the tattered sleeve of her T-shirt to examine the slice down her bicep. "You need stitches."

"I'll get my car keys." Felicity started to rise, but Ronnie jerked her back down.

"No. I don't do hospitals. *Ever.* It's hard enough at the clinic. Anyway, this is just a surface cut. I can wrap it."

"I'll stitch you up." Tom gently released her arm, leaned down, and reached under the daybed to retrieve the remaining first aid supplies Ronnie had used to save his cat life. He carried everything to the booth.

Felicity's head turned to follow him. "You know how to do that?" Was there anything he *couldn't* do?

Ronnie tried to stand. "I'll suture myself."

Felicity pressed on her knee until she sat again but noted the raw fear in Ronnie's eyes. The idea of relinquishing control to someone else was probably terrifying for her. "You're left-handed, Ronnie, and it's your left arm that's hurt. If you won't go to the ER, then let Tom help."

She closed her eyes in surrender and gave a slight nod.

Felicity joined Tom at the booth table, whispering, "You *can* help, right? You actually know what you're doing?"

"Yes."

"How?"

"Until now, the Acolyte has always won. I never said she came through uninjured." Tom slipped his hands into a pair of latex gloves.

"Wait, we don't have any numbing stuff! You can't just sew up someone's arm without Novocain or lidocaine or, shit, I don't know— hemorrhoid cream or *some* sort of anesthetic."

Tom grabbed a beer out of the refrigerator, opened it, and handed it to Ronnie. "She's a trained warrior." Tom's matter-of-fact statement sounded almost like a compliment. Maybe it was.

Ronnie gulped down the entire bottle and handed the empty to Felicity. She gave Tom a quick nod. He ripped open a sterile laceration kit and crouched beside Ronnie, wiping dried blood with gauze and antiseptic and examining the edges of the bright red gash in her rich mocha skin.

Felicity focused on not throwing up, proof there were some skills the necklace didn't automatically bestow. Taking a few deep breaths, she sat on the floor on the other side of Ronnie and took her right hand again. "Squeeze. Hard." And Ronnie did.

Their patient remained deathly still, staring straight ahead, and Felicity was reminded of when the roles were reversed. Just last week, Ronnie had stitched up a Zen cat who stared out the window. Now the cat was tending to her.

The pain must have been considerable, but Ronnie didn't make a sound. Felicity was in awe of her control; the only outward sign of the pain was a lone tear that streamed down her cheek to drip into her lap.

While Tom closed the gash with a row of neat stitches, he tried to distract her with small talk. "I'm guessing you were deployed to the Middle East. What part?"

"You wouldn't know it."

Clearly, Ronnie was in no mood for small talk.

Tom concentrated on his work in silence. Once the wound was closed and bandaged, Ronnie got a shot of antibiotics and swallowed some over-the-counter ibuprofen with another beer. Felicity, too, felt deserving of a beer since she hadn't fainted or puked. As Tom cleaned up, Felicity applied gauze bandages to Ronnie's neck, then settled her in the daybed with the extra blanket.

"Can you grab whatever's in the freezer, Tom?"

An instant later, he stood over them with the familiar bag of baby peas and the infamous panini. "No ptomaine worries?"

"It's hard for me to throw anything out, all right? I never know when it might come in handy." She snatched the items and placed them where they could do the most good. The peas went on Ronnie's eye, and the panini against her swollen knuckles.

"Whatimeisit?" Ronnie was groggy from the pain and shock.

"Almost three."

"I gotta go back to my apartment at dawn."

"No." Tom made that pronouncement from the kitchen sink, without turning their way.

"I need my laptop."

"No."

"But I think I found who was texting Misty."

Tom and Felicity shared a shocked glance.

Ronnie tried to sit up, and Felicity pressed her down again. "Stay still."

"I must have dozed off while running the directory match, and when they broke in, my computer fell between the bed and the wall. The blocked number's been scraped up by now, for sure."

"Directory match?" Tom asked.

"To trace who owns the phone number. I need the laptop."

"Still no." Tom picked up Ronnie's left hand. "Make a fist, please."

"Stop poking and prodding the poor girl," Felicity said. "I'll go get the laptop."

"I'm checking for nerve damage, and you are the last person I'd let anywhere near there, Felicity."

Ronnie sighed in frustration. "Well, *somebody's* got to get it."

"Understood, but they knew you weren't telling them the whole story about the phone, so once they've nursed their wounds, they'll be back to watch the place."

Felicity tried again. "Then it makes perfect sense for me to go. You said yourself that Apep doesn't know there's a new Acolyte, right? And even if he *did* know, I'm not exactly standard Acolyte material. I'll be back in a…"

Tom grabbed Felicity's wrist. "No. His men are watching Ronnie's apartment. You wear the *usekh*, the one thing he needs to come into his full power."

"If I wear a scarf…"

"You can't be seen anywhere near the place."

Felicity sighed. "And he's actively looking for you, right? So you can't go either."

"Exactly."

"Then who…"

"I'll figure it out tomorrow. For now, we all need to sleep." Tom adjusted the blanket over Ronnie's shoulder, then pointed toward Felicity's bedroom. "Go."

"You're so freakin' *bossy!*" Felicity stomped to her bed, too tired to argue, and was asleep as soon as her head hit the pillow.

She awoke to a strange cry. At first, she wasn't sure what it was, but then remembered Ronnie was there and could be in pain or having a nightmare. Felicity jumped out of bed and moved quietly through the darkened trailer, her eyesight sharp. She reached the daybed just as the wounded warrior settled back into sleep, her injured left arm draped around a huge grey cat with unusual black markings, stitches vaguely visible along his side.

CHAPTER TWELVE

"No warm-up," Felicity said. "Let's just do Step Three. That's the lance, right?"

An irritated Tom picked up the long, metal spear from the grass beside him, the razor-sharp metal menacing in the morning light. Sometime between Ronnie's arrival and when they'd woken at seven, a plain brown box had been placed on the stoop. Inside were the lance, knives, and fetters. Just seeing the medieval-looking implements of torture made everything seem more real. And imminent. And terrifying.

"Step Three of vanquishing the god of chaos: Taking a Lance to Smite Apep." Tom expertly twirled the four-foot-long, blade-tipped pole in his nimble fingers, then offered the dull end to Felicity.

She reached out, grabbed it, and almost lost her balance. It was heavier than it looked. By a lot. "What the hell is this made of, solid iron?"

"Yes."

Felicity tried to raise the tip above her head and almost fell over. "It's too long."

Tom ignored her whining. "The incantation—in English—is: *Horus has taken his lance, thrusts into Apep.*"

"That's a little clunky, isn't it?"

"It's better in Egyptian, which *someone* refuses to learn."

"Fine. Horus takes the lance…"

"*Has taken his lance!*"

"That's super present perfect passive voice, but hey, you're the boss."

"Felicity…"

"*Horus has taken his lance, thrusts into Apep.*"

"Finally! Now, thrust with the lance, quickly, throwing your whole weight forward. Like this." Tom mimicked the maneuver, slowly the first time, then faster with each repetition. It was impressive to see. Tom was powerful but moved like a dancer.

Felicity did just as Tom demonstrated and ended up on her hands and knees in the weeds, the lance point stuck in the dirt. She yanked it out, got up, and lifted the lance in triumph. But she began to tilt backward, dropping the weapon in time to right herself. When she dared check in with Tom, he was staring at the sky and mumbling in one of his languages. She bet dollars to donuts it was more cursing.

"Russian again?"

"Greek." He gathered his composure. "We'll have a lance made that's lighter and shorter. Let's move on to Step Four."

"Is that the little knife? I think I can handle that."

"Step Four is Fettering Apep." Tom produced a length of chain with a weighted end. He swung it to produce enough momentum to wrap the chain around his wrist, cutting through the air with a whistle. "This is real simple, Felicity. You just wrap it securely around one of Apep's wrists while saying the incantation: *They who should be bound are bound.*"

"*They who should be bound are bound,*" she repeated, taking the chain from Tom. She was pleased to find it wasn't unmanageably heavy or even very long. But this was not all good news. "Wait a second. If I need to lasso him with this short chain, I'll have to be close to him. But I don't want to be close to him."

"By this point, you will have performed the first three steps, and he'll be substantially weakened. The risk will have been reduced."

Right. Because by then she would have dribbled on him, nudged him with a cat toy-enhanced left foot, and stumbled into him trying to lift thirty pounds of iron. The poor guy didn't stand a chance.

Felicity swung the chain slowly, back and forth. "You know, I've been thinking. Apep always knows the plan of attack, right? Six moves in the same order, over and over. I can't believe you've managed to win for two thousand years! Are you that good, or is Apep a halfwit?"

"Apep is most definitely *not* a halfwit."

"Then you're that good."

"I am."

"That's what they all say." It was Ronnie, limping around the side of the trailer. Her face looked much better than the swollen pufferfish Felicity had expected, but she was hurting.

Tom spun around. "You should be in bed."

"I need to get my laptop. I told you."

"And I told you, *no.*"

Ronnie looked past Tom to Felicity. "Your cat seems to think he's in charge of damn near everything."

Felicity shrugged. "He's not my cat, and, unfortunately, when it comes to all things Apep, he sorta is."

"But you're the one who's putting her ass on the line. So shouldn't you be in charge?"

The heavy chain pulled on Felicity's wrist.

"Hey! Are we havin' a party?" Tasha's voice originated from the other side of the trailer, her determined footsteps moving over gravel and weeds and heading directly for their training spot. Felicity adjusted her scarf and hid the fetter behind her back, hoping Tom had concealed the lance and knife.

Tasha rounded the corner. "Party all night! Party all morning! Party all the time! Seems to be the new normal around here!"

She didn't look to be in a partying mood, however. "You're up early, Tash."

"Not by choice, I assure you. And Jim is extremely upset. We need to talk."

Felicity felt she deserved a lot of credit for not rolling her eyes. Perhaps an Emmy or an Oscar. Maybe even a cash prize for not saying something along the lines of *Did the widdle pickpocket pinhead get his fee-fees hurt?*

Instead, she said, "Of course. Let's step inside."

They climbed up the metal steps, and Tasha pulled the door shut, tightly, keeping her voice low. "You know how hard Jim works..."

"What's he do again?" Felicity couldn't resist. Besides, she really didn't know what Jim did, if anything, to support himself, other than steal petty cash from his girlfriend's wallet.

Tasha ignored her. "We were up late watching a movie..."

"*Last of the Mohicans?*"

"Jim doesn't care for those kinds of movies."

"Movies with heroes? Or just the kind with DDL in the lead role?"

"He likes movies with car crashes and explosions. We watched something called *Furiously Faster* or something, I don't remember, since I fell asleep halfway through. Anyway, my point is that we got to bed late and then Jim gets woken up in the middle of the night because *someone's* pounding at your door! And honestly, Felicity, I just wanted you to know…that was extremely insensitive."

Felicity nodded. "Did you happen to see Ronnie out by the garden? My vet tech friend?"

Tasha frowned. "I mean, I noticed her but didn't look at her closely. Why?"

"It was Ronnie banging on the door. She came here in the middle of the night because a couple of criminals with knives broke into her apartment and tried to slit her throat. So, yeah. She was desperate for help and bleeding. Sorry for interrupting Hair Gel Jim's beauty sleep."

Tasha squinted. "What did you just call Jim?"

"Rest assured, the next time a friend is attacked, I'll tell them to wait until morning."

"I didn't know, *OK*? I'm sorry." Tasha looked lost, then scowled again. "But what did you call Jim?"

"You didn't know because you didn't ask. You just jumped up, ready to defend the asshole in residence. And yes. You heard me. Hair. Gel. Jim."

A muffled *thump* on the stoop made them jump. It was followed by a low, croaking *Mmraah-ah-eeeow*.

Felicity opened the door, expecting Mojo but then saw he was already inside. She glanced down at a huge seal point Siamese wearing a bright orange, custom-made backpack.

For an instant, Felicity was too stunned to react. She sensed her own cats scurrying behind her just before a hush fell over the trailer. A quick glance confirmed that her cats had assumed the position again, stiff and alert, eyes glued to the newcomer who was sauntering in like he owned the joint.

Tasha and Felicity watched the buff and black male Siamese stroll through the bedroom, inspect the bathroom, look under the booth, and then head toward the daybed, all without making a sound or acknowledging anyone's presence. It dawned on Felicity that this cat was looking for something... or someone.

"Lissie? What the...?"

"Could you give me a second, Tash? Maybe you could go back to the house?"

"Hell, no! You wanted me to ask? Fine! I'm *asking*. And your time is up; you're going to tell me everything, right now, about whatever Looney Tunes shit you've gotten yourself into. And while you're at it, you'll explain to me what it is with you and random cats. Did you attach a homing beacon to the roof? Send out catnip smoke signals?"

"This isn't a random cat, and I'll tell you the truth, though I recommend you be seated when you hear it." Felicity gestured to the booth and waited for Tasha to slide in. Then she opened one of the little windows on the junkyard side and called out, "Tom, someone's looking for you!"

Tom and Ronnie came in a moment later. Tom immediately placed the knife, fetter, and the blunt end of the lance in the kitchenette sink, then propped the pointy end of the spear against the wall. Tasha's eyes widened at the sight of the weaponry, and she gasped once she got a look at Ronnie's bruises and cuts, but her attention shifted to the Siamese now sliding his front paws forward across the linoleum and bowing in supplication before Tom. Then he lay on his side at Tom's feet.

"Oh, good. It's here." Tom unhooked the backpack, lifted it from the cat, and nodded to the beautiful creature. "*Dua netjer en ek!*

Em heset net Bastet." Tom opened the front door and the cat jumped to its feet, leaping over the threshold and clearing the porch railing in one smooth maneuver. It disappeared into the woods.

Felicity's cats instantly relaxed. Ronnie joined them on the daybed. Tasha sat in stunned silence, her bottom lip hanging loose.

"What's in the backpack?" Felicity asked.

"It's from Alexander."

"What's wrong with FedEx?"

"Not for this." Tom unzipped the backpack. The first thing he pulled out was a men's leather wallet. He smiled. "Great! He recovered my wallet. I can drive now." He slipped it into the back pocket of his jeans.

The next thing he pulled out: multiple stacks of what appeared to be freshly minted hundred-dollar bills. He handed them, one stack at a time, to Felicity, who began to feel extremely woozy. She clutched the bundles to her chest, arms trembling.

"Da *fuck?*" Tasha whispered.

Moments later, Felicity was hunched over the table, the stacks of hundred-dollar bills fanned out before her. It was all she could do not to hyperventilate. Tom had just explained that each half-inch bundle contained ten thousand dollars. There were eight of them. Even Felicity managed *that* math.

She kept touching the bills, like they would disappear if she didn't maintain physical contact. Her brain raced as fast as her breath. "I can pay off the hospital," she mumbled to no one in particular. "The doctors. The bill collectors. The landlords. I can get a lawyer to deal with Rich."

"Alexander's got that covered, remember?"

She looked at Tom. "Right! I forgot!" She glanced at Ronnie "I can pay *you* back! I can pay the vet bills!" Next, she looked to Tasha, who sat in rigid silence across the table. "I can catch up on my rent! Can you believe it?"

Then she glanced at the cats. "I can pay for Boudica's oral surgery and finally get Mojo fixed!"

Merrrooowww? Mojo's green eyes shot to Tom, who patted the cat's big head.

"Sorry, buddy."

"Felicity. Renee. Cheshire." Apparently, Tasha had recovered the ability to speak.

Felicity prepared herself.

"What the complete and utter absolute *fuck* is going on in this Airstream?" She whipped around to look at Ronnie, who gave a shrug. Then she glared at Tom, who seemed unsure whether it was his place to speak.

"Go ahead," Felicity said, knowing she couldn't put it off any longer. "Do your thing."

Tom stepped toward Tasha and proffered a bow—head bent, back flat, and arm sweeping. "I am Tubastet af-Ankh, *hem-netjer-tepi* of the Ever-Living Goddess Bastet, temple guard of Per-Bast, warrior, and trainer of Acolytes." He stood tall and produced his most charming smile. "Can I ask you a couple of questions?"

Tasha looked flummoxed. "Uh…"

"Is Felicity Cheshire your lifelong best friend?"

"Well…"

"Do you trust her? Are you sure she has a compassionate heart? That at her core she's a courageous, honorable, and loving woman?"

Tasha opened her mouth to speak, closed it again, thought for an instant, and finally said, "Sure."

"Good," Tom said. "Please keep that in mind as I explain to you, in detail, what the complete and utter absolute fuck is going on here in this Airstream."

"You don't really believe this load of crap, do you?" Tasha paced up and down the center aisle, picking furiously at her cuticle.

Felicity understood why it would be hard for her best friend to process these developments. Tasha believed in things like assets and allocations, high credit ratings and low mortgage rates. It wouldn't be easy for her to accept what she was hearing.

"Tasha, there's eighty grand in cash right here on the table. You held it in your own hands. You checked to make sure it's not counterfeit. You saw a cat deliver it."

She shook her head, refusing to listen.

Felicity tugged at the neckline of her T-shirt. "This ancient Egyptian amulet is fused around my neck. You tried yourself to remove it but couldn't."

Tasha's poor cuticle was getting a workout.

"You see how Ronnie's been cut and beaten because Apep wanted Misty's phone."

Tasha crossed her arms across her chest.

"Hey, Tom," Ronnie interjected from her spot on the daybed. "Why don't you just morph into a cat? That oughta put an end to Tasha's doubts."

"I'm not a circus act, Veronica, and I don't give a shit if she believes. Her belief isn't critical to our mission." Tom directed his formidable scowl at Tasha. "But I won't let you be an obstruction."

Tasha tipped her chin to look him in the eye. "May I remind your highness that you're a guest on my property?"

"And may I remind *you* that your entire reality—your property, your existence on this earthly plane, and all that you treasure, including your insipid assface of a boyfriend—will come to an abrupt and violent end unless Felicity performs her sacred duty?"

"So you say."

"Jim will die. You will die. All things you love will be annihilated, whether or not you believe what I've told you."

Ronnie popped to a stand. "See ya. I'm going back for my laptop."

Tom blocked the Airstream door.

"You're pissing me off, cat. Step aside."

The door banged. Everyone jerked in surprise.

"Tasha, sweetheart? Are you in there? Are you all right?" Jim pounded again.

Tasha stared at the ceiling and breathed deeply. "Hey, Big Bear, I'll be right out!" Her voice had gone high and squeaky again, and Felicity repeated the words back to her in silent horror: *Big Bear?*

Tasha waved her off, reaching for the door. Tom stepped aside.

"Wait!" Felicity jumped from the booth, grabbing Tasha by the shoulders and whispering, "*You* can go to Ronnie's, grab the laptop and some clothes for her." She glanced at Tom and Ronnie. "Tasha can do it!"

They showed no enthusiasm for her plan.

"Think about it! She can take *Big Bear* with her in case the bad guys are still watching the place." *Finally, Jim might be good for something.*

"It could work," Tom said.

"Would you do that for us, Tash?"

Ronnie was already writing down her address and exactly where Tasha would find the items she needed.

"But what do I tell Jim?"

Felicity grasped her bestie's hand and squeezed. "Tell him my friend got jumped and she's afraid to go back to her apartment. Ask him to be the hero, to protect you and defend a helpless young woman."

"*Sheee-it,*" Ronnie said.

Tasha looked baffled.

"He can be your DDL for the day!"

Tasha perked a bit. "OK, but..."

"Here's my keys and the list." Ronnie pressed the items into Tasha's hand, explaining which key was to the apartment door and which fit the building. "Park a block away," she whispered. "Go in the back door. It's daylight so you won't have to turn on any lights, but lay low so no one can see you moving around once you're in the apartment. I think I left my blinds open."

Jim rattled the door handle. "Tasha? What's going on in there?"

"Just a second, Jimmy! I'm helping Felicity with something!"

"Keep your eyes peeled," Ronnie said. "If someone's got the place staked out, get a good look at the car and the occupants. Get a license plate number if you can. A photo would be even better if you can manage it safely. But most important, don't let anyone follow you here."

"*Tasha!*" Jim resumed banging.

"Thank you." Felicity wrapped Tasha in a tight hug, whispering into her ear. "I know this is bonkers, but please, *please* believe me. I hate that I had to lie to you. I never want to do that again."

Tasha nodded, worried. "I'll try, Lissie, but this... this is some pretty far-out shit, even for you."

They eavesdropped from inside the trailer as Tasha convinced Hair Gel Jim that he needed to save a damsel in distress, skipping the part about the damsel being a US Marine. Once they were in Tasha's car and on their way to the apartment, Felicity coaxed Ronnie into the bedroom, convincing her to lie down.

She'd barely pulled the bedroom door across when Tom was breathing down the back of her neck.

"We need to perfect Step Four."

Felicity didn't respond because she was focused on the money strewn across the banquette table. "I wish I could put this in the bank for safety, but I don't have an account anymore. They kicked me out because I bounced too many checks."

She picked up a stack of bills, put her nose to the paper and sniffed. "I couldn't deposit this much cash without getting flagged by the Feds, anyway. They'd peg me as a drug dealer."

Tom chuckled. "Don't worry. It'll be safe here in the short-term, and I'll ask Alexander to set up an account for you and handle any inquiries."

"Tom?" She returned one bundle to the table and picked up another. "This is an obscene amount of money, and it's downright scary that all you have to do is call your supernatural attorney friend and suddenly all my worries are gone."

"He's not supernatural." Tom pursed his lips. "The Rigiats are law-abiding people, and their resources are the fruits of millennia of careful investment. It's Alexander's duty to provide earthly support and counsel for our sacred mission."

"Good for him." She stacked all the piles of cash on top of each other and admired her creation. "Maybe I should pay off all my bills right away before I face Apep. That way, if things don't go well, I can die debt-free."

"Whatever you want."

"You know what I want?" Felicity looked up at Tom, suddenly

pissed off. "I want someone else to wear the necklace and fight Apep for the earth's survival. But we don't always get what we want."

Tom watched without comment as she slipped several bills into her purse and began hiding stacks of cash through the trailer—under the booth seats, in the tiny freezer, in the silverware drawer, in back of the cupboards, in her snow boots, and under the sink in the box of scouring pads. When she was done, she struck an exaggerated superhero pose in front of him, feet apart, chin up, fists on hips.

"Back to fettering, Tuba-uber-trainer?"

He shook his head and muttered to himself. "*Abbiamo bisogno di un miracolo.*"

"What was that?"

"I said you're doing great!"

Such a terrible, terrible liar.

CHAPTER THIRTEEN

Felicity fettered until she could fetter no more. Tasha and Jim had returned with the laptop and Ronnie's necessities, and Tasha now moped on the flat rock by the garden, making helpful observations while Felicity practiced. Hair Gel Jim had taken off on his Harley, angry about something.

Ronnie was inside the trailer, booting up the laptop. She promised she'd have directory match results for them soon.

Felicity just wished she'd hurry the hell up because Tom had already made her practice the spitting from Step One and the squat-turn-kick of Step Two, and Felicity's lips were tingling and her quadriceps were seizing and he'd just used the words "sit" and "up" in a sentence and she didn't know how much more she could take.

"Guys!" Ronnie poked her head out the Airstream door. "I got it!"

They rushed inside.

"I traced the number to a privately held Portland tech startup called Viper Applications." Ronnie launched into her briefing before they'd even shut the door behind them. "It's on Hawthorne Boulevard, and they specialize in cybersecurity. They've been in business just over two years. Check out this logo."

She spun the laptop around so Felicity and Tom could see the screen.

Felicity stared at the animated graphic of a malevolent serpent slithering through the letters *A P P*, its fangs dripping with venom. "Not very subtle, that's for sure."

"Well, at least it doesn't say, 'Yo, my name's Apep'!"

Tasha offered this take from her spot on the daybed, where she sat cross-legged, absently stroking Gumbo's head. Felicity had never seen Tasha touch one of the cats. Ever.

"You good, Tash?"

She shrugged. "Jim's gone off to get a beer with his conservation friends. It'll keep him out of the way for a bit."

Felicity knew there was much more to that statement, but they'd have to discuss it later. Right now, the mother of all puzzle pieces was staring at them from the laptop screen.

"Actually, that's exactly what it says." Felicity smiled. "That's how you write Apep's name in Egyptian hieroglyphs, right Tom?"

"Yep."

Felicity grabbed the stolen library book from the booth. "That's the first thing I looked up in here. The word *Apep* begins with the image of a snake followed by two phonograms for the letter *P*, with the *A* sound implied."

"That's him." Tom stood close to Ronnie's shoulder as he peered at the screen. She didn't seem to mind this time, probably because with four adults and twelve cats in the Airstream, personal space was pure fantasy.

"How do you go about ending the world with computer

applications?" Tasha wondered aloud. "Unless it's with dating sites. Talk about human suffering! Ha!" Tasha's bitterness was born of experience. Felicity had never asked the name of the site where she'd unearthed Jim. Was "Assholes Only" a thing?

"Pestilence." Tom leaned against the kitchenette sink.

"Apep's text message." Felicity stared at Tom. "We assumed he meant a human disease, but what if he meant..."

"He meant a computer virus." Ronnie spun the laptop toward her and began clicking away on the keyboard. "A Trojan Horse. Maybe a rootkit. I can't find a client list, so he might not yet have his fingers in anybody's pie. But I remember seeing some buzz about Viper on one of the deep web hacker forums I belong to. I'll have to go back and find it."

"Deep web?" Felicity asked. "That doesn't sound very safe. Or legal."

A smile curled at the edge of Ronnie's lips. "There's a hella gray area in cyberethics. Sometimes the ends justify the means, right Felicity?" Her fingers flew along the keys. "There are black hat hackers who want to cause havoc and steal money. Then you've got white hats trying to stop the havoc and thievery. The secret is to know who's who—I mean *really* be sure— and not make enemies of any of them. I'll let you know what I dig up on our little snake friend."

Felicity was truly impressed with Ronnie's ability to carry on a conversation while typing.

"I worry that Apep's software carries some kind of replicating, completely undetectable malware. It's technologically possible. All he'd have to do is alter an established virus enough to avoid detection, and a black hat could use something like that to bring the world to its knees."

Felicity's stomach cramped. "You mean like power grids, air

traffic control, and banks?"

"Or…" Tom said, his face tight and grim, "…he could just launch the missiles and be done with it."

"Excuse me." Felicity pushed past Tom into her bedroom, closed the door, and slipped into a clean shirt and her trusty crocheted scarf. Upon her return she said, "Knowing who he is and where he's located is our only ace in the hole. C'mon, Tash. Road trip!"

"Where're you going?" Tom's eyes flashed with anger. "We haven't even started Step Five."

"We'll get to it, but right now, we have the advantage, so we need to run with it. You said it would be best if we could choose the time and place of battle, right?"

"It would."

"And you want me to be calm, right?"

Tom raised an eyebrow.

"So let me go collect information and context. Do reconnaissance. He knows you, Tom. Ronnie was seen by his goon squad. But me? I'm invisible. That's not hyperbole. People don't see me. They run into me on the street because it's like I'm not even there."

Tom shook his head. "I don't like it."

"Duly noted, but you said the necklace doesn't work like GPS. He can't track me in real time, right, and he's already picked the coast as his target?"

"Yes, but…"

"Then you stay here and help Ronnie dig through the digital dumpster. Let's roll, Tash."

"Uh…"

"Hawthorne Boulevard, Tasha. Ronnie said the offices are in the Hawthorne District. You know what else is in the Hawthorne District?"

"Shopping!" She jumped up.

Felicity reached into the silverware drawer, pulled out three hundred-dollar bills from under the forks, and handed them to Tasha. She shoved another ten in her purse. "We'll just blend in with the Wednesday afternoon crowd. Maybe I can get myself a few nice turtlenecks."

"A new scarf might be good." Ronnie didn't look up from the laptop.

Felicity gave Tom an assuring nod. "We'll be fine."

He didn't look assured. "Call if there's a problem. Don't put yourself at risk. And please, Felicity, remember that you are nowhere near ready to battle Apep. You can't face him without me."

"No argument from me on that one."

"And, seriously, call if you'll be late," Tom added. "We don't want the kittens to worry."

Tasha found the cutest pair of athletic shoes, with the words Fuck Off and Die stamped every which way across the white canvas uppers. She said she wasn't sure where she'd wear them—definitely not the office—but she was confident the perfect occasion would present itself.

Then they casually strolled east, across the street from the address for Viper Apps. It was nothing special, just one of the many two-story, red-brick storefronts along the funky boulevard. It looked lifeless, boring. The windows appeared to have been painted a dull gray on the inside.

"That's it?" Tasha seemed disappointed. "That's ground zero for the evil empire?"

There were two simple numbers on the utilitarian front door, which looked thick enough to be bombproof. Other than that, there was no signage, no venom-dripping logo, or any other indication of what went on inside. Above a doorknob was an industrial-looking keycard reader. The one thing that did stand out to Felicity was the number of security cameras. They hovered over the door, perched on either side of the entrance, lined the roofline, and were bolted to the outside window surrounds.

She noticed Tasha gawking at the building.

"Look straight ahead," Felicity snapped. "Don't turn around and stare like that. Laugh like something's funny."

Tasha laughed and merrily swung her shopping bag.

They were going to have to up their spy game.

They stopped for a late lunch at a cozy, hipster diner across from Viper Apps. Felicity pulled Tasha to the table right in front of the window.

"What are you doing?" Tasha looked confused.

"Upping our spy game. We need to see whether anyone goes in or out." She shot a glance at the building across the street. "And we're having lunch. I'm starving."

While they looked over the menus, Felicity had the feeling that they, themselves, were being spied upon. She casually glanced around at the other patrons, at the passersby, and at Viper Apps, but saw no one looking their way. She decided to shrug it off. Tasha seemed oblivious so maybe it was just her imagination.

"Thanks for getting Ronnie's laptop."

"No problem."

"What happened?"

"Let's order."

They both chose fancy, twenty-seven-ingredient salads. The whole process felt decadent to Felicity. There she was, sitting in a big-city cafe with cloth napkins, having lunch with her best friend—a lunch she'd happily pay for. It was so much more civilized than soup and peanut butter. If she remembered correctly, the last time she'd been to a nice restaurant was the night before her divorce papers were served. Felicity had thought it was just a pleasant dinner out with her husband. Only Rich knew it was the last supper.

The waitress came by to fill their iced teas, and when she left, Felicity looked Tasha straight in the eye. "Tell me what happened at Ronnie's place."

"Nothing, really." Tasha tried to dismiss it.

"Then why does it sound like something?"

"I have no idea."

Felicity sighed.

"Fine. It's really nothing. It just felt…"

"Spit it out, Tasha! Did Jim spray paint the walls? Pee in her plants?" Felicity felt her eyes widen in comprehension. "Oh, God. Did he *steal* something?"

Tasha waved away the question. "He was just a little *nosy*, is all. Picking up stuff that wasn't on the list, opening drawers, checking out all the electronics. It just felt *wrong*. I know I keep using that word when it comes to Jim, but it's the only thing that seems to fit."

"Sounds wrong to me. Sounds sleazy. Like maybe he was casing the joint."

"Oh, come on, Felicity. It wasn't like that." Tasha stabbed a piece of artisanal lettuce and a crescent of heirloom tomato. "Can we just drop it?"

Felicity dropped it, but her mind was all over the subject. She detested that jerk. She didn't trust him in the slightest.

They finished their salads, shared a slice of gourmet cheesecake, and dawdled over their iced teas as long as they could. Still, no one had gone in or come out of Viper Apps.

Felicity couldn't stop smiling while paying the bill. It had been far too long since she'd been able to treat herself to anything, and now she could even treat her BFF.

They hit a few consignment shops in the district. Felicity found two lightweight blouses with high necks. At a quirky import shop, she fell in love with a festive, woven linen scarf made in, of all places, Egypt! She bought it without looking at the price tag, something she hadn't done... ever.

They crossed the street and walked up the block toward the Viper Apps building. Right next door was a quirky boutique with dream catchers, crystals, and tarot cards. She pulled Tasha inside and watched her friend wander among the shelves of candles, herbs, goblets, and reclining Buddhas.

Felicity stayed toward the front, staring out the window. That odd feeling was back. A person, a *man* was watching them. She could feel his energy, though she could see no one particularly interested in their comings and goings. The attention didn't feel threatening. Just the opposite, in fact. Felicity sensed they were being watched *over* instead of just plain watched.

By now, nothing should strike her as strange, but this was very strange, indeed.

Felicity had never been inside an occult store. In fact, she could only guess at the purpose of most of the stuff she was seeing. As she examined a small black cauldron, she felt an unmistakable pull to the back of the shop, as if she'd been grabbed by a tractor beam. She put one foot in front of the other until she stopped, then looked down into the glass display case. Right there, centered on a black velvet cloth, was a silver bracelet with an all-too-familiar theme.

Felicity's mouth fell open. She brought a hand to her breastbone.

"May I help you?"

A handsome young man smiled at her. If it weren't for the kohl eyeliner and facial piercings, he could have been Brad Pitt.

She pointed.

"You'd like to see the Bastet bracelet?"

"Yes," she croaked.

He used a key to unlock the back of the case, then placed the bracelet on a satiny pad on the glass countertop. "Would you like to try it on?"

"Absolutely."

Felicity slipped it over her left hand. It fit perfectly. But she was confused. "Why do you have Bastet stuff here?"

He shook his head as if he didn't understand her question. "We carry items dedicated to many of the world's most revered goddesses: Isis, Hecate, Ishtar, Danu, Gaia, Bridget, Artemis, Devi, Quan Yin, the Morrigan, Freya."

"Whatcha got there?" Tasha peeked over Felicity's shoulder. "Hey! Is that *her*?"

"It's her," Felicity whispered.

"Holy crap. What are the chances? We should all get one— you, me, Ronnie, and Tom."

Felicity couldn't look away from the dazzling solid silver encircling her wrist, the majestic, throned cat at its center, lapis lazuli scarab beetles as bookends. "Do you have more of these?"

"I doubt it, but I can check."

When Felicity realized the handsome young man had not budged, she looked up, sheepish. "Sorry." She slipped the bracelet from her wrist and handed it back to him.

"We don't usually carry more than one of each piece." He placed the jewelry back into the case and locked it. "They're handmade. I'll look, just to be sure."

"That's really gorgeous, Lissie."

"It is, isn't it?"

The young man returned holding a box, the surprise plain on his face. "I can't believe it, but there were three more. That never happens. They're not exact duplicates; each design is a little different. Do you want to see them?"

"Yes!" Tasha and Felicity said in unison.

And the miracles kept on coming. Felicity paid 780 dollars plus tax *in cash*. Felicity already wore her bracelet. Tasha made her selection and slipped it on her wrist before they exited. The remaining bracelets were tucked safely inside the zipper compartment of Felicity's purse.

Their plan was to walk a couple more blocks, turn around, and then make one last pass by the Viper Apps building, looking for details they might have missed. Their plans got derailed just two storefronts away.

"Tasha Romero?"

Coming down the busy sidewalk was an extremely well-dressed woman with shoulder-length, brown hair styled in loose curls. She was a stranger to Felicity, but, clearly, Tasha knew her.

"Mrs. Wiegand?" They moved toward one another and shook hands.

"Please, call me Sheri."

"Sheri, this is my friend Felicity Cheshire. Lissie, Sheri Wiegand is the Realtor that Jim and I met with last week."

"Oh." Felicity shook the woman's perfectly manicured hand.

"How odd running into you in Portland!"

"We're just here for the day, doing some shopping."

"I can't resist these eccentric little places either. But I'm actually in town for a meeting. I'm representing a buyer interested in one of these commercially zoned historic buildings."

Tasha smiled. Felicity smiled too, not sure how much longer the three of them could keep smiling in silence. But Sheri kept the conversation going.

"I know it's only been a few days, but have you had time to think over my marketing plan for your land?"

Tasha looked vaguely sick. Felicity knew that in her heart, her best friend had no desire to sell her family inheritance, so why didn't she just say so?

"Your plan is impressive, Sheri, and you know your stuff. But honestly, I'm still in shock. The land's worth way more than I ever dreamed."

That was why.

"The market is insane, especially along your part of the coast. That's what I was telling Jim when we first discussed the possibility of working together." Sheri smiled widely, completely missing the way Tasha had just stiffened from head to toe.

"Really? When was that?"

"Pardon?"

"When did you first talk to Jim about my land?"

"Oh. I sold his friend's home last fall, and I ran into the two of them at the Holiday Fair."

"The *Christmas* Holiday Fair?"

"I never miss it. I adore all the precious arts and crafts, and those homemade baked goods are to die for! It's part of what makes Pine Beach such a charming seaside town. But yes, I started chatting with Jim…"

Felicity could barely breathe. Either this lady had a rotten memory or something truly awful was going on because Tasha didn't meet Jim until February. He'd moved in by the beginning of April.

They hadn't even known one another at Christmas.

"...so when he mentioned that eyesore of an old junkyard was closing down at the end of summer..."

"The junkyard's closing?"

Sheri blinked in discomfort. "I thought you knew, Tasha. In fact, I assumed that's why you were interested in selling. I figured you two had discussed it and agreed that now was the perfect time to sell."

"Musta slipped his mind." Tasha's voice had iced over, but the ever-bubbly Sheri was just warming up.

"I guess it's still a bit hush-hush. I first heard about it from Jim, but I've since learned that it's been in the works for a while. Old Newton is retiring and moving up north to be with his daughter, and the town convinced him to let a conservation group buy it cheap, pledging to clean it up and turn it into a nature preserve. Apparently, Newton has a thing for tufted puffins or something, so he agreed to the terms."

"Conservation?" Tasha was motionless.

"Anyway, Jim mentioned that you owned the land nearby, and here we are! I hope you'll let me help you with your sale."

Tasha nodded and somehow managed to squeak out a response: she'd be sure to call Sheri when she'd made up her mind. And with another megawatt smile and a little wave, Sheri continued on her way.

Tasha charged ahead without saying a word. Felicity ran to catch up and stayed by her side.

"Where are we parked, Lissie?"

"Down here. We're going the right way."

"Good."

They waited for the light at the crosswalk.

"Christmas," Tasha said. "I didn't even know that fuckface at

Christmas. He was talking with a Realtor about *my* land at Christmas, implying that we were in a relationship."

"I heard." Felicity took Tasha's hand. They kept walking.

"We met on a dating site just before Valentine's Day."

"I know."

They walked in silence another block.

"I thought he was romantic, maybe a little over the top with the flattery, but I thought he was just awkward and immature."

"I know."

It began to drizzle as they crossed the street, but they just kept walking, the sound of their shoes on the wet pavement keeping cadence.

"But he's a liar, Lissie. A grifter. He targeted me. I'm not his love. I'm his *mark*."

"I could kick his ass for you now."

Tasha stopped, spun to Felicity. "I don't doubt you could. But this is my job to do. And I'll do it. Because I'm not some pathetic, desperate, middle-aged woman."

"You never were."

Tasha fiddled with the new bracelet on her left wrist, her eyes scanning the rooftops. When she glanced down again and looked Felicity in the eye, there was a glint of determination, of clear intent. Tears rolled down her cheeks, rivulets of mascara pooling at the corners of her mouth. "I'm part of a goddess posse now, aren't I?" She held up her left arm. "And I've got the bracelet to prove it!"

Felicity wiped Tasha's tears and gave a little laugh. "Damn right. We're Bastet's Badass Goddess Posse now, and we have everything we need to take care of business."

Tasha's smile collapsed, as did her raised arm, and the tears came in earnest. "My God, Lissie. I fell for it. *Again*. What am I gonna do?"

"First off, you'll take out the trash and clean house."

Tasha nodded, sniffing.

"And once you've dumped that sleazoid lowlife into the hazardous waste bin of dating mistakes, you'll help me save the world." Felicity pulled Tasha into her arms and squeezed her tight.

It was late by the time they gathered around the Airstream to study Felicity's sketch of the Viper Apps location. Everyone's bracelets sparkled under the wagon wheel chandelier—all but Tom's, anyway. He'd flat-out refused to wear it and shoved it back at Felicity.

"I don't do jewelry. Ever. Only the *usekh*."

"Yikes. Fine." She put it back in its box and stuck it in the kitchenette catch-all drawer.

"Oh, c'mon, Tom! Don't you want to be part of the Badass Goddess Posse?" Tasha asked.

"Not me. Maybe there's someone else who can wear it."

"Party pooper." Tasha took a sip from her mug of tea. Her eyes remained red and swollen from crying the entire long drive back to Pine Beach, and though she'd managed to put on a brave face since they returned, she'd fooled no one.

They bent their heads over the sketch.

"It's basically a no-frills bank vault, locked up tight," Felicity said. "It looks like every other building on the street. Nothing notable about it."

"It was a letdown, honestly." Tasha said. "I expected something a little more, you know, *sinister*. The guy's allegedly some creepy monster, a destroyer god of chaos, right?"

Tom scowled. "Not alleged."

"My bad." Tasha slurped her tea.

Felicity pointed to the sketch again. "We drove through this back alley on our way out, since I figured walking there would look suspicious. All we saw was one narrow steel door and a few more cameras. Not even a garbage dumpster or a mail slot. But there was one thing." She glanced at Tom. "I swear someone was watching us. Keeping an eye on us, really, and though it didn't feel threatening, it was disconcerting."

"Oh. That was Alexander." Tom spoke matter-of-factly. "I asked him to keep an eye on you while you were in Portland."

"*What?* You sent him to spy on us? Doesn't the guy have more important things to do?"

"Not really. Helping us is what he's trained for his whole life."

"Next time, give me a heads up, would you? *Please?*"

"Sure."

"So, what else?" Ronnie asked, tipping her head to the sketch.

"Not a damn thing. Like I said, it was plain and small. A big nothing."

Ronnie shrugged. "You don't need a fancy office to mess with the syntax of established malware."

That was a surprise to Felicity. "I pictured a whole team of expert programmers."

"Nope," Ronnie said. "Just a few computers and couple of sweaty INCELs."

Tasha chuckled. Tom frowned again. He was especially grumpy tonight.

"But Apep can't do this alone, right?" Felicity pressed for more details. "He must have coconspirators."

Ronnie shook her head. "The software engineers probably don't even know what they're working toward, Felicity. If you break up something into small pieces and give each person just one task, then there's no conspiracy. It's just a bunch of worker drones putting in their eight hours and one black hat lurking in the shadows, waiting to assemble the bomb from all the components."

The distinctive roar of Hair Gel Jim's Harley Davidson put an end to their discussion. Everyone watched Tasha stand up, take a deep breath, and pull her shoulders back. Her hands shook as she set down her mug.

"I'll go with you." Felicity slid out of the booth.

"I'm fine, Lissie."

Tom touched Tasha's forearm. "I'd ask you if you're OK, but it's obvious you're not. Anything I can do to help?"

"Nah. It's my mess, and I'll clean it up."

"What the hell's going on?" Ronnie pushed her way out of the booth.

"Look, it's no big deal." Tasha looked to Felicity before she continued. "I found out today that Jim isn't who I thought he was, that he's a liar and a con man, so I need to kick his ass out."

"That happens to be my specialty," Tom said.

Tasha chuckled. "Not sure why you'd bother yourself with somebody's earthly concerns, Tom. You've got enough on your to-do list."

"You are one of us, Tasha. One of the..."

"Posse," all three women said.

"Exactly. And no member of the posse goes into battle alone." Tom opened the trailer door, gesturing for Tasha to walk through. "Want me to bring the lance?"

That got a laugh from Tasha. "That would be fun, but I'd like to stay out of women's prison if you don't mind."

Ronnie snickered.

"But you might want these." Felicity reached behind her,

grabbed the shoe store bag, and held it out to Tasha.

"Oh, my God! You're so right!"

Tasha sat on the daybed, ripped off the shoebox lid, tore through the tissue paper, and quickly laced up her Fuck Off and Die athletic shoes.

"Time to take out the trash," she said.

It was normal for him to become a part of an Acolyte's life, to mingle with her family, and, on occasion, venture into her larger community to meet her friends. But he'd always been careful to keep his distance so he could form an objective understanding of time and place, customs, taboos, hopes, and fears. Each time, he stayed only long enough to accomplish his mission and then he left, the same warrior priest he'd always been, until the start of the next cycle.

This latest visit had been anything but normal. Misty McAlpine of Clackamas was the product of a splintered and self-absorbed society, one with as much meanness of spirit as decadence, where people focused on lack while drowning in a flood of riches. He soon discovered just how unsuited his new Acolyte was for the task.

Misty believed it was all about *her*. It was her fatal flaw, and all of humanity may have to pay.

"I promise to make this short and sweet," Tasha announced, her arms swinging as they marched side by side across the lawn toward her house, its windows glowing yellow with electric light.

"How can I help?"

"Be my silent backup, then follow him out. Make sure he leaves and lock the gate behind him."

"Got it."

His thoughts weighed heavy on his spirit. He'd made too many mistakes this time around, crossed too many lines. Misty died in his arms. He came perilously close to death himself and was forced to find a replacement Acolyte, but instead of a maiden brimming with potential, he found himself with an older woman cobbled together by a lifetime of loss, missteps, and an instinct for survival.

For the first time, his Acolyte lived a solitary existence. Every young woman who had come before—serf or queen, weaver or field worker, of fine lineage or of the lowest caste in the poorest region— had belonged to a family. As he now understood, Tasha, the woman who walked with purpose beside him, was Felicity's family. Along with Felicity's domesticated cats. Ronnie, now, too.

And himself.

Somehow, within the span of a week, he had gone from veterinary patient to taciturn commander, from mentor to brother, and from roommate to trusted auxiliary posse member.

This trip had been filled with unexpected twists. This cycle's Rigiat had become a true friend, and the Acolyte's friends had become a goddess posse.

And now it was too late for him to turn back, to try to force this mission into the mold of the past. This time, he was not simply invested in his Acolyte's success in battle. He cared for Felicity Cheshire as a person and found himself invested in her life and happiness. It complicated the training process. He'd let her modify the language, the schedule, the mood. Had he been too easy on her? Was there a way to push her harder, move her along faster, without her shutting down completely?

He cared for Ronnie too, the iron-tough beauty with the damaged warrior spirit. And Tasha—well, he was helping her dispose of her assclown boyfriend, right?

He wondered if the bonds he felt with these women—the *attachments*—would be the costliest mistake of all.

They reached the front door. Tasha pulled it open. Jim was stretched out on the couch, his filthy boots upon the furniture. When he saw she was not alone, he jolted upright, then stood.

"Whaa..."

"This is Tom."

"Yeah. The Satan worshipper. We've met."

"Guess who I ran into in Portland today?"

Jim shrugged. "I don't know. Is this some kind of game? What's going on?"

"Sheri Weigand."

Though Tom had no idea what Tasha had discovered about Jim's true character, it must have something to do with the Weigand woman.

Jim seemed equally oblivious. "Yeah. *And?*"

"She told me how helpful you were all the way back in December, telling her the junkyard was closing and being purchased by a conservation group. You know where I'm going with this?"

Panic crept into Jim's eyes, but he pushed it down. "Baby. Come on. You know that's bullshit." He took a step toward her. "We didn't start dating until February. Why would I talk about you to some real estate agent before we even met?"

"I know, right? I wondered the same. But then I figured it out. You planned to screw your way into convincing me to sell, and then you planned to steal a bunch of my money."

"Babe!" He reached out for her.

Tasha straight-armed him. "You used me. You thought I'd be an easy target."

"I love you. Whatever you imagine I did. I didn't do it. Believe me..."

"We're done." Tasha took out her mobile phone, set the timer, and placed it on the coffee table. "You've got five minutes to collect as much of your shit as you can carry on your Harley, and then you're outa here. I'll send word when you can collect the rest."

"But you *love* me!"

"Four minutes, fifty seconds."

Jim's expression switched up fast. It went from that of a man unjustly accused to one consumed with rage. His upper lip curled.

"You stupid, ugly, old *bitch*."

That did it. He stepped in front of Tasha. "You now have four minutes and thirty-six seconds to do as she says."

"Or what?"

He shook his head, feeling pity for this insect of a man. No blows were required. He simply widened his stance, lowered his chin, and glared until Jim scuttled like a roach down the hallway, retrieving an armful of clothing, a few toiletries, and a six-pack from the refrigerator, shoving everything into a small duffle.

"You're boring, Tasha." Jim reached the door. "You're an uptight control freak who couldn't handle a free spirit like me."

"I think the term is free*loader*."

Jim spun around and pointed at her. "And your roots are showing!"

He followed Jim out the door, as Tasha had asked. Once the motorcycle had sped through the gate, he secured the padlock. He turned back to find Ronnie and Felicity on the front stoop of the Airstream.

"Hope you were gentle," Ronnie said.

"Is she OK?" Felicity asked.

"She's fine, but I think she needs her posse."

CHAPTER FOURTEEN

The rain had pounded against the windows all day. By afternoon, the storm pressed heavy and dark against the daylight. Because outdoor training had not been an option, they'd worked in Tasha's house, pushing furniture against the walls to create space in the center of the living room. Ronnie lay on Tasha's sofa, fresh ice packs on her eye, hand, and stitches, while Tasha stomped through the house, conducting a room-to-room sweep, determined to eliminate any sign that Hair Gel Jim had ever set foot on the premises.

"I've been thinking." Tasha threw another armload of clothes into a cardboard box. "You know how you've always said I should renovate this place?"

Felicity nodded. She'd long encouraged Tasha to invest some money into her house—get rid of the old carpet, cracked linoleum, and burnt-orange drapes. Maybe get some professional landscaping done too. The house might have started out as a classic World War II-era Pacific Northwest cottage, but it had been stuck in the '70s for as long as either of them could remember.

"I think it's time. I'm talking a whole gut job, down to the studs, with new electric, plumbing, a new roof, fix the cracked foundation. I'm totally serious. It's time."

Felicity was astounded. When she'd suggested that Tasha clean house, she didn't expect her to take it so *literally*.

"And everything will be exactly the way *I* want it. I'll choose all the finishes. Colors and fabrics. Tile. Light fixtures…" She disappeared down the hallway, returning with a plastic milk crate of Jim's shoes. She dropped it on the floor with a thud. "You know what else I've been thinking of doing?"

Felicity made a quick glance toward Tom. He hadn't been paying the slightest attention to Tasha's manic resolutions. Instead, he stood with his hands hanging limp at his sides, watching Ronnie sleep, lost in thought.

Hunh.

"My hair." Tasha announced. "No more touch-ups! I'm just going to let it grow out in all its white-witch glory. Fuck anyone who doesn't like it."

"It will be beautiful."

"And if I look like a hideous hag, that's fine too. Ain't nobody's business but mine, know what I'm sayin'?"

"I do."

"OK. I have to strip the bed. Maybe burn the mattress." She disappeared down the hall again.

This time, when Felicity turned to Tom, his jaw was tense and his eyes fierce. He looked right at her. "Let's get back to it."

Except for that lost-in-thought interlude with Ronnie, Tom had been laser-focused on training all day. He homed in on every little word, the tiniest subtlety of execution. Felicity understood. Time was running out. And though it was obvious to all that she had improved in strength, agility, confidence, and endurance, she had not perfected steps one through four. She wasn't even close. And there were two steps they'd yet to cover.

"The shorter, lighter lance should arrive today," Tom said.

"That's good."

"Now listen carefully. Step Five for defeating Apep: Taking a Knife to Smite Apep." Tom handed Felicity the eight-inch weapon. Its blade was flint, and its wooden handle had been carved elaborately with hieroglyphs. She recognized the story they told: *Bastet, the daughter of Ra, once again slays the serpent of evil and chaos!* Felicity examined the blade carefully, noting how the precise flaking of the flint had made it razor sharp.

The knife wasn't heavy. In fact, it fit quite comfortably in her hand. She made a slashing motion through the air. "I've got this, Tom!"

"Here's the incantation: *Seize, seize, O butcher, fell the foe with thy knife.*"

"No problem." Felicity bent her knees a bit and willed herself to become supple and quick. "*Seize, seize, O butcher, fell the foe with thy knife!*" She slashed the blade in the air again, added a fancy spin, and then stabbed forward with a grunt.

"Careful with that, Felicity."

"You go, girl! That was awesome!" Tasha carried a load of sheets to the washing machine off the kitchen.

Felicity gathered herself, nodded in response to Tom's warning, and then took a few steps forward. She wielded the knife like a sword, holding it far in front of her. She thrust viciously. "Seize! Seize, you bastard!"

"Not like…"

Felicity attempted to execute a turn but lost her footing. In an instant, Tom shot forward and yanked the blade from her hand just as she toppled to the carpet.

"Thanks. Whoa." As Felicity got back to her feet, Tasha's landline telephone rang. Ronnie woke up blinking. They could hear Tasha pick up in the kitchen.

"Hello?"

"You could have stabbed yourself," Tom hissed, his mouth a thin line of anger. "Or you could have broken the blade! Do you have any idea how difficult it is to source caramel-colored chert?"

"I have no idea what chert is, let alone why it has to be caramel-colored."

"It's a sedimentary rock with high quartz content."

"OK. But *why?*"

"Because. That is how. It has. *Always. Been. Done.*"

"Of course." Felicity was preparing to point out how he resorted to the same answer for all her questions when Tasha poked her head out of the kitchen. "Lissie, it's for you."

Felicity grabbed the living room extension, noting that Ronnie now sat up. Her bruising seemed a bit better in the lamplight. "Hello?"

"Felicity?"

It was a breathy, hesitant voice that she didn't immediately recognize. "Yes?"

"Hey. It's Bethany."

"Bethany?" Felicity couldn't think of a single reason Bethany would call unless something had happened to Rich, and she didn't think her luck was that good.

"I hope this isn't weird for you. You know, that I'm calling you. I don't want it to be awkward."

"It's fine."

Tasha was holding out her hands and mouthing the words,

What the hell? Felicity had no answer for her and shook her head.

"I couldn't find a phone number for you, but I knew you lived on Tasha Romero's property, so I called her. Sorry if this is a bad time. Is it… you know, a bad time?"

Bethany sounded more unfocused than usual. Also, she was near tears. "Is everything OK?"

"Oh, yeah. Sure. But I was just wondering if I could maybe come over. To your place. I… just… uh, Rich will be out with clients all evening, and I thought…" Her voice faded.

Felicity gave a quick glance around the rearranged room—to Tom holding the ritual dagger, to the stitched-up Ronnie on the couch. And thought of the state of her trailer, with chains on the daybed, an iron lance leaning against the wall, her scraps of paper taped to cupboards, and the twelve cats. "You know what? How about I come to you? Will that work?

"If you're OK with that. Won't it be hard for you, you know, to be *here*? Where you used to live?"

"It's fine, Bethany. I can be there in about half an hour."

"That'd be super sweet of you. Bye."

Felicity replaced the phone into the cradle, baffled.

"Was that who I *think* it was?" Tasha unceremoniously dumped a pile of Jim's comic books on the dining room table.

"Yeah. The new Mrs. Richard Hume, Esquire. And she wants me to come over."

Tom grabbed his loafers from the corner.

"You don't have to come."

He sighed, then shot her an irritated glare. "Yeah, I do."

"I don't need a bodyguard."

"Apep is getting ready to strike. Are you ready to face him?"

"Right. Put your shoes on, and I'll grab my keys."

The faux farmhouse appeared dreamlike in the rain, and when Felicity pulled to a stop in the driveway, she gave herself a moment. The last time she'd been here, it was to collect her belongings. How determined she'd been on that day, absolutely refusing to succumb to the undertow of grief, loneliness, or loss. With the help of her attorney and Tasha, she'd packed the rented panel van with the barest essentials, the things that belonged to her alone, and left behind anything from a marriage gone to rot.

On that day four years ago, she'd carried off sixteen large boxes, a few sentimental pieces of her mother's furniture, and a heavy awareness lodged deep in her belly. She now understood that her marriage had been as faux as the architecture. The sense of mourning she felt was for the loss of a fantasy—her dream of the home and family that could have been—not the reality of life with Rich.

She cut the engine and looked at Tom.

"I'm sorry," was all he said.

"For what?"

"It's got to sting a bit, coming back here."

Felicity shook her head. "The only sting is knowing my assets are trapped in the roof shingles and sheetrock and hardwood flooring of this monstrosity."

"Alexander's on it."

"Will I ever meet my new lawyer?"

"One day, I hope."

If I manage to save the world.

Bethany greeted them at the door, her big smile fading the instant she saw Tom. She asked, politely, that they wipe their feet on the welcome mat, then gestured for them to come inside. She looked tired. Not her usual perky-perfection self. She clutched another sleek

248

water bottle—this one a leopard print—but the matching scrunchie had slipped halfway down her ponytail and pieces of blond hair stuck out every which way. Her blue eyes were red-rimmed and her cheeks blotchy.

"Bethany, this is my nephew, Tom. He's visiting and very protective of me. I hope you don't mind that he came along."

"It is a dark and stormy day, Auntie. You know how I feel about you driving alone in bad weather."

Felicity cringed. Tom was a terrible actor, and she thought he came off more psycho than sentimental. Bethany didn't notice.

"It's super sweet that your family has come to visit. All the way to Oregon! It's nice someone worries about you. Cares about your safety." Bethany sank into the nearest of two substantial linen Chesterfield sofas—brand new, Felicity noted—then dropped her face to her hands and burst into tears.

Tom wandered into to the kitchen. Felicity sat down beside Bethany and reached for her hand—stopping herself partway. Was it appropriate to physically touch your ex-husband's new wife? What was the etiquette here? "Are you OK, Bethany? Is everything all right with the baby?"

"I want to go home, but there's no home to go to."

Felicity glanced around the room, confused. The place had been completely redone since she'd been asked to leave the premises. What was once eclectic chic was now an ultra-modern oasis of creams and whites, elegant in a picture-perfect way, but sterile. Rich had removed every trace of her. Which brought her right back to her initial point of confusion. "Aren't you already home?"

"No, not here. Not Pine Beach." Bethany straightened and pulled her face from her hands. The poor girl looked shaken to her core. "Can I tell you something? Something, you know, super personal?"

Felicity had a feeling that etiquette was about to the be the least of her concerns. "If you need to."

Bethany sniffed and raised her chin. "*I don't even like him!*"

That outburst must have been in reference to the only *him* they had in common. "Rich?"

"I didn't mean to get pregnant. I swear. I figured I'd have years to decide whether I wanted children."

"Things don't always turn out the way we planned."

"No kidding. Can I tell you a secret?"

Though fearing the depths they were about to plumb, Felicity offered an encouraging smile.

"I was ready to break up with him. And I mean, the exact day I found out I was pregnant. I'd written down what I was going to say."

Felicity did her best to look objective yet concerned.

"I can't raise a child alone! I'm not even sure I can raise one at all!" Bethany wiped her tears and tugged on her spandex T-shirt, tight around the gentle pooch of her tummy. "I'm sorry to dump this on you, but, you know, you're the only friend I have here."

"I *am*?" That was downright heartbreaking.

"You've always been super sweet to me, when you have every right to hate me. The truth is, I don't have anyone else. My family disowned me when I dropped out of Lehigh Valley Community College and ran off with a boyfriend—that's how I ended up on the West Coast—and I just needed to tell someone the truth."

"Oh, Bethany. I'm sorry."

"And, well, I figured you of all people would understand why I don't even *like* Rich and, oh my *God*, he's running for mayor now! He's on my case about looking perfect, not gaining too much baby weight! He wants me to smile and shake hands and do interviews and remember old people's names *and what am I gonna do?*"

Felicity was ashamed of herself. She'd judged this girl… woman… girl/woman… so harshly. She'd been jealous and bitter. Yes, Bethany was young and perky and pretty and pregnant, but she also was alone, afraid, and married to Richard Hume. If anyone was deserving of pity, she was.

Felicity's thoughts went to Circe, the beautiful Siamese mix found dumped at a loading dock, insecure and lost. Bethany was Circe in human form. And since when had Felicity turned her back on a stray in need?

She put her arm around Bethany's shoulder and gave her a gentle squeeze. "It's going to be all right, honey. The important thing is that you are honest with yourself about how you feel and what you want."

"I know, right? Like the sign says over the office door: *You have a right to be happy!*"

Felicity tried not to snort laugh. She managed to hold it in for a whole three seconds before it escaped. Bethany pulled back in surprise, then sputtered out her own guffaw. The two of them continued laughing, in earnest, until Bethany's tears started again.

Suddenly, she heard a low growl. Strange. Was it coming from outside? She decided to ignore it and patted Bethany's forearm. "You don't have to make any decisions now, honey. You have time to figure things out."

Bethany looked up, hopeful. "You think?"

"I do. And I'm going to help you."

"Thank you, Felicity!" Bethany threw both arms around her neck and hugged tight, a floral-citrusy cloud embracing them both. "You remind me so much of my mother before she disowned me!"

The low growling intensified, abruptly turned into a sharp *yip!*, and was followed by an otherworldly, lunatic laugh.

"Felicity." She turned to see Tom, his hands resting protectively on the back of the sofa, scowling as he stared out the windows. "We have an issue."

The upstairs master bedroom—also remodeled—featured a new second-story balcony that overlooked the generous backyard. Standing here at the railing with Bethany and Tom, she noticed that it offered the perfect vantage point from which to admire the new in-ground pool, hot tub, tennis court, and outdoor kitchen. Apparently, Rich had put all the money he'd stolen from her to good use. He'd built a resort, right here in Pine Beach, while she'd been on food stamps.

Beyond the backyard bacchanal, shadows dappled the lawn. The rain had turned to a fine mist. Dusk crept in.

Then the shadows moved.

And yowled.

"Jackals." Tom kept his voice low.

"Don't be silly." Bethany turned to him and gave a little laugh. "Maybe coyotes is all."

"I hate jackals." Tom practically spat the words.

Felicity was curious. "Is it a cat thing, or…?"

"I need your phone."

"It's in my purse on the sofa downstairs."

Tom nodded, then disappeared inside.

A particularly loud series of yaps unnerved Felicity, and she decided it would be wise to get Bethany off the exposed balcony, and the sooner the better. "Hey, have you started decorating the nursery yet?"

Bethany's eyes lit up. "Yes! Would you like to see it?"

"Absolutely."

Bethany led the way through the master bedroom and down the hall. "I had it painted a pale yellow. We don't know if it's a boy or a girl yet, of course. But I found the most adorable teddy bear fabric that's a perfect match."

In Felicity's time, this room had served as Rich's home office. Now, it was about to become a joyful and welcoming child's room.

Felicity waited for the stabbing pain and grief to hit. Instead, she felt only a twinge of regret. She'd put so much time, energy, and love into this house, but had been denied the one decorating duty she'd most coveted: she'd never had the chance to paint a nursery a pastel yellow, or sky blue, or blush pink.

Bethany picked up a furniture catalog. "This is the crib I like best. It's kind of a sleigh bed design, see? And there's a matching changing table and dresser combination."

"That's lovely."

Bethany shook her head. "You probably think I'm nuts; one minute saying I don't want my husband and didn't plan on a baby, and the next I'm picking out cribs and teddy bear fabric."

Felicity smiled. "Not nuts. Just hormonal and unsure what the future has in store. Which is completely understandable."

Tom rushed into the room, slightly breathless. "It's worse than I imagined. The house is surrounded."

Bethany frowned. "By the coyotes? We should call animal control or something, right?" She began flipping the pages of the catalog again.

Tom lowered his voice. "Ronnie checked police scanners and news outlets. They're nowhere else in the area. Just *here*."

"Is it me? Did I attract them?" Felicity hated the possibility that she'd put another innocent person in danger.

"Not entirely." Tom's gaze shot to Bethany's belly pooch. Luckily she was still focused on her catalog.

"*They're here for the baby?*"

"What about the baby?" Bethany remained oblivious.

"Can we shoo them off somehow?"

"No." Tom pulled Felicity into the hallway, his voice barely audible. "They await their master."

"Who the hell is that?"

"Wepwawet. Like Mahaf, he can straddle the realms for his created purpose. Mahaf ferries the dead. Wepwawet is the opener of the ways."

"What ways?" Felicity checked to be sure Bethany had returned to her catalog. "I read that jackals are associated with death, that they're involved in funerary rites. You're saying he's coming here to open the ways to death?"

"Exactly. Wepwawet and his minions are here because they sense this is where mass death will begin, just like Mahaf did. In the meantime, there's nothing the harbinger of death enjoys more than snuffing out a new life."

Felicity's stomach dropped.

"Should we call animal control now?" Bethany glanced up.

Felicity knew they had no choice; they had to get Bethany out of there. They couldn't leave her behind to be ripped apart by a pack of ravenous jackals. And for sure, Bethany needed to be long gone by the time What-the-What showed up, because Felicity had seen an illustration of him in one of the reference texts at the library, and he was disturbing as all get-out.

A loud crack of thunder split the night air. The whole house shook, and the lights flickered. Felicity looked out the bedroom window in time to see the entire sky flash white and then pulsate with an eerie, purplish glow.

The jackals howled in unison. Bethany slapped her hands over her ears. "Can somebody tell me what's going on? This is getting scary!"

Felicity went into the nursery and pried Bethany's hands from her ears. "Bethany, sweetie, have you seen the movie *The Mummy*?"

"The one with Tom Cruise?"

"Any of them, really."

"No. I can't handle scary movies like that."

"Super," Felicity said.

"Look, Rich told me you'd gone over the deep end and were nothing but a loopy old cat lady, but I didn't believe him because I hardly believe anything he says." Bethany sat cross-legged on the king-sized bed. "And now you're telling me the queen of cats asked you to save the world? Seriously? So Rich was right? You're catshit crazy?"

Felicity popped up the handle on Bethany's rolling suitcase and summoned her patience. "Bastet is more than a queen. She's a goddess. Now what else do you need? We've got underwear, pajamas, three outfits, seven scrunchies, your makeup bag, your toiletry bag, and two pairs of shoes. Anything more? Last call."

"I guess that's it, but…" The howling, yipping, and growling started again, and Bethany shot to her feet. "They sound closer. Are they getting closer? I don't understand what ancient Egypt has to do with Pine Beach, Oregon, but I bet this isn't a problem back home!" She hiccupped from all the crying. "Evil demons never show up in Lehigh Valley."

"That you know about," Tom said, entering the bedroom.

The roof rumbled. Everyone's gaze shot to the ceiling. The chandelier in the master closet swayed.

"Time to go. *Now.*" Tom gathered Bethany and ushered her down the hall, down the stairs, to the front door. Felicity was right behind, dragging the suitcase.

"My water bottle! I need my water bottle!"

Felicity grabbed it from the coffee table and shoved it into the side pocket of the luggage.

"All right then." Felicity heard the sound of jaws snapping on the other side of the door. "What's your plan? How do we get out?"

"You tell them to let us pass."

For a moment, Felicity just stood there, staring. "Wait. *That's* your plan? Me? *I'm* the plan?"

"Exactly."

"I'm sure immortal warrior priests have more experience with these sorts of things."

"Felicity, I don't hold rank here. I don't have the power to face Wepwawet. You do."

"That's it? I just stroll on out to the monster and his carnivorous kickline and politely ask them not to rip our faces off on our way to the car?"

"No polite asking. You've been bestowed with the *usekh* of the Ever-Living Bastet. You don't ask for anything. You *command* them to give us safe passage."

"I'm not really the commanding type."

"What's going on?" Bethany tried to wriggle free of Tom's protective grip. "You're both nuts!"

Tom turned his stone-cold glare on Felicity. "Either you become the commanding type immediately or this young woman and the child in her womb will die."

"*Hello?* What?" Bethany had turned a lovely shade of moss green. She made strange little urping noises, like she was trying not to heave.

Clearly, this was no time to panic. And yet, it was the perfect time to panic. Because until now, the idea of dying in a battle with an ancient Egyptian evil entity had been theoretical. Now it was imminent. And personal. Because her objective wasn't so much to save humanity in general, but to save Bethany specifically, who was now staring at her while looking dangerously close to hurling all over the plush, cloud white carpeting.

"Now, Felicity!"

"Fine! I'll do it. I'll command." She rolled the luggage toward Bethany. "You're in charge of your bag. Do whatever Tom says, no matter how bossy he sounds. He wants you to be safe. Understand?"

She nodded, which triggered another gag reflex.

Felicity stared at the door. She put one hand on the latch and ran the other hand through her humidity-frizzled hair. This was it. Rubber, meet road. Whatever she would need to defeat What's-his-What, she'd better already possess it because there was no time to go out and try to find it. The jackals were circling.

But then again, when hadn't they?

Breast cancer did its damnedest to take her out. It failed. Rich buried her alive in deceit and cruelty. She'd clawed her way to the surface. Infertility and bankruptcy and homelessness and joblessness and food stamps—none of those things had defeated her.

Then she remembered the day in front of the bakery, when that guy on the phone walked right into her. How long had she been invisible to the world? Unimportant? Taken for granted and underestimated? She'd been just another middle-aged woman with sagging skin, surgical scars, and failing joints.

Fuck that.

Something stirred in her. She felt it ignite along the soles of her feet, rooting her to the earth itself. The force tingled as it raced to her toes, up her ankles and calves. All the rage and loss coalesced and roiled like lava, past her knees, thighs, and hips. It caught fire in her belly, rushing through her chest, sparking against the necklace, racing down her arms and through the bracelet to her hands, then shooting with a *whoosh* into her mind.

For the first time ever, Felicity knew who she was. She wasn't the sum of her struggles. Nor was she the labels others gave her—pitiful, cat lady, hoarder, crazy old broad, pathetic, unstable, not normal.

Everyone had been wrong about her, and that was bad. But the true injustice was that she'd been wrong about herself.

She would no longer allow anyone to define her. Never again.

She was Felicity-Fucking-Cheshire, and she was enough.

She ripped the soft Egyptian cotton from her shoulders, balled it up, and shoved it into Tom's chest.

"Hold my scarf."

She pressed down on the front door latch and spoke to Bethany. "Stay behind me until I tell you to run."

Bethany whimpered. "No, no, no. I can't do this."

Felicity glanced over her shoulder. "You'd be surprised what you can do when you have no choice."

She opened the door.

The creature was taller than Mahaf, but he was leaner. Meaner. He had the head of a wolf, edged with white fur, and he wore what looked like a soldier's uniform from a forgotten time. His eyes glowed a fluorescent amber. He bared his teeth.

The book's illustrations hadn't done him justice. He wasn't just disturbing. He was gruesome.

Despite this, Felicity stepped onto the front porch. The jackals squeezed in, the circle closing tighter. The night air was alive with growling, yowling, and yipping. Creatures trampled on the roof above them, lurked in the bushes beside them, gathered in battle positions on the lawn. She heard the unmistakable *smack!* of drooling jaws.

"Lord Wepwawet." Felicity expected that she would have to shout to be heard over the canine cacophony, but somehow, that wasn't the case. Her normal speaking voice sliced through the ruckus.

The wolf-headed creature assessed her face, then his neon glare found the gold *usekh* around her neck. His hand shot into the air, and he held it there, rigid. Every jackal went silent. The mangy creatures strained and struggled, as if they tugged against invisible chains and could come no closer.

"Who dares utter my name?"

Felicity knew he was speaking to her, and she understood him perfectly well. But her ears had only heard a deep garbling, an animal sound that her brain had somehow translated into language. That was disconcerting.

She stepped down, pausing on the bottom porch stair. She looked up at his grotesque face. "I am Felicity Renee Cheshire of Pine Beach, Oregon. I am the chosen Acolyte of the Ever-Living Goddess Bastet." She descended to the front walk, which provided a straight shot to the driveway and her car. She felt Tom and Bethany behind her on the stairs.

It was showtime.

"I demand safe passage for myself and my companions. Make it so!"

Well, crap. She'd just used Captain Picard's line from *Star Trek: The Next Generation*!

The deity must not be a fan of cable reruns because he didn't flinch, not a muscle or a tuft of fur. The jackals tugged at their invisible shackles, ready to pounce, yearning to sink sharp fangs into soft flesh.

"*Demand?*" The low, rough voice rumbled through her mind. He was one scary son of a bitch, and this was the exact moment when the old Felicity would have apologized and backed down, and to what end? All three of them would've been torn into to bite-sized jackal treats.

But that surge of power held rock-solid within her, and she took another confident step. "Yes! I command thee, Lord Wepwawet, Opener of the Ways. I *command* that you ensure our safe passage. Do as I say!"

Felicity kept moving, one foot in front of the other. She heard Bethany's panicky breath in her ear.

Then, out of nowhere, Felicity remembered something Rich once said. He'd come home from court to brag about how he'd faked his way to winning over the jury. "Life is simple, Felicity," he'd said. "If they sense the slightest hesitation, they'll devour you. You gotta dazzle 'em with bullshit."

Ah, yes: Lord Richard Hume, Opener of the Ways of Bullshit.

She actually laughed out loud.

The harbinger of death tipped his wolf head, perplexed by her outburst. She took another step. Because she was a queen. Of truth. Of kindness. Of laughter. Felicity had been chosen to wield the powerful amulet of a high goddess. And this knowledge was her passport, bestowing upon her the absolute right to keep walking, head held high.

The jackals foamed at the mouth, their deadly focus squarely on the young mother. Thank the Goddess that Bethany was safely tucked between Felicity and Tom—at least she hoped Bethany was safe.

One of the jackals exploded with a strangled laugh. Another gnashed its jaws. Others howled out a chorus of outrage. Felicity walked on.

The gold encircling her neck tingled. The silver at her wrist hummed. No hesitation. No weakness. It was she who held rank here. And then she understood—the necklace and the bracelet amplified her power; they didn't bestow it.

The power was hers.

Now just inches from Wepwawet and his jackal frontline, Felicity didn't alter her pace. She pressed forward. The pungent scent of feral animal stung her nostrils. She walked right into them...and passed right *through* them.

She gulped in the damp air.

What just happened? Had they physically parted to allow passage? Or had the creatures suddenly become insubstantial, as thin as a lingering nightmare? It didn't matter.

"Run!"

Tom and Bethany were right behind her. It took just seconds for everyone to scramble into the car, Bethany and her suitcase in the back. Felicity was halfway down the driveway before Tom managed to slam his door shut.

For a moment, the only sound within the car interior was labored breathing. At the first stop sign, Bethany poked her head between the front bucket seats.

"You're not crazy at all, are you, Felicity?"

"Just a few more bites. Please." Felicity spooned Szechuan beef with broccoli onto Bethany's plate. "You and the baby have been through a lot tonight."

He leaned back in the chair at Tasha's dining table, which had been cleared of Jim's stuff so they would have room to eat. He watched Felicity fuss over the wife of her unfaithful ex-husband, a young woman who carried the child Felicity could never conceive.

His Acolyte had surprised him that night. Ordinarily, he didn't like surprises, but in this instance, he was ecstatic. They'd survived Lord Wepwawet and his jackals. Somehow, Felicity had done it. She *believed* she was capable of command and then took it.

It had been an astonishing thing to witness.

Of course, there was still a shitload of work to be done with the steps to defeat Apep, but for the first time, he had caught sight of the warrior goddess within Felicity. For the first time, he saw at least the potential for victory over Apep.

"She's different. What happened?" Ronnie sat to his right, devouring a plate of orange chicken with expertly controlled chopsticks. He considered stealing a nibble but decided to refill his own plate.

Of all the unique pleasures found in this trip to the earthly plane, American Chinese takeout was definitely in his top ten. How this ancient cuisine had become tastier—with modified, modern cooking methods and ingredients from another continent—was nothing short of a mystery. Ordinarily, he didn't like mysteries.

Mysteries like Veronica Davis of Pendleton. There was a lot beneath the surface with her, and it bothered him. But most of all, it bothered him that he was bothered by her.

"I see the difference too, Veronica."

"You know, I've mulled it over and decided you can call me Ronnie if you want." She popped another piece of chicken into her mouth and locked her gaze on his. She had just bestowed upon him the title of friend. She knew it. He knew it. And he relished it.

Though he shouldn't. But he did. Which was something he'd rather not examine too closely.

"Thank you, Ronnie. What did Felicity tell you about what

happened tonight?"

She shrugged. "Just that you guys were attacked by a pack of drooling supernatural jackals and had to spill the whole backstory to Bethany before she'd agree to leave with you."

"That about covers it." He helped himself to another egg roll, more shrimp fried rice, and a bit of the beef. "The original Acolyte's defeat set into motion a whole series of events that I hadn't anticipated. Tonight could have been a disaster if Felicity hadn't..."

"What?" Ronnie cocked an eyebrow and lowered her voice to a whisper. "What'd she do?"

"Well, Felicity became."

"Became what? A *cat*?"

He laughed, enjoying how it released the tension in his chest. That was another distinct pleasure during this visit. He had laughed more since arriving in Pine Beach—and under the direst of circumstances—than in the last thirty-one Apep regenerations combined. "No."

"Then explain."

"I'm not sure I'll find the right words."

Ronnie propped her chopsticks on the edge of her plate and scowled. Her bruises were fading. He'd checked her stitches earlier and found she was healing nicely. And he liked her hair the way she had arranged it tonight. It was the way she'd worn it when she'd saved his life, two full puffs of curls, one at each side of her head. The style gave her the appearance of a lighthearted sprite, a nymph.

"You're fluent in fourteen languages, dude."

"And all without an accent."

That made Ronnie laugh. "So find some words. What happened with her tonight?" She placed an elbow on the table, then cupped her chin in her hand. She looked up at him, her dark eyes dancing with intelligence, humor, and tease.

He looked away and took a bite of an egg roll. Eventually, he said, "I think Felicity stepped into herself tonight, fully, as if a cage door was opened and she was suddenly free."

"Hunh." Ronnie closed one eye.

He laughed again, then tried another approach. "You know the necklace has never been bestowed upon someone like Felicity."

"Yeah."

"I think it's created some sort of new... *alchemy*. Strange things are happening; events are unfolding in unusual ways. This is new territory for me. Sorry if I'm not explaining it well."

Ronnie nodded, chin still in hand. "You done good, Tubastet-af-ankh, *hem-netjer-tepi*."

He pulled back, shocked at the sound of his name and title emanating from Ronnie's lips. He had grown accustomed to the "Tom-this" and "Tom-that" from his new friends.

"I Googled the pronunciation." Ronnie suddenly straightened and stared at Felicity across the table. "Whoa. OK, *that's* weird."

He followed her gaze.

"Am I seeing things or has the center stone changed color?"

"*Pizdets!*" The blue of the sapphire had deepened, intensified, and taken on a richer undertone that he had never seen before. How was that possible? The stone's color had never changed, Acolyte after Acolyte, visit after visit, century after century. Why now?

Ronnie pressed close. "Did the necklace somehow activate tonight? Is that what caused her to bust out with her bad self?"

He considered that, but decided the truth might be even more astounding. He dipped his head toward Ronnie and whispered his answer. "Actually, I think Felicity's bad self has changed the necklace."

Tasha appeared from the hallway. "Sewing room's all made up

for you, Ronnie. You're in the guest room, Bethany. There better be some fried rice left or I'll have to knock some heads."

Ronnie lifted her iced tea glass in Bethany's direction. "I guess it's time to officially welcome you to Tasha Romero's Home for Wayward Wenches!"

He nearly choked on his Szechuan beef.

Tasha piled her plate. "Wayward *goddesses*, Ronnie. Please."

"I don't consider myself wayward," Bethany said, looking around the table, wide-eyed. "I mean, sure, I'm two thousand miles from home, pregnant, married to a pimply old man I don't even like, and I can't decide whether I'm crazy or if all of *you* are crazy, but I don't think *wayward* is the right word."

Tasha cleared her throat and took a seat.

"Not that you guys are old. Or crazy. I always say the wrong thing!" Bethany dropped her forehead into her hands.

Felicity hated to nag, but Bethany had barely eaten, and the young woman and her baby were her responsibility now. In fact, the more she thought about it, the more she worried about how all this would look to Rich.

She'd basically kidnapped his pregnant wife, which would fit quite neatly into his crazed-with-jealousy theory.

"Are you sure you don't want more to eat?"

Bethany shook her head, rubbing her face back and forth against her open hands. She'd been sitting like that for at least five minutes.

Felicity glanced at Tasha, who shrugged. She looked to Tom, who tried to smile. Ronnie rolled her eyes.

"Bethany, are you all right? I'm worried about you." Felicity was aware that she spoke with the same voice she'd used to rescue Circe from the loading dock and coax the terrified, emaciated cat to eat. But it'd obviously worked since Circe was thriving. So Felicity decided to push the plate in front of Bethany one more time. Finally, Bethany looked up, grabbed the fork, and took another bite, though obviously still in shock.

"Was that real, Felicity? Was any of it *real?* Because nothing about it made sense."

"You'll get used to it, honey," said Tasha, now the voice of experience.

"But there's a lot ahead of us," Felicity added. "You'll need to stay strong. Especially when Rich calls, which will be soon."

"Oh, God."

"It'll be all right," Ronnie said. "We got your six."

Bethany appeared dazed. "You sure it's safe here? They can't get to me and my baby? Maybe you should take me home so I can tell Rich what happened."

"*NO!*" Four voices answered in unison.

"Rich is not equipped to comprehend something like this. And he can't protect you." Felicity took a breath. "He will get angry and lash out, but you will survive, just as I did."

Tom stood, walked around the table, and crouched down next to Bethany's chair. "I've protected this house and land with a sacred ritual. No harm will come to you here."

"You *promise?*"

"I promise."

Just then, the junkyard Rottweiler exploded in a barking frenzy. Everyone jumped, even Ronnie. Then the dog segued into a nice, long howl.

"Are they after me again?" Bethany's big blue eyes welled with tears. "Did they follow us here? I thought you said…"

"It's just a pet dog," Tom assured her, his voice steady. "Not jackals, Bethany. Just the big, old dog who lives next door."

"Holy shit," Felicity muttered. Her heart pounded so fast and hard that she feared it would leap from her chest like in the movie *Alien*. "I'll tell you one thing. I will *not* miss that sound when they close down the junkyard. I've had enough of that damn Rottweiler."

"Or the sound of the car crusher engine," Tasha added.

"You're definitely not going to sell?"

Tasha smiled at Ronnie's question. "You were asleep when I mentioned renovating instead of selling, but yeah. The money's tempting, but I'm staying put."

"That is a bomb-ass decision, Tasha. Hey, when you have a minute, can I get my key ring back?"

"Oh." Tasha shook her head. "Don't be mad, but in all this chaos, I can't remember where I left it. Maybe it's still in my car."

"No worries. I'm not going anywhere for a while. I told Dr. Nguyen about the break-in, and she gave me two weeks' sick leave."

"You should be completely healed by then," Tom said.

Bethany's cell phone rang. She grabbed her water bottle with a shaking hand and took a big swig, then glanced at the screen. "It's Rich. I can't do this."

"You can," Felicity said. "We're right here with you."

Tom rose from his crouch at Bethany's feet. When he returned to his chair, Felicity couldn't help but notice the glance shared between Ronnie and the cat-turned-man.

"Hello, Rich."

Bethany scrunched her eyes shut as she listened, finally speaking, her voice small. "I… the thing is, I'm not coming home. At least not now. No, as in *days*." She listened. Her brow furrowed. She bit her lip. The room was filled with the rise and fall of Rich's indistinct ranting.

Felicity grabbed Bethany's free hand and squeezed.

"Actually, Rich, I'm *not* happy. I need to figure out some stuff and need space to do it. I'm staying with a friend. That's not…it doesn't matter who."

Bethany squeezed Felicity's hand in return. She looked up and tried to put on a brave face, but they all watched Bethany's eyes grow huge. Her head snapped to attention.

"You don't get to talk to me like that. I won't let you threaten me. No, actually, I *don't* owe you anything, and I don't care who you get to answer your office phone tomorrow. What? Nuh-uh. I don't want any part of that; *you're* the one running for mayor, not me, so you can sit with the editorial board and answer…"

Felicity rubbed her forehead. Dear Goddess, this exchange was painful to hear.

"The *washer setting*? Are you stinking kidding me right now? You're a lawyer. You can figure out how to turn a knob. Really? OK, I'm done. I'm blocking you after this call. I'll get in touch in a few days."

Bethany hung up and powered down her phone, double-checking that the screen had gone black. She looked up, shaking her head. "What a complete dick! I deserve so much better."

Felicity stared at Bethany in awe. It had taken her twenty-plus years and a court summons before she could even think about uttering those words.

"Hey, Ronnie?" She couldn't take her eyes off badass Bethany. "Can you run to the trailer and grab…"

"The fourth bracelet." Ronnie scooted her chair from the table and stood. "Already on it."

CHAPTER FIFTEEN

Bethany was settled into Tasha's guest room, and Ronnie was already asleep on the pull-out couch in Mrs. Romero's old sewing room, which, though not exactly five-star accommodations, had to be better than the Airstream's ancient daybed.

Felicity sat on her little metal porch looking up at the clear night sky. She'd switched off Tasha's floodlights and the stars blazed overhead, vivid and alive. It seemed so peaceful tonight, as if all was right with the world.

She knew better, of course.

Tom opened the door and stepped outside. "Mind if I join you?"

"Please do."

He settled into the folding chair. They sat side by side in easy silence for several long moments. As she gazed at the sky, Felicity listened to the slow and deep pattern of Tom's breathing, half expecting it to transition into a mesmerizing purr, like Boudica's. She turned to him, thinking maybe he'd fallen asleep.

Tom was staring at her, his mismatched cat eyes shining in the darkness.

"It'll be nice for you to have the daybed to yourself, huh?"

He gave a noncommittal nod. "Thank you for taking such excellent care of everyone in your orbit."

Felicity smiled. Clearly, neither of them would be addressing how he'd spent the last couple of nights in cat form, curled up against Ronnie. She suspected that Ronnie wasn't aware of the sleeping arrangements.

"That's kind of you to say, Tom."

Felicity leaned her head back for more stargazing. "What's it like? The Realm of the Gods?"

"Ineffable."

She waited for him to expound on that, but, as any English teacher knew, explaining what one meant by ineffable would be at odds with the word itself. Besides, he wasn't in a particularly chatty mood. He was *such* a cat. "Do you miss it?"

"Sometimes. But I know I'll return."

"How does that work?" She turned in her chair to face him. "Let's say I manage to destroy Apep. Do you just immediately take off?"

"You *will* destroy Apep, and I'll hang around long enough to release the necklace and say my goodbyes."

A familiar heaviness lodged in Felicity's chest. It took a second to give it a name: *loss*. "I'll miss you when you go. Is that a weird thing to say?"

Tom laughed. "Not at all. I'll miss you, too, Felicity Cheshire of Pine Beach, Oregon. And that's new for me, I've got to admit. I'll miss Tasha, Bethany, Ronnie, and all the cats, even Gumbo, the imbecile."

She snorted. "Don't let him hear you say that."

"Oh, he knows he's a dullard compared to the others, but it doesn't bother him in the slightest. Maybe that's the blessing within the curse."

"That's deep."

Tom laughed again. He'd been laughing a lot in the last couple of days, and she found the sound soothing to her soul.

"You really think I can do it, Tom? You think I can beat Apep?"

He was silent for twenty-two seconds. Felicity was sure of the duration of the cone of silence because she'd ticked off the seconds in her head. At the twenty-second mark, her palms began to sweat.

"Yeah," he eventually said. "After seeing how you faced Wepwawet, my answer is yes. But only if you give me everything in the coming days. You need to commit to training harder than ever before. I fear our time is up."

"I'm all in, Tom. I'll give it everything I've got."

"I am glad to hear it."

She stood up. "Want a glass of wine?"

He nodded. Felicity went inside to pour two glasses. Mojo followed her when she returned outside, and, once she got settled, he jumped in her lap.

"Felicity, I know it's none of my business, but have you talked to Cassius?"

"Who?"

"Your Roman dairy farmer."

"Oh, jeez. No. That was a one-off. I'm kinda busy these days, in case you haven't noticed."

"I simply wondered."

Felicity took a sip of the merlot they'd picked up at Safeway. "And *I've* been wondering…"

271

He laughed. Yet again.

"I bet this world seems dirty and smelly and dangerous to you, compared to the Realm of the Gods."

"Sure, but compared to other visits to the mortal plane, it's paradise. As a woman from a modern, industrialized nation, you'd be horrified by the conditions I've experienced in the past."

"It's not like the Airstream is a castle or anything."

Tom tipped his head and grinned. "Felicity, actual castles were inferior to your Airstream, by a lot."

She snort laughed.

"But to answer your original question, I do not miss the God Realm when I am on earth, but sometimes, while in the Realm of the Gods, the earthly plane tugs at my heart, at my memory. Humanity will always be home."

"*Home?* But isn't..."

"Remember that I was fully human until the fall of the temples. I was in Bastet's service as a human, as was my mother before me and her mother before her and so on."

"The women in your family were priestesses?"

"Oh, yes. For many generations, until my mother died giving birth to me. I was raised by my grandmother."

"I didn't know. I'm so sorry."

"Thanks. It was a long time ago."

Felicity made sure to pause the conversation, careful not to rush past something so devastatingly personal. Eventually she asked, "How exactly did you become immortal?"

She winced, worried she'd pushed him too hard and he'd just walk back inside to sulk on the daybed. But he answered.

"When the Romans came, it was clear to Bastet that the time of free and open worship had ended. The Ever-Living Goddess granted me my new form so I could continue to serve her in both realms."

"How does that feel, Tom?" Felicity heard the quiet awe in her own voice. "How does it feel to not worry about failing knees and arthritic fingers and a dimming mind? To be free from the hell of aging?" Felicity whispered her next question in the intimacy of the darkness. "What *is* forever, anyway? What is existence without the press of time? How do you *feel?*"

After a moment, he let go with a deep sigh and whispered his answer: "Tired. Mostly, I feel tired."

It rained again in the morning, so Felicity and Tom trained in Tasha's house. The living room furniture remained shoved against the walls, but Felicity immediately noticed that the mounds of Hair Gel Jim's belongings had grown overnight, still piled on top of the dining room table. How much crap could one parasitical man possess?

Thrown on top of a shoebox full of junk was the bottle of Passion's Fire spray perfume and the cheap pair of earrings that had turned Tasha's earlobes green.

Tasha'd had a productive evening.

Tom pulled off his shoes and took a wide stance. Felicity did the same. They went through a series of breathing and centering exercises, followed by stretches. That morning, Felicity managed eight legit pushups—no girl elbows required—and recorded a personal best with twelve sit-ups.

"If only Mrs. Frankel were alive to see this day," Felicity said.

After reviewing the incantations for steps one through five, Tom decided it was time to forge ahead.

"Step Six of defeating Apep…"

"Sorry. Am I late?" Ronnie appeared from the hallway. She was barefoot and wore a pair of cutoff shorts and a USMC T-shirt. "Let me grab a cup of coffee and I'll be right back. Go ahead, didn't mean to interrupt. Just want to watch. Ignore me."

Tom seemed bothered by Ronnie's sudden appearance. He probably didn't want an audience. "The sixth step…"

"What is the sixth step, again?"

"Can I finish my sentence?"

"Sure."

"Putting Fire Upon Apep." He reached into a side pocket of his cargo shorts. "This is a flint, and this is a striking stone."

"I knew it! I've always told myself that all the shit I had to learn in Girl Scouts would come in handy one day."

Tom ignored her. "You'll use these to spark a ritual fire." He reached into another pocket and pulled out a small bronze box. "And you'll carry that flame into battle with this."

"Can't I just use matches?"

"She should be able to use matches." Ronnie brought her coffee mug to the couch. She curled up on one end, blowing over the hot liquid.

"I have a couple of Jim's lighters." Tasha passed through on her way to the kitchen, pointing to the overflowing shoebox on the dining table. "Look under his socks."

"I like those long fireplace lighters." Bethany leaned against the hallway arch in a summer pajama set. She looked cute as a button. Felicity's eyes were drawn to the Bastet bracelet dangling from her left wrist. It looked good on her.

"That'd work!" Tasha hollered from the kitchen.

Tom closed his eyes, gnashed his jaw, then opened his eyes again. "The incantation for this final step is longer than the others so please pay attention." He cleared his throat. *Fire be in thee, O Apep. May the Eye of Horus have power over the soul and the shade of Apep.*

Felicity repeated it to herself several times until she felt confident that she had it memorized. "Fire be on thee…"

"*In* thee," Ronnie said. "Tom distinctly said *in thee*."

Tasha leaned against the dining room table, cradling her coffee mug. "I'm team Felicity on this. It should be *on*. Unless he's supposed to catch fire on the inside first, you know, like spontaneous combustion."

"*In* is the correct translation from the ancient Egyptian," Tom snapped. "Let's continue. This step includes footwork. Watch me carefully."

Felicity watched him, over and over, and gave it a try. She wasn't a total klutz, but there was one particularly tricky combination of right foot, left foot, right foot where she couldn't seem to nail the timing.

"You're spending too much time on your left foot." Bethany joined Felicity in the middle of the room, standing with her back to Felicity. "Watch." Bethany executed it perfectly.

"Do it again, but slower." Felicity copied each move Bethany made and began to catch on.

"Let me guess—varsity cheerleader?" Ronnie smirked behind her coffee cup.

"Please." Bethany waved her off. "I'm not some dumb blonde who spent high school drooling over beefy football players. It was even sadder; I was captain of our competitive dance team, which meant I spent four years drooling over hunky gay dancers."

The room stayed awkwardly quiet until Felicity giggled. Soon, all were laughing.

Except Tom. "Why is that funny? What's funny about wanting something you can never have? The more time I spend with the women of Pine Beach, the less I understand women as a species. Can we please focus?"

This made them laugh all the harder, but they eventually got the giggling under control. Bethany continued to demonstrate the footwork, explaining how Felicity could improve weight distribution by staying on the balls of her feet. The tip was quite helpful. Tasha joined in, adding a bit of country and western flair to her moves, followed by Ronnie, who couldn't resist any longer. Soon, the whole Badass Goddess Posse was dancing and chanting the incantation in seamless perfection.

Tom took a seat on an old recliner pushed against the wall, and Felicity swore he looked as obstinate as Valkyrie. He'd managed to reproduce that aloof-yet-irritated expression, the one aimed in Felicity's direction whenever she tried to get the cat to move.

"Let's add a spin!" Bethany demonstrated.

Felicity placed a hand on Bethany's shoulder. "I don't think Tom wants us to change the steps."

The women stilled, then turned to Tom.

"It has always been done in exactly the form I demonstrated." Tom pinched the bridge of his nose. "No one has ever tried to add or subtract from the precise movements."

Tasha put her hands on her hips. "But where's the power come from, Tom? Is it from following exact words and steps or is it from Lissie herself, what she thinks and feels and why she's doing it in the first place?"

"Her *intention*," Ronnie concurred. "Who cares if she gets a step wrong or adds a twirl? What really matters is that her heart is in the right place, right?"

Tom stood. He moved confidently into the center of the room and gestured for everyone but Felicity to take a seat on the couch, then waited for them to get situated. "Ladies, thank you for your assistance."

He moved stiffly, drained of whatever patience he'd had. "Yes, Felicity's focus must be on defeating Apep. That is essential. But it's also essential that she follow the steps precisely. It is the only method that's ever worked. Now…" Tom opened the little bronze box. "You'll have to be close enough to Apep to blow the embers onto him. Like this." He demonstrated.

Felicity took the box and was about to practice when something dawned on her. "Will he be a man or a snake?"

"*What?*" Tasha looked to Felicity for clarification. She hated snakes. A lot.

"Oh. I didn't mention that? Turns out Apep can take human form or become a giant, hideous snake thing."

"You mean literally?" Tasha shook her head. "Hell, no."

Ronnie shrugged. "It's a theme. Tom can turn into a cat."

"So everybody says." Tasha was unconvinced. "I've never seen it happen."

"Oooh!" Bethany bounced on the couch. "What kind of cat?"

"The extremely handsome kind," Ronnie said. "A large, gray Egyptian Mau with distinct markings. His fur is plush and soft."

"He sounds super cute."

"To tell the truth, I think he's better looking as a feline, though he does have the same gorgeous, mismatched eyes."

"Can we please focus?" Tom seemed embarrassed by Ronnie's description of him.

Felicity had been unable to let the question go because she would be the one standing up to Apep, and she needed to know exactly what she'd be dealing with. "If he shows up as a snake, how big will he be?"

Tom had reached his limit. "What the fuck difference does it make what he looks like? All that matters is that he's defeated with use of the *correct fucking steps!*"

"Someone's been spending too much time with Felicity," Ronnie said.

Tasha looked woozy. "Well, it matters to me. I don't do snakes."

"Then you can stay outside when it all goes down, be our lookout," Ronnie suggested.

"*Enough!*" Tom was so angry that his face had gone purple, and the veins stood out on his neck. "There will be no posts or lookouts. No one will be involved in the battle but myself and the Acolyte."

"Yeah, not happening." Ronnie stood up and walked to Tom, arms crossed. "We're a team now. Just the other night, you helped Tasha deal with Jim, and do you remember what you said? I sure do. *No member of the posse goes into battle alone.*"

"I wasn't talking about the battle with Apep."

"Does it matter, Tom? A battle is a battle, and in my squad, we've got each other covered. *Semper Fi*, dude."

Tom leaned in, bent at the waist, and went nose to nose with the slightly shorter Ronnie. "This is not your squad, Marine. It's not even your business. Step aside and let me do my job."

"Beg to differ, cat. This is the twenty-first century. Sure, we'll use your old weapons and say your catchy little phrases, but we will also develop a full course of action—planning and practice before mission deployment."

While this exchanged occurred, Tasha had tiptoed her way away from the couch and stood beside Felicity. Bethany was alone on the sofa, perched at the edge, hands gripping the cushions and her mouth agape.

Tasha leaned into Felicity. "She's pretty impressive in full-on warrior mode."

Suddenly, Bethany popped up from the couch and stood next to Ronnie, straightening the collar of her summer pajama ensemble. "I'm with her!"

Tasha hopped over to stand on Ronnie's other side. "Me, too, except for the giant snake part."

Felicity was stunned. Only days ago, she'd believed that Tasha had betrayed her, that she was losing her only friend. And now she had her own band of champions? "You guys. I am so... I don't know even what to say."

Tasha turned her way. "I hear a *but* coming."

"The thing is, Tom is right. This is *my* destiny, *my* battle. I can't risk your lives."

Bethany pouted.

Ronnie didn't. "There's a flaw in that reasoning. So listen up, both of you." She pointed to Tom and Felicity. "If Felicity fails, we're all dead anyway. I prefer to go down fighting."

"Me too," Tasha said.

Bethany bit her lip. "I'm super scared, but I'm with them."

Ronnie looked up into Tom's eyes and made sure she had his attention. "Your time here has been a clusterfuck from the get-go. Your social influencer Acolyte got herself killed. *You* almost died. Then you hand over the necklace to the first female you lay eyes on; in other words, *nothing* has followed the old script. So we're helping you. End of discussion."

Tom took a step back, his anger fading. He glanced at Felicity, then at Tasha and Bethany. Eventually he answered Ronnie. "I'll hear your suggestions, Lance Corporal, if you swear to me, on your honor, that during the battle itself you will stay in the background and allow Felicity to carry out the steps, *alone and exactly as written.*"

She sighed. "Fine."

They gathered around the coffee table, glued to Ronnie's laptop screen.

"This is the interior of the Viper Apps building, at least the plan filed with the City of Portland's Bureau of Development Services."

Bethany was impressed. "How'd you get that?"

Felicity patted her hand. "It's better we don't know."

"Actually, this is public record. No hacking required." Ronnie pointed to the screen. "This corner office—the largest enclosed space on the second floor—is likely Apep's."

"Agreed," Tom said.

"No elevator," Ronnie continued. "Access is via two separate stairwells, one that exits out front and one to the back alley, which is good. What isn't so good is Google Earth's street-level view of both of these exterior doors." Ronnie pulled up a split-screen image. "I've blown it up."

Tasha pointed. "That's the card reader we saw!"

"Brand-spanking new, too, both front and back. Never seen anything like it and can't find anyone else who has, either. Probably custom."

"Can you hack it remotely?" Tom asked.

"I tried. It isn't tied into a remote access server, which means we'll need a physical card to get inside."

"Why do we have to go inside?" Bethany played with her scrunchie.

"We don't, necessarily." Ronnie clicked again to display an image of the alley. "We could watch the building, catch Apep coming out, and follow him home."

"Not an option." Tom leaned over her shoulder, but Ronnie

did not complain. "He'll be mostly healed from his wounds by now, and his senses are so advanced he'd immediately know he's being followed."

"So we have just two advantages at this point," Felicity said. "We know where his office is, and he doesn't know there's a new Acolyte. The last thing we want to do is tip him off to either."

Tom agreed. "Following him home would be pointless anyway. It will be a protected space, and he'd have the advantage."

"Can't we just wait for him to come out and attack?" Tasha looked hopeful.

"Surprise is good," Felicity said, "but it's probably not wise to confront him near innocent bystanders."

"Correct," Ronnie said. "We'd risk both collateral damage and interference from the public. Can you imagine some do-gooder stepping in to defend Apep?"

"Decision made," Felicity said. "We get a keycard, get upstairs, and catch him off guard. Then we drop the wrath of the Goddess on him."

"And while Felicity's unleashing the six steps, can you destroy the Trojan Horse?"

Ronnie patted Tom's hand. "If you get me inside, I'll bring it all down."

"But how do we get a keycard?" Beautiful Bethany seemed baffled. Beautiful and baffled. But she had a valid point.

Ronnie leaned back in her chair and tapped her foot, thinking. "Apep knows all the tricks. Let's say we somehow get our hands on a Viper Apps employee keycard; the instant that employee realizes it's missing, the whole system shuts down. All our effort would be for nothing. We can't go that route."

"But how would we get in without using somebody's card?"

Bethany asked.

"We make our own."

Tom shook his head. "I am afraid you've lost me, Ronnie."

"We're all lost," Tasha said.

"No. This could work." Ronnie got up and paced, thinking. After a long moment, she spun around. "I know a guy. I'll need a couple thousand bucks in cash and a ride to a meetup point."

"No problem—for the ride, anyway," Tasha said.

"I'll handle the cash," Felicity said.

"We'll scan the card instead of stealing it, then extract the data to fabricate our own. It's gonna be tricky though; whoever does this will have to be nearly invisible. You've got to get the keycard, scan it, and get it back to the employee before they notice anything happened."

Felicity cleared her throat. Everyone's eyes went to her. "This sounds like a job for an invisible woman of a certain age."

Felicity parked her Saturn on a residential street a mile or so from Viper Apps and stayed put while Tasha took her post. Since Apep had tracked the *usekh's* accumulated energy to the coast, Felicity was safer near Apep's office than at home in Pine Beach. Still, they decided not to risk Felicity being captured in security camera footage.

Their plan was for Tasha to monitor the building and call Felicity when they had a likely employee target. Tasha snuck through someone's yard and crouched down in the hydrangea bushes lining the opposite side of the alley. From there, she could keep an eye on the small employee parking area. It had taken some convincing, but Tasha had agreed to dress the part, to look as nondescript as possible. For the first time in memory, she'd left the house without makeup, jewelry, or anything form-fitting.

"It's like I'm going out in public naked," she'd complained.

But she'd chosen a pair of loose jeans, a baggy T-shirt, a baseball cap, and her **Fuck Off and Die** athletic shoes for her important job.

She called Felicity about six p.m. to report that no one had left and nobody walking or driving along the alley had even glanced her way. "So what are *you* doing, Lissie?"

"Just reading my hieroglyphs book."

"Sounds exciting."

Shortly after seven, Felicity received a text. It was a license plate number. Tasha called immediately, her voice frantic.

"Hurry! A silver Prius just turned left at the light. His bumper sticker says: My other car is a Tesla!"

"Got it."

"He's a dumpy, nondescript white guy. It looks like the keycard's on a thing around his neck!"

"I'll keep an eye out."

Felicity hung up, tossed her book onto the passenger seat, and drove off. She caught sight of her target at a light, three vehicles ahead. And that's when reality struck: she had absolutely no clue how she'd pull this off. It was madness to try. She prayed that this man lived alone, but what if he was headed home to a wife and baby? Or lived with his mother? Would he immediately change out of his work clothes, giving her an opportunity to scan the card? What if didn't? She hoped he lived in a single-level house because she couldn't imagine how she'd shimmy up a tree or drainpipe to gain access to a second story.

She blamed herself for this predicament. After all, it had been only a matter of time until she evolved into a legitimate felon. And to think how innocently it had started, taking Rich's raincoat. And now—breaking and entering! And *scanning!*

Perhaps she should have considered the costs when she'd

chosen a life of crime.

Her phone rang. Tasha again.

"Do you see him?"

"I can't talk and drive. I'll call you when the mission's accomplished."

"OK. But everyone else is leaving. There's just one car in the back now. And I see a shadow moving in the corner office."

"Just stay put until I call."

"But what if you get arrested? Who's gonna drive me back to Pine Beach? I won't be caught dead taking public transportation looking like this."

The Prius pulled into the Fred Meyer grocery store.

"Gotta go!" Felicity hung up and followed, straining to keep an eye on the fellow who exited the car. He was a fairly short, nerdy type, and Felicity watched with glee as he pulled a lanyard from his neck with some kind of work ID dangling from the end, then shoved it in the pocket of his khakis. It was now or never, she knew, hoping Bastet's necklace gave her added stealth or daring or just a set of giant, hairy balls, because she was going to need all that and more to pull this off.

Felicity parked, went inside, grabbed a cart, and tossed in random items until she found the nerdy man gawking at row upon row of frozen pizzas. She pretended to be enthralled with the ingredient list for a microwaveable vegetable medley while simultaneously easing her way behind him, getting into perfect position. She slipped her hand into her pants pocket and palmed the scanner. It was the size of one of those mini calculators that come with a new wallet. She'd practiced the maneuver several times back at Tasha's house: *Press one side of the card against the scanning plate, keep it still for at least five seconds, then flip the card over and do the other side. Make sure it doesn't slide around or lose contact!*

She waited, trying to steady her nerves, when he finally selected a pizza, flung open the freezer door, and smashed her right in the face.

"Oh!" She staggered. "Oh, heavens!"

He grabbed her. "God, lady! I didn't even see you there! Are you all right?"

"I don't know." She clutched at his shirt for balance. "Hold on." Then she grabbed his belt. "I'm seeing stars." She looped her finger through the lanyard protruding from his pocket and fell to the ground, catching herself on her hands before shoving them under her stomach. She found the lanyard pinned to the floor under her belly button.

"Oh my God! Do you need an ambulance?"

There was only one card on the lanyard. It could be a Fred Meyer frequent-shopper card for all she knew, since she couldn't see it, but she slipped it from its plastic sleeve and pressed it to the scanner plate.

He tried to pull her up.

"Stop! Please don't touch me. I just need a moment to catch my breath."

Shit. There had to be ten people milling about now. She flipped the card over and counted to five, then managed to insert the card back into the lanyard sleeve.

"Please stand back. I'll get myself up. I have orthopedic issues."

Nobody listened. The crowd pulled her to her feet. Dozens of eyes stared at her with pity and concern. The poor computer programmer was red-faced. "I am *so sorry*, ma'am," he said. "I hope you're not injured."

She placed a hand on his forearm. "I'm fine. Please don't give it another thought."

He bent down, scooped his lanyard from the floor tiles, and mumbled, "You sure you're OK?"

"Fine. Just fine."

Felicity abandoned her cart in front of the tofu display, made a beeline for the front door, and was back in her car and onto Hawthorne Boulevard in under a minute.

She pulled up to the curb of the Cup and Saucer Café, immediately waving Tasha to the driver's side.

"Did you get it?"

"If I didn't, then I've just made a spectacle of myself for nothing."

"I thought you were going to be invisible."

"Had to improvise. You're driving." Felicity hopped over and squeezed into the passenger seat.

"Why?" Tasha got in behind the wheel.

"I want to review my incantations and read my book some more."

"It's distracting to drive at night with the overhead light on."

"I have to study."

Tasha sighed. About fifteen minutes out of downtown she said, "It's so weird. I've been back and forth to Portland more in the last couple of weeks than I have in the last couple of years."

"Tell me about it."

"If we live through this, we really need to get out more."

Felicity nodded, knowing that was a big if.

"Fabulous work. Really."

Ronnie had connected the scanning device to her laptop, and everyone stared at a digital signature displayed on the screen. She shook her head. "Don't know how you pulled this off, Felicity, but we've got it."

"It wasn't pretty, that's all I can tell you."

"I'll email this to my buddy who'll fabricate the card. It'll be ready to pick up tomorrow on our way to the Viper Apps offices."

"Sounds like a plan."

Felicity was weary to her bones. She had a raging headache. All she wanted was to seek refuge under her decadent comforter for a solid ten hours of blissful oblivion. But when she announced her intention, Tasha protested.

"We're ordering pizza for our planning session!"

"It's pretty late."

"Why don't you lie down in the guest room until it comes?" Bethany put her hand on Felicity's elbow and guided her down the hallway. "Let me get you a cool cloth for your head."

A moment later, Bethany placed a soothing cloth on Felicity's forehead and pulled a blanket up to her shoulders. "Have a nice rest; we'll wake you when the delivery guy arrives."

"That's sweet of you, Bethany."

"Want me to leave the hall light on?"

"Sure. Thanks."

Felicity lay there, staring at the circa 1973 light fixture on the dim ceiling, until finally, mercifully, her eyelids grew heavy...

She gasped. This pain. A dense agony deep in the tissue of her breasts, throbbing through the network of muscles and tendons and nerves and bone. It shouldn't be there. No. They'd gotten it all! She'd beat it!

She glanced down at her naked body, watching in horror as her left breast began to contort. Then her right. Beneath her skin something crawled, grew, forced her vulnerable flesh into misshapen masses until both breasts were twisted and deformed.

No!

It was back. She'd endured hell for nothing.

She heard Tom's words: *Evil is a cancer. If the smallest speck remains, it can, and does regrow.*

She watched it spread through her body, grotesque and excruciating. Her legs became too distorted and heavy to move. Her tumor-clogged lungs burned in a sucking struggle for air.

Someone laughed at her. It was a cruel and mocking sound, and it poured into her open wounds like acid.

She tried to run, but her legs were useless. The laughter became a living thing, a wisp of malignant darkness that trapped her like a fly in a sticky web. Immobile. Useless.

No! She had so much to do.

Spit, left foot, lance...

Fetter, knife, fire...

The necklace squeezed her throat. *I can't breathe.* Tighter. *I'm trapped.*

She had to fight! She had to free her warped and swollen legs from the spiderweb or everyone would die.

Her feet began to fade away. No! All of her was fading now. She was becoming invisible, from her knees to her hips to her belly. How could she fight if she didn't exist, if she was nothing but a worthless collection of invisible atoms, if she was...

Gone?

Her breasts vanished. Then her heart. Heavy footsteps approached.

"Food's here!"

Felicity shot up in bed. No idea of the time or place. Head pounding and heart slamming, doom tightening and twisting at her windpipe.

"Holy shit, Lissie." Tasha stood in the doorway, taken aback. "Were you having a nightmare or something?"

"Something," she muttered.

CHAPTER SIXTEEN

During Felicity's nap from hell, everyone had gathered around the coffee table and opened the pizza boxes since Tasha's dining table still served as Hair Gel Jim's trash heap.

"I sure hope that's all of his stuff, Tash." Felicity rubbed her eyes and sat cross-legged on the floor.

"I left the loser three messages today, and I swear if I don't hear back by tomorrow, it's all going into the car crusher."

Ronnie snorted with laughter.

Bethany grabbed a plate. "What kind would you like, Felicity? We've got a pepperoni, a veggie special, and a bacon and pineapple."

"Which should be against the law," Ronnie snapped.

"Pepperoni would be great." Felicity accepted the plate from Bethany, pleased to see that the mom-to-be's plate held three pieces. It was a relief to see Bethany eating.

Tom sat on the end of the sofa, snarfing down a giant slice he'd folded in half.

"Tom?"

He shook his head, managing an emphatic *no* even with his mouth full. Once he'd swallowed and dabbed at his lips with a napkin, he set Felicity straight. "Pizza is *not* Italian food. Don't even go there. Egyptians invented the concept of baking flatbread with stuff on top."

"Sure, Tom."

"Hey. I almost forgot!" Ronnie went into the kitchen and returned with a six-pack of bottled beer. "For you, cat."

Tom accepted the cardboard carton and slipped one bottle out to examine the label. He stayed frozen for a long moment, so long that Ronnie grew restless. She seemed about ready to bolt from the room when Tom looked up, his eyes huge with wonder.

"How...?" he shook his head, incredulous. "You found beer made with ground pistachios! I don't even...thanks. This means a lot."

From his reaction, Felicity figured it had been a long time since he'd received a gift.

Ronnie shrugged. "No biggie. If it's beer, somebody in Portland brews it."

"That sounds kinda gross," Bethany said, just before she took a sip from her leopard print water bottle. Felicity noticed that she'd changed into a pretty mock turtleneck angora sweater and a matching pink scrunchie. It must have pained her that the only water bottle she'd brought along did not match.

Ronnie tapped her palm to the coffee table. "All right. Time to review our C of A."

Felicity looked around, realizing she was the only person not familiar with the acronym.

"Course of action," Tasha said with a knowing bob of her head.

"So, Tasha, tell us what you saw tonight."

"Sure." She straightened. Felicity couldn't help but notice that she looked younger without all the goop on her face. "I left the alley about 7:30 p.m. to meet up with Felicity, and by then there was just one car left in the small parking lot. A brand-new black Rolls Royce. I kid you not. Everyone else had gone for the day, and the only light I saw was in the second-floor corner office."

"So that was probably him," Ronnie said.

"No question about it." Tom raised his beer bottle in a toast before he took a long, thirsty swig. "Apep's predictable in some ways. He's always got to have the best of everything in any given time, from a golden chariot to a black Rolls Royce. The more exclusive the better."

"You think he's staying late to nail down the last-minute details?"

"I think time's up, Ronnie. We'll strike tomorrow night, once his workers have gone. Felicity, your lighter lance will arrive in the morning, giving us a whole day to practice with it."

"Great." She took a bite of pizza, dipping her head to hide her expression. She wished she'd never gone into that guest room for a nap because now she couldn't shake the uneasiness of the nightmare. It clung to her, oppressive and unsettling. She still carried the awful feeling of being trapped in that dark corner, trying to remember the order of the steps: *spit, left foot, lance, fetter, knife, fire.*

"You start, Tasha." Ronnie pointed. "What's your role?"

Tasha smacked both hands to her knees. "Bethany and I will pack a duffle with all the weapons on the checklist and carry it inside the back door of Viper Apps. We will leave it at the bottom of the back stairs."

"Then what, Bethany?"'

"I'll watch the back door while Tasha takes her post at the front. She'll call out to me if she sees anyone coming, and I'll do the same."

"Good." Ronnie seemed pleased. "I'll take point and lead

Felicity and Tom up the back stairs, then immediately get to work on disabling the malware. Quiet as a mouse." Ronnie pointed at Felicity. "You ready to save the world?"

Felicity felt like a doe in the high beams. "Of course. Spit, left foot, lance, fetter, knife, fire. Got it."

"And the incantations?" Tom's voice was sharp with anxiety.

Tasha answered. "Believe me, Tom. She's got it. That's all she did tonight on the way to Portland and back, like a football cheerleader: *Rise thee up! Fell thy foe! Ra, Ra, Ra!*"

Bethany nearly choked on the contents of her water bottle.

Tasha continued. "And that was when she wasn't reading her boring hieroglyphs book."

"The structure and grammar of hieroglyphs is fascinating."

"Spoken like a dedicated English teacher." Tasha saluted Felicity with her glass and drained the remaining iced tea in one swallow.

A loud knock at the door gave everyone a jolt.

"Are you expecting someone so late?" Tom asked.

Tasha shook her head as she went to the front door to look through the peephole. She gave a thumbs up. "It's Jim. Finally."

Everyone relaxed as Tasha swung open the door. "It's almost eleven. You should have called."

He said nothing, just offered her a wide, blank smile and pushed his way past Tasha into the house.

"Hey! I didn't say you could come in."

"Is that any way to talk to your Big Bear, Tash?" Jim finished wiping his hands on the once-white hand towel he carried, summing up the group around the coffee table. Then he tossed the towel directly into the open veggie special box.

He grinned. "Ooh, a pizza party! Fun! And the gang's all here!"

His grin disappeared, and he turned and walked to the dining table loaded with his stuff.

Felicity stared at the dark yellow stains on the towel, her mind scrabbling for why it was important. Her every sense told her she needed to stay alert. *Think.*

Jim didn't touch his belongings. He made no move to carry anything to the truck that Felicity saw parked outside. In fact, Jim barely glanced at the display of all his earthly belongings. He turned to Tasha. "You always thought I was stupid, didn't you? Always so sure you were the smart one."

"Get your shit and go." Tasha pointed to the door.

"But it turns out *you* were the stupid one, my darling, my sweetheart, believing the loads of bullshit I shoveled your way, day in and day out, as if a guy like me would *ever* go for an ugly, old, white-haired bitch like you. But you were desperate for love, weren't you, schnookums?"

"Get the fuck out!" Tasha's fists clenched in rage.

But Jim didn't move. His eyes were glazed. He was high on something. "Yeah, *the gang's all here.*" The way he repeated the words was truly bizarre. He still made no move to take anything to the truck.

He produced another disjointed, creepy smile, and reached into his pocket for... keys. Ronnie's key ring. He held it up like a trophy.

"Shit," Ronnie said under her breath.

That's when it clicked into place. Felicity glanced sideways at Tom, careful not to move.

"He's erased the *Wadjets,*" Felicity whispered, panic surging.

She jumped to her feet, her brain putting the puzzle pieces together. Apep's men were watching Ronnie's place. Jim had her keys. He went back to the apartment to clean her out. They saw him,

294

probably threatened him, and then cut a deal with him. Jim worked for Apep.

The front picture window exploded, glass spraying everywhere, and Felicity peeked over her forearm to see the junkyard dog from next door flying into the room. Everyone screamed and covered their heads as the dog slammed to the carpet, blood running from its muzzle and front legs. But it sprung up, scanned the room, and found its target: Tom.

Felicity threw herself on the dog's back. She'd only seen the beast from a distance and heard its deep bark, so she was shocked at the animal's size, maybe close to two hundred pounds. It growled and barked and frothed at the mouth, then lunged at Tom, not the slightest bit concerned that Felicity had draped her full weight across him. The dog shook her off, throwing her into a pile of glass.

Tom was fast. He grabbed a dining room chair and swung it at his attacker, keeping the dog at bay.

"Felicity! Get your weapons!"

That was the moment Jim threw Tasha across the dining room, then rushed Ronnie, who'd been helping Tom beat back the dog. Jim grabbed Ronnie by one of her puffs, and slammed her against the wall so hard that her head cracked the plaster. Bethany let go with a nonstop scream.

"Run, Bethany!" Ronnie managed to deliver a few well-placed knees to Jim's groin and an elbow directly to his nose, but he didn't react. It was as if he hadn't felt the impact. And that's when Felicity suddenly understood: the dog and Jim were not themselves. Something—*someone*—controlled them.

The dog now stood on Tom's chest, its huge jaws resting on his throat. Tom's eyes flashed at Felicity: *go*, they instructed her. Just then, Jim yanked a zip tie out of his pocket and roughly bound

Ronnie's wrists behind her back. Felicity scrambled in the glass, finding her footing, then snatched Bethany with a bloody hand. "Come on! *Now!*"

Bethany kept screaming, too shocked to move, so Felicity lifted her up from beneath her arms and rushed her toward the kitchen. They had to step over Tasha, who was limp but breathing. They'd almost reached the back door when Jim was on them. He'd moved impossibly fast for a normal human being.

That was when Felicity realized she was getting her first taste of Apep's power. She nearly vomited.

Jim ripped Bethany from Felicity's hold, threw her over his shoulder, and carried her, kicking and screaming, back into the living room.

Felicity bolted out the back door. She knew what was coming—*who* was coming—and knew she couldn't risk getting zip-tied or she'd be of no use to anyone. She crouched low in the darkness against the back of the house, slipped silently around the corner and up the side yard, past the chin-up bar, toward the front bushes, trying to slow her breath.

Sounds of chaos erupted from inside. Growling and screaming. She nearly sobbed. Her friends were being attacked in there, and she had to save them; she had to *do* something! But she could not let herself get flustered. She had to stay calm, focus, move slowly, plan, adapt. *Do not rush, Felicity.* Because she knew that's exactly when she'd fuck up. And if she fucked up, she'd get everyone in the house, and on the planet, killed.

Felicity took a few more silent steps, willing her heart to calm. She could do this. She had to do this. She was ready. She would retrieve her weapons and wait for Apep's arrival.

That's when she heard a whisper float upon the darkness. A

rich baritone, silky, inviting. She recognized the distinct cadence. The words had a familiar melody. The voice mumbled. No. It *chanted* an ancient Egyptian incantation.

Felicity hunkered lower, now on elbows and knees, inching closer. She dared to raise her head enough to peer through the front bushes just as a man in a suit emerged from the dark and into the porch light.

Apep.

He stepped inside Tasha's small house.

"Enough."

Felicity raised her head to see over the railing and through the smashed front window. She nearly melted at the sight—they were alive. Jim had zip-tied everyone's hands and ankles and then gagged them. The three women were slumped on the floor, propped up against the faded couch. Bethany was slumped forward, her keening heartbreaking to hear. Ronnie was battered and bloody, but her eyes burned with fury. Tasha was dazed. Her whole body shook. Tom had been isolated, placed against the matching love seat a few feet away.

Only then did Felicity assess her enemy. He was not at all what she'd envisioned. He was tall but lithe, handsome, filling out a custom-tailored suit that skimmed his wide shoulders and narrow waist. His dark, thick hair was swept away from his face, and his jaw was clean-cut and squared. He could have been the hero in a romance novel if it weren't for the fact that he was a fiend of the underworld, evil incarnate, the source of chaos and destruction, and the eternal foe of the Ever-Living Bastet.

Jim and the dog were now glassy-eyed and propped against the dining room wall like mannequins. They were Apep's playthings, his puppets.

She'd known from the start that Jim would get his, but she

wouldn't wish this horror on anyone, even him.

Apep surveyed his surroundings with overt disgust, then let his gaze settle on Tom. "How the mighty have fallen. Not quite the palatial comforts of the temple, eh Tubastet-af-ankh?"

Felicity glanced over her shoulder at the Airstream, where her weapons were neatly laid out on the booth table, in proper order. She could *never* reach the trailer without being seen. Apep's senses were highly advanced, Tom had said. And if a grunt like Jim had moved at the speed of light, how quick would Apep be?

Her only advantage was that Apep still did not know she existed.

He walked the length of the living room with grace. He was relaxed, as if he had all the time in the world. Apep spoke to Tom yet gestured toward the three women. "I'll let your little friends live, at least briefly, and I promise them a painless death, but only if you surrender your mistress's *usekh*."

Apep stopped before Tom, staring him straight in the eye. "After all, this is not our concern, is it, priest? What have these humans ever done for our kind? They no longer serve. They keep no festivals, observe no rituals, make no offerings. They no longer even believe. And yet your mistress adores them so!"

Felicity shivered. The sound of his voice made her blood ice over.

"Are you not weary of this eternal battle you wage with me, priest? Hmm? The endless cycles of training and fighting, blood and pain? And even after you win, you never manage to find the flesh I leave behind, and so I am *always* reborn. Again and again. So tiresome. Do you not see the futility?"

Tom could not respond, of course. He was gagged. Felicity saw his entire being vibrate with the desperate desire to lash out.

"And now, suddenly, an opportunity! You can end it all, tonight."

Apep reached out to stroke Tom's black hair, his hand gentle, his voice low and intimate. Her enhanced hearing allowed her to hear his soft whisper, "Let us put this degenerate species out of its misery. It's no more than they deserve for their disobedience. Then we can all return to the paradise of our rightful realm, for eternity."

Slowly, in a movement almost a ritual in itself, Apep removed the gag from Tom's mouth. "Surrender the *usekh*. I can smell it. I can taste it. I know it is near."

Tom met Apep's hot stare. "It is out of your reach."

Apep drew back, astonished. "You have bestowed it again?" He backhanded Tom across the face, his wrath charging the air with electric static. "I should have killed you in those tunnels, made sure you were *dead*! I shall not make that mistake again!"

Felicity winced. A thin stream of blood trickled from the corner of Tom's mouth. She had to cover her own mouth to stop a whimper from escaping, and only then did she realize she was smeared with blood, her hands and arms were darkened with it, her skin sparkling in the porch light with embedded razor-sharp shards of glass.

Apep straightened, turning his attention to the three women on the floor before him. "Not quite the strength and vitality I'd expect, but I assume you were desperate. This will certainly make my job easier."

He stepped to Bethany, forced her chin up, then ripped open her pretty angora mock turtleneck, exposing her bare chest. He was stunned to see her throat was unadorned. "Not the young one?"

He moved to Ronnie, grabbed her around the throat and lifted her to his eye level as she struggled to breathe. "The strong one, then. She reminds me a bit of you, Tubastet, a frustrated, fading warrior."

He squeezed under her jaw with one hand as he tore open her T-shirt. Nothing. He dumped her, let her collapse to the floor in a heap.

Apep looked at Tasha. "*This* one? How sad that you were reduced to begging a dried-up hag to serve your once proud mistress." He reached down, yanked Tasha up onto her feet and shredded her blouse with a single hard jerk, revealing another bare neck and chest. Apep's face fell. He shoved Tasha to the floor beside the others.

He spun on Tom, kicked him in the side so fast Felicity almost missed it. "Where is your mistress's champion? Where *is* she?"

Tom remained expressionless. He said nothing.

"Have it your way." Apep reached into a deep interior pocket of his suit jacket and pulled out a long, ritual knife much like the one back in the trailer, a trailer that might as well have been a thousand miles away. The knife was flint, like hers. Deadly sharp.

Apep removed his jacket, folded it neatly, and draped it over the back of a dining chair. He did the same with his tie, his movements precise and unhurried, so out of place in the shattered setting. It brought him pleasure to draw out the cruelty.

He turned to Tom. "You are aware, of course, that you suffer from the same weakness that afflicts your misguided mistress."

Apep snagged Bethany by the upper arm and hauled her to her feet. She cried, big, racking sobs, eyes closed. Her legs trembled. "You possess a fondness for humans that, luckily, I do not share." He pressed the blade to Bethany's soft cheek.

Felicity's time was up.

"Here I am."

She stood tall, opening the top buttons of her shirt as she walked through the door, revealing the golden *usekh* that encircled her neck and rested upon her shoulders.

Apep spun around, flabbergasted. Bethany wrenched out of his hands and threw herself onto the sofa. Apep paid her no attention. His eyes were glued to Felicity.

She didn't cower, didn't so much as flinch under his unrelenting stare.

Apep took a step toward her and laughed.

She wasn't sure what to do when he began to howl with laughter, nearly doubling over with hilarity. She thought about hightailing it to the trailer while he was distracted, but he sensed her edging toward the door.

All amusement vanished. He shook his head. "Oh, no. No running. I'd catch you like a cat catches a mouse, and what fun would that be?" Apep stepped toward her.

Felicity stepped back.

"Really, Tubastet. I thought the hag was pathetic. This one is even older!"

"Same age, asshole!" Tasha screamed from behind her gag.

Apep glanced at Tasha, then again at Felicity. "Truly? Well, what's that old saying? *It's not the years, it's the mileage?*" He moved another step toward Felicity. She took another step back.

Apep sighed, as if bored with an unpleasant chore. "After all the honorable battles and worthy champions, it seems a shame to end it all with one so worthless. Should I strike her down quickly, Tubastet? That seems the most merciful approach, don't you agree?" Apep smiled at Felicity, his perfect, white teeth gleaming. "And do not fret, priest. I shall not hold this insult against you when your lifeless heart is weighed."

Apep faked a strike toward Felicity. She flinched back in terror. He laughed again. "How truly desperate you must have been, old friend, to choose this one. She is far too elderly to possess a pure spirit and a pure body. Or, no, wait…"

He gave Felicity a slow once-over.

"Perhaps she *is* a maiden. I mean, look at her, who would want *that*?"

Felicity's flesh went cold. She took another step back and suddenly, her body felt like lead, her limbs like concrete. She was trapped.

Like a fly in a sticky web.

It hadn't been a nightmare! It had been a warning, a premonition. Felicity couldn't catch her breath. The monster was right. There was no way she could do this. Who had she been kidding?

Apep simply turned his back to her. That was the threat level she posed to him. *None.* And everyone in the room knew it.

"Why so quiet this evening, Tubastet?" He crossed to Tom, pulled his head back by his hair, and laid the flint blade to his throat. "Do you wish for a mercifully quick kill for your champion? Or perhaps I should have a bit of fun first. I could fuck her, give her a thrill, before she dies?"

Apep dropped Tom's head and returned to Felicity. "Oh dear, you look worried. Is that for yourself or have you grown fond of the overgrown feline? If so, you are one in a long line of maidens whose lust for him goes unrequited. He gets his fair share of pussy, certainly, but ever the obedient priest! He never touches his mistress's Acolytes." Apep's smile dripped with pity. "So tell me, chosen one. Which of your friends do you think he is fucking behind your back?"

The accusation was ridiculous, yet it still got under her skin. She felt raw, laid bare, completely helpless. She looked at Tom, frantic. He shook his head *no*, but turmoil had fouled her thinking. She'd lost focus.

"Your choice, champion." He gestured dramatically to the room, like a circus ringmaster. "Do I slay the priest before I defile your old body, or should I spare him so that he may watch?"

Felicity tasted bile on the back of her tongue.

"Perhaps I fuck one of your friends first. The young, pretty one or the strong one, but certainly not the hag." He extended his hands. "Well? What will it be, old girl?"

Old girl.

The words ricocheted in her head, designed to wound, then lodged at the back of her throat. Not just Apep's words. Rich's, too, the man who had discarded her because she was old. He'd walked away without a backward glance. Because she…

NO! Her chest vibrated beneath the necklace. Her left wrist tingled. She risked a quick glance at the Bastet bracelet, smeared with blood but shining through. It was a reminder. It pulled her back to what was true.

Rich hadn't discarded her because of who she was. He did it because of who *he* was: a cheating, self-obsessed, amoral bastard. And those liabilities were not hers to carry. Not for another second.

She felt a surge of authority. The deceitful douche standing before her was just another Rich, using the same tired weapons, words intended to be fatal—*but only if she let them.*

Felicity would not. Never again. She was a queen. And she would defeat this monster.

She stood taller, centered herself to the earth, and took a deep breath of energizing air. She looked to Tom, bruised, bloodied, and bound, but he smiled. And he said the words she longed to hear. "Bastet has chosen well."

"SILENCE!" Apep spun on Tom, backhanded him again, so hard that the love seat nearly toppled over.

Felicity rushed him. "*Be thou utterly spat upon, O Apep.*" She pursed her lips as Tom had instructed. Nothing. Not a drop of saliva survived in her desert-dry mouth. She tried again. And failed to collect even a hint of moisture.

Apep twirled in her direction. "*English?*" Then back to Tom. "You think *English* will work? How ridiculous." He opened his arms wide. "But please, go right ahead. I'll be a good sport. Do it properly, oh champion, or die trying."

Felicity needed water. She needed a drink of water. She made a dash for the kitchen, but Apep blocked her way. "I am afraid this is a come-as-you-are war."

Apep laughed. She backed away. Felicity felt—truly, physically sensed—his oily laugh attempt to slither its way under her skin, into her bone. She focused, visualized the necklace's energy encircling her, protecting her. In her mind's eye, she hurled the laugh back at him.

He raised one eyebrow. "*Touché.* You have a modicum of defensive skill." He tipped his head in Jim's direction. "At least more than the bad boyfriend and the mutt. Perhaps this will be more entertaining than I'd anticipated."

Felicity continued to back into the living room, scanning, looking for a way to carry out Step One, all the while working her tongue and teeth, trying in vain to gather saliva. Tom's beer was upended on the carpet, drained. The other bottles remained capped. Tasha's iced tea glass was empty.

Then she saw it—Bethany's ever-present water bottle. It had been knocked off the coffee table and lay on its side just under the couch.

Felicity glanced at Apep, who slowly tracked her every move, amused as he stalked her, confident that she posed no threat.

Felicity dove under the coffee table and grabbed the water bottle. Apep's fingers instantly encircled her ankle and he dragged her out, laughing again, but she ignored him and focused. She sprung open the push-button bottle valve and tipped it into her mouth, collecting a huge gulp.

It took only a nanosecond for her tastebuds to discover that it wasn't water. It was some hideous concoction, gritty and bitter with suspended bits of grass or dirt or something else disgusting that was probably meant to nourish a developing baby.

Without thinking, Felicity spit the vile stuff everywhere, just as Apep flipped her onto her back.

The laughter stopped.

Felicity blinked in disbelief. She'd sprayed the gross green smoothie all over Apep's dress shirt! No longer amused, he grabbed the mustard-stained hand towel and briskly swiped at the spots of thick goo.

Felicity sat up, amazed. She willed her voice to carry, sharp and clear. "*Be thou utterly spat upon, O Apep.*"

He dropped the towel and looked down at himself, surprised to watch tiny pinpricks of light develop in the fabric, spreading to create a clear spray pattern. Each and every miniscule droplet began to glow and then burn through the fabric of his expensive shirt.

Felicity was just as shocked as he was. But only for an instant. It wasn't over.

It had only just begun.

CHAPTER SEVENTEEN

Spit, left foot, lance, fetter, knife, fire.

Felicity reviewed the list in her head. Next was her left foot. She popped to a stand, only to feel that familiar tsunami of panic. She stared down at her canvas lace-ups. Which one was her left? She closed her eyes for an instant, seeing the purple-feathered cat toy in her memory. She knew this. She knew which foot was which! There would be no bloody tutus today.

The footwork came automatically. She remembered everything and never lost her balance once. She performed everything just as she'd been taught, found her center of gravity, and struck out with her left foot.

Apep snatched her heel and yanked up, fast and hard, throwing Felicity into Tasha's entertainment center. Her back hit the TV, which came crashing to the floor along with the contents of every shelf. Felicity thudded to the carpet, Tasha's entire DVD collection raining down on her head. Just as she readied herself to stand and fight, Apep knelt across her ankles, completely immobilizing her legs.

"Now what, champion?" It was a taunt.

He was heavy, and he knew exactly how to deliver maximum pain. Bolts of agony raced up her legs, and she felt a growing numbness at the base of her spine. She had to act fast. Felicity's eyes went to the smoldering bits of his dress shirt, and she remembered what Ronnie had said, that intention counted.

Felicity's intention counted.

The idea came suddenly.

She twisted around, dragging her hand through Tasha's DVD collection, grabbing what she needed. She hurled it with all her might at Apep's chest, saying, "*Raise thee up, O Ra, and crush thy foes!*"

"What do you think...?" Apep's voice trailed off. A glowing mark materialized on his chest, the exact rectangular shape of a DVD case. Then the pin-prick burns left by Step One glowed again, brighter now, as did the new rectangle, and the fabric burned away. An audible sizzle filled the room.

"*NO!*" Apep jumped to his feet, swatting desperately at the burns, obviously feeling pain. "This is not possible!"

Felicity's eyes scanned to the DVD case she'd thrown. It was just one of the many editions of *My Left Foot* that Tasha owned—her favorite DDL film and his first Oscar. Felicity turned, rummaging through the pile, and found the 25th Anniversary Director's Cut. A classic.

She flung it at Apep, hitting his flank, buying herself a few precious seconds while he screamed in agony.

Spit, left foot... lance was next.

Apep charged her, enraged, but she scrambled out of the way. He stumbled on the jumble of DVDs, losing his balance, arms whirling.

Where was she going to find something that could stand in as a lance? Tasha's fireplace poker had been stored in the garage for the season. Would a pencil work? Anything sharp and made of iron? A skillet?

She forced herself to remain rational, to keep in mind that her intention counted, just like Ronnie had said. Ronnie said that! *Ronnie!*

Felicity faked to the left and zig-zagged to where Ronnie sat bound and gagged, realizing she'd just used one of the spins Bethany had taught her. She knew that she had merely an instant to reveal her plan to Ronnie, but when their eyes locked, Ronnie nodded. She already understood.

Apep charged. Felicity gripped Ronnie's shoulders and pulled her upright until she was balanced on her hobbled feet. They made a half-turn together, getting in perfect alignment. Ronnie bent her knees, bounced once, then propelled herself up and forward while Felicity shoved with all her might.

Ronnie ducked her chin and braced for impact. She head-butted him. Hard. Apep lurched back, unbalanced, his hands cupping his skull.

Felicity spoke the incantation. *"Horus has taken his lance, thrusts into Apep!"*

Ronnie rolled away from the stumbling Apep and took cover against the far end of the sofa. She nodded to let Felicity know she was OK, but that was a lie. Ronnie would have to get checked for a concussion, her hatred of hospitals be damned. No one could crack heads like that and not be hurt.

Felicity watched in fascination as Apep's forehead, cheeks, and jawline—down to his throat—crackled and crumbled. She could smell burning flesh. She watched what looked like flames licking under his skin, fingers of fire spreading just under the surface. The whites of his eyes glowed hot.

She was already planning her next move. *Spit, left foot, lance.* Fetter was next.

Apep cried out in rage and anguish. "You did not use a lance!"

"But I did. Allow me to introduce you to US Marine Corps Lance Corporal Veronica Davis."

"Heresy!" Apep staggered, his smoldering head cradled in his hands. Every spot Felicity had attacked pulsated with heat and flame. He had slowed down considerably but had not stopped. He remained as deadly as ever, and three steps remained. If Apep stopped her at any point before she'd completed the incantation for the sixth step, he would reign victorious.

Felicity knew it would take a miracle to get through three more steps. She hurt. Glass stabbed her flesh. Her legs shook, and her back was about to spasm. Yet she had no choice but to go on, to keep moving. The world needed her. Tom believed in her.

"The fetter!" Tom called out. "Fetter him, Felicity!"

"No more from you!" Apep lurched toward him, blind with anger and pain, and rammed his fist into Tom's face.

He flopped over. Out cold.

Felicity felt the blow as if she'd been struck. Tom suffered, and she wanted more than anything to go to him, rescue him. Again.

That would have to wait. She needed a fetter. Tom had explained that binding Apep's wrists together wasn't required; she simply needed to encircle one wrist and speak the correct words. But why only one wrist? How was that a hindrance in battle? She'd never gotten an answer to those questions, and as her eyes scanned the room, looking for a reasonable substitute for the chain that was coiled neatly on the Airstream's booth table, she had an epiphany.

Nothing about this ritual was literal. The power was in the allegory.

She spotted a belt atop a pile of Jim's crap and ran for it. She grabbed and turned, but Apep was quicker, even in his increasing decrepitude. He ripped the thin leather strip from her hands, cutting into her palm. The pain nearly blinded her. But she refused to let it drag her under. She had to keep going. Stay on point.

Apep charged. She leapt aside, just past his reach, onto the couch. And she saw it. In one move, she snatched at Bethany's ponytail and yanked off the scrunchie, then jumped down. She didn't attack.

She waited for Apep and his smoldering, stinky body to come barreling at her, then grabbed his arm and slid the scrunchie over his hand, using his own forward momentum to send him smashing into the hallway arch.

She was out of breath. She could barely get enough air to speak the necessary words. In a scratchy, winded voice, she said, "*They who should be bound are bound!*"

The sound that emanated from Apep was otherworldly. He leaned against the arch, holding his wrist out before him, his face contorted in disbelief as the scrunchie burned. All the earlier wounds flared up, and he writhed against the pain. "These are not the correct steps!" His voice was desperate.

It was a hideous thing to see. Flames shot from the scrunchie up Apep's bare arm, across his bare torso, the shirt now burned away. Felicity saw his flesh glow like red-hot molten lava beneath an undulating, charcoal-black crust of skin. The deformity spread up his neck, onto his face.

"Not the correct weapons! You have not correctly fettered me! *This cannot be!*"

"Then you should have paid attention in middle-school English class because I just realized that it's all a fucking metaphor! Well, except for this, which I'm doing just because I can." She kicked him in the groin as hard as she could. It also began to glow, to burn.

Apep bellowed, a deafening cry of anguish and fury not of this world.

Felicity raced to the other side of the room. *Taking a Knife to Smite Apep*—that was next. He'd threatened Bethany and Tom with a flint blade. Where was it? He no longer carried it, did he? It had to be here somewhere.

She searched desperately, knowing time was short, that Apep was wounded and furious and was slowly burning up from the inside out, but that didn't stop him. He was blundering his way toward her. She dropped to her knees, looked under the couch, and swept her arm underneath. Nothing. She shoved her hand behind the cushions, Bethany staring at her with bug eyes. Nothing. She jumped up, kept scanning, searching, growing desperate.

That's when she spotted it under the dining room table. *Damn!* Apep stood between her and the knife! Felicity knew it would be stupid to try, even in his weakened state.

Taking a Knife to Smite Apep. How many times had she studied those words in her hieroglyphs book? *Taking a Knife...* oh.

Hold up.

Felicity turned to snag the pizza cutter, gripped the red plastic handle, and prepared to strike. Apep grabbed her from behind, wrapping her in his arms. She felt the heat of his burning flesh singe her back.

She struggled, twisting a half-turn in his grasp.

"And now, champion?" Apep pressed his scorched lips to her neck, just above the gold. His whisper oozed into her eardrum, into her brain. "You have no knife, old girl. It was a valiant attempt, but you are defeated."

No. She refused to let his words hit their mark. She would not allow doubt to enter.

Not today, Apep.

She had managed to maneuver the pizza wheel to a location near his stomach. She couldn't see. It was just a guess. But it was all she had.

He laughed.

"Hey, snake eyes. You know those priestly texts you like so much? Turns out the hieroglyph for *knife* isn't just a noun. It can be modified into the verb *to cut*."

He laughed harder.

Felicity rolled the pizza cutter across his flesh with all her might. Apep released her, recoiling and convulsing. He screamed in anguish as fire and blood poured from his gut. Flaming blood—the most horrific thing Felicity had ever seen. His entire body was engulfed in it.

She staggered backward. She still had to speak the incantation. "*Seize, seize O butcher, fell the foe with thy knife*! Boom!" Felicity dropped the pizza cutter like a microphone and managed to add, "Never fuck with an English teacher."

Apep writhed and twisted. The sound of his cry changed, and Felicity watched Jim and the junkyard dog collapse, unconscious.

Oh, no. Oh, shit.

Apep thrashed wildly as his suit trousers and socks burned away and crumbled to the carpet in a pile of soot. For an instant he was naked, the luminescent wounds like tattoos on his hard-muscled, charred body. But in the next breath, his flesh dissolved and rearranged itself into something hideously twisted, black, and deformed. He was becoming a snake.

A huge, hissing, black cobra.

Felicity raced for the fireplace. Matches. The final step was

Putting Fire Upon Apep. She didn't need the ritual bronze box or the ember; she just needed fire.

But there were no matches. Of course, there weren't! The same reason why there had been no fireplace poker—it was summer!

Felicity circumvented the still manifesting snake and made her way to the dining room, throwing open the buffet junk drawer. There had to be a lighter. She ripped out the drawer. Dumped the contents on the floor. On her hands and knees now, desperate. How could there be no lighter?

Wait. Tasha said there were lighters in Jim's shoeboxes. Felicity dove onto the mountain of Jim's junk on the dining table and began digging. Ball caps. Magazines. Pens. Boxer shorts. Jeans. Vests. Leather chaps? Shavers and deodorants and antibiotic ointments and hair gel. Felicity unearthed those cheap earrings and even cheaper perfume, but no lighter.

She felt the scorching heat first, then the snake wrapped around one leg, then two. She glanced down. Huge mistake. She could see the monster growing in circumference and length. She felt it become heavier, stronger. Damn it, she just needed one match! Would the world end just because she couldn't find one single fucking match?

She kicked and squirmed, loosening the snake's hold enough to make a dash for the door. The snake slapped around her legs again and coiled tight, then slammed her onto her back on the dining table.

It knocked the wind from her. She recovered, then flailed and kicked and screamed. She balled her fists and pounded at the scaly skin, but the monster only compressed her tighter, slithering himself higher and higher up her body.

Felicity saw Ronnie rolling herself along the floor, inching closer, but what could she do still bound and gagged? Apep easily batted Ronnie away with his beefy tail, slamming her against the wall again.

So much pain and damage. Felicity had put Ronnie and Tasha and Bethany and Tom through so much, and here she was, about to fail.

And still, Apep grew. Thicker. Longer. Deadlier. Gone was the charred human skin. He was a glossy, sleek serpent of chaos, a supernatural killing machine.

Oh, Goddess, I need help. Felicity's eyes surveyed the room. Tom remained unconscious. Ronnie lay against the wall, unmoving. Tasha was squirming on the floor, her eyes squeezed tight as she struggled to free herself. Bethany simply stared into space from the couch, immobilized by terror.

Felicity wrestled, pounded; she wouldn't go down without a fight. She'd completed five steps. She couldn't just give up. *Think. Think!*

Oh, shit. The cobra poked under her arm, then squirmed around her torso. Suddenly, she was face to face with a huge snake head, its eyes a glowing yellow with reptilian pupils, black slits.

The monster flared its hood and opened its mouth to expose two fangs, dripping with venom.

"*Gkngiiiiiisssssssshhhhh.*"

Felicity leaned away from the grotesque sound. Time was up. She had just seconds. *Think, Felicity!*

She had no fire. Fine. What else could defeat a snake in battle, or at least occupy it while she found a goddamn lighter?

Bastet could. Because Bastet was a goddess...and a cat. Bastet could defeat the snake because she was part cat.

Cats.

She struggled to get enough air in her lungs. The snake squeezed tight and continued to hiss. Out. In. The monster's hissing sounded like a bellows, like breathing.

"*Gnshiiiish, huiiiissssh. Gnshiiiish, huiiiissssh.*"

Felicity closed her eyes and pictured her cats in the trailer. Mojo and Alphonse, Scratch and Sniff, Rick James and Teena Marie, Gumbo, Valkyrie, P-Diddy Kitty, Circe, Melrose, and finally Boudica. The image sharpened into focus, as if she were right there with them. Felicity observed from above, noting what each was doing, which ones groomed, which played, and which slept.

She floated higher, vaguely aware her life was being squeezed from her, that she was, in fact, dying. Dying so close to success. It was a shame. And now her lungs burned, seized in on themselves, useless without air, and she sensed herself floating away, her beloved cats receding below.

Her body convulsed so hard that the *usekh*'s bell tinkled.

Just then, Boudica crooked her head to stare above. With her one good eye, she peered straight up, as if she saw Felicity hovering, near death, along the curved ceiling of the Airstream. As if she could hear the bell.

With her last bit of strength, Felicity whispered: "*Come.*"

Her awareness snapped back to Tasha's living room, where she was about to die and let everyone down. Sadness swept over her… everything and everyone she loved. Gone.

Apep was toying with her. He would loosen his grip to give her another taste of oxygen and then bring her back just long enough to cut off her air again, all the while flicking and whipping his hideous forked tongue against her face. But she would die bravely, without begging or sobbing. She'd done more and gotten farther than she had ever imagined possible. At least she had that.

As Felicity took a painful, shallow breath—knowing it could be her last—Boudica leapt through the broken window. The other eleven cats were right behind her, clearing the windowsill and immediately joining the fight. The kittens ran to Tom, licking his face to revive him, while everyone else ran straight for Apep.

They jumped on him, claws sharp, biting and tearing through the scales. They hissed and yowled, cried and growled, and even when Apep was able to flick one away across the room they came right back, never lessening their attack, a unified force of flying fur, until finally, infinitesimally, the coils began to loosen.

Felicity took a giant gulp of air. Then another. Oxygen flooded her bloodstream. She was alive, alert. Her beloved cats had gone to battle for her, fought by her side.

She got one hand free. She could do this. She could complete the final step, and she suddenly knew how.

She reached behind her, blindly patting her hand along the piles of Jim's stuff, eventually finding the Holy Grail. Her fingers curled in place. She placed her index finger upon the trigger.

She whipped her arm around. Aimed. And squirted Eau de Butt Crack all over Apep.

She kept going, pumping over and over and over until she had emptied the entire bottle of Passion's Fire into his hideous snake face.

"*Fire be in thee, O Apep.* May the Eye of Horus have power over the soul and the shade of Apep!"

And then, he simply burst into flames.

Felicity shoved him away and barely escaped the tongues of fire shooting from his slick, black scales. One last time, the serpent of chaos opened its mouth wide and hissed, then let out an almost human scream, piercing and tormented.

Felicity could stomach no more, rushed to Tom, Boudica beside her. She knelt down, and he pried his eyes open. She pulled him so that he sat up. "Tom!" She grabbed the pizza cutter and hacked away at the zip ties around his wrists. "Tom, answer me! Wake up!"

She heard Boudica yowl and spit. Felicity jerked around just as Boudica hurled herself over Felicity's shoulder... and directly into the flames shooting from Apep's head. His fangs had been inches from Felicity's neck when Boudica pounced, and now Felicity could only stare in horror as those needle-sharp fangs sank deep into Boudica's fur. The cat went limp.

"NOOOOOO!!!!!!" Felicity grabbed a chair and pummeled the snake until he released the cat, but Felicity kept hitting and screaming; over and over she beat him until the flames accomplished their job, consuming his flesh, and an empty snakeskin collapsed to the floor, made of nothing but air and ash.

Felicity picked up the scorched Boudica in her burned and bloody hands, but it was too late. Her beloved cat was gone.

Tom was already freeing Ronnie, who then worked on untying Bethany and Tasha. Felicity simply stood in the middle of the ash heap, cradling her dead cat.

Her insides were numb. She felt nothing.

Tom crossed to Felicity and gently placed his hands on her shoulders. "You saved the world, Felicity Cheshire."

She shook her head. "It was Boudica. She saw me. Heard the bell. She knew I needed her!" Felicity gulped down a mouthful of air. "Boudica saved me. She saved us all."

The numbness lifted. Felicity felt a wave of grief rumble and roll and hit her so hard that her knees buckled. She held Boudica tightly against her breast, rocking her as a mother would a baby, as if she could love her back to life again.

She sobbed. She held her dead cat, curled in on herself, and let it all out, everything strapped down and muzzled and beaten back over the years. It spilled out gently at first. Then it pushed, roared its way into existence. Everything raw and real that had been silenced within her was finally set free.

As she howled with grief, Felicity became aware of a strange sensation. The necklace had begun to pulsate against her breastbone with a deep, concentrated rumble. She tucked Boudica into the crook of her arm and raised her free hand to the necklace, astonished as the vibration built and the gems under her palm began to glow.

"Oh my God; Lissie, what's happening?"

Tom took Boudica, gently laid the dead cat on the floor, and helped Felicity to her feet. Everyone gathered in stunned silence to watch each individual gem in the necklace shoot out a finger of light, every color and shade, bursting into bright beams that twirled and danced and merged together, drifting downward to embrace Boudica. The light lifted her little, burned body, and the beams began to spin her, slowly at first, then faster and faster and faster as the light intensified, until all exploded in a blinding flash.

Boudica was gone. The necklace returned to normal.

"What just happened?" Tears rolled down Felicity's cheeks. "Where did Boudica go?"

Tom wiped away her tears and pulled her into his arms. "Home. She's gone home."

CHAPTER EIGHTEEN

As Felicity watched first light creep across the lawn, she decided it was a good thing that Tasha had decided to renovate. Her house and everything in it had been half-demolished and fried to a crisp, courtesy of one flaming chaos serpent and a couple of easily manipulated minions.

They'd returned from the emergency room. Everyone was exhausted and starving. Someone mentioned ordering Chinese takeout. Ronnie indeed had suffered a concussion and was still angry that Felicity had insisted she be examined. Bethany was unhurt but not talking much, which caused Felicity to worry that she'd been badly traumatized. Tasha had a sprained an ankle, had broken several fake nails, and had lost her remaining bottom incisor in the melee. Tom had suffered two bruised ribs and a broken nose, requiring a manual realignment and gauze-packed nostrils, which he resented.

Felicity walked away with minor burns and lacerations after having been forced to endure two hours of nurses picking glass from her forearms and hands. As a bonus, every muscle and tendon in her body ached, and her hair had been singed so badly that the nurses had to cut several inches off the back.

But all in all, they'd been lucky.

Ronnie had cleaned up the poor Rottweiler and they'd returned the dog to his owner, who apologized profusely for his pet's out-of-character behavior. It turned out the creature was named Fluffernutter, and was a lovebug when not demon-possessed. The junkyard proprietor wrote a check on the spot to pay for replacement of Tasha's picture window.

Hair Gel Jim was fine. He was embarrassed, claimed to have the world's worst hangover, and could not stop telling Tasha how sorry he was for the things he'd done. Like how he tried to steal from Ronnie, how he'd removed the *Wadjets*, and how he'd cut a hole in the fence so the Rottweiler had access. Oh, and he apologized for running a long con on Tasha with plans to steal some of the profits from the sale of her land.

"But I swear, that's all I remember doing."

Felicity snorted in disgust.

"What did Ronnie need all those electronics for anyway?" He held an ice bag to his forehead. "The big guys gave me a hundred bucks to tell them where the chick from the apartment went, then they took me to their boss, some guy in a fancy suit, who described the Satan worshipper to a T and gave me another hundred to show him where he was."

"You're a class act, Jimbo." That was Ronnie.

"I think he might have drugged me!"

Bethany rose from her spot on the sofa, pointing to Jim. "You're a terrible person." She'd broken her silence. "I don't know you from Adam, but I think we should hand you over to the police. A man like you should be in jail."

Tasha had been sweeping ashes with a cordless vacuum but got queasy when she found the occasional bit of charred, scaly snakeskin. She turned it off and sighed. "Listen, Jim. Take your shit and leave. And never—hear me when I say this—*never* come back here again."

Jim stood a little unsteadily and gathered up most of his clothes from the table. He didn't seem to notice or care that he dropped a few items.

"The weirdest part is that I swear I saw the cat lady kick some giant snake's ass! Was there really a giant snake? Or was it all a drug dream?"

Tasha picked up a fallen sock and shoved it onto the pile in his arms. She spun him around to face the door. "It was all one giant nightmare. Now get thefuckoutahere."

While Tom and Tasha nailed plywood over the window, Felicity returned to the trailer and her cats. After their courage in battle, every one of them had huddled in the Airstream to mourn for their friend. Felicity hadn't had a chance to speak with them since.

She began their usual breakfast ritual, trying not to cry again for the missing Boudica.

"You are all heroes." The cats gathered 'round, listening attentively. There may have been a time when Felicity wondered if they understood her, but no more. Tom had been correct; she had two-way conversations with her cats. They understood each other perfectly. And there was no shame in that. "You saved me," she told them. "You saved the world. I am immensely proud of every single one of you."

She kissed and petted each kitty and added a little extra food, which seemed vastly inadequate. But they purred, rubbed against her, licked her cheeks, and climbed all over her when she sat on the floor. Eventually, she noticed how much Scratch and Sniff had grown in the last two weeks.

"Look what big boys you've become! I've been so preoccupied, I didn't even see it! Forgive me."

Mew-mew, they replied in stereo.

He hugged Tasha goodbye.

After a few moments, she pushed herself away, wiping tears from her eyes and shaking her head. "Sorry."

"No need to apologize."

"Thank you for helping me with Jim. Thank you for... you know... everything. You're a good man, Tom. A good man-cat. Whatever you are."

"Thank you, too," he said. "You are a very strong woman, Tasha. Have fun with your remodel and keep an eye on Felicity for me."

She grinned. "It might be the other way around from now on."

"It just might."

He approached Bethany. She'd revealed herself to be far more resilient than she looked. "I wish you all the best with the baby," he said.

"I appreciate that."

"And with Rich."

"Yeah." She chewed on her lip.

"Remember that you have a posse to help you."

She nodded, saying nothing, then looked away quickly. Before he could prepare, she threw herself into his arms and squeezed tight. "Thank you! I'm going to miss you, Tom!"

He chuckled. "I'll miss you too."

He dreaded this last one, and turned to see Ronnie standing near Tasha's front door. She inclined her head. "I'll walk with you."

He followed her across the porch, down the steps, and into the yard, where she turned to face him. Ronnie's older bruises now blended with her newer ones. She'd had the hell beaten out of her, more than once, but she stood tall and straight, ready for whatever came at her next.

Ronnie shoved her hands in the pockets of her tactical pants. He thought it was a sign that she wasn't the hugging type.

It was probably for the best.

"Thank you for everything, Lance Corporal Veronica Davis of Pendleton." He bowed, like he had in her tiny studio apartment, and straightened to find she'd turned away to stare at the trees. He saw her shoulders tense, but she rallied, as she always did, and turned to look him in the eye.

"My buddy and I are driving to Viper Apps today. We're gonna shut the whole thing down, then leave an anonymous tip with the authorities."

"Thank you. For everything." There was so much more he wanted to say, but he faltered.

"Pick a language, dude," she said, trying not to smile. "You've got fourteen to choose from, amirite? Unless all that was complete bullshit."

He did as she asked, speaking the simple, surprising truth of it all—that she would remain in his heart, a part of him. Always.

"*De tha se xcháso poté.*"

"Back at ya." Ronnie swallowed hard and kicked the toe of her boot in the weeds. He expected her to make one last smart-ass comment and be on her way, but without warning, she sprung up on her toes, grabbed the back of his head, and drew him down to her.

Ronnie's mouth crushed his, her lips supple and slippery, opened just enough to allow the hot tip of her tongue to brush against his. Her firm hand remained in control at the back of his neck.

It lasted just a flash, a breathless instant, and in a different time and place this kiss would have been a clear invitation. Ronnie was offering herself to him. And in any other reality, he would gladly accept, make this magnificent warrior his own, and give himself to her alone.

But the kiss ended. He took a big gulp of air—kissing with gauze-packed nostrils had left him light-headed—as she stepped back, averted her eyes, and let her hand slip away from the nape of his neck.

"Ronnie..."

She shook her head, raising her liquid brown eyes to him. "Later, cat." With that, she spun on her heels and marched inside. She was gone.

Mrrrowww!

As Tom walked through the Airstream door, Mojo ran toward him, weaving in and out of his ankles.

"You were fierce, my friend. A true soldier." Tom bent down and scratched behind his ears. "In fact, all of you were courage personified. It has been a great honor to know you."

He straightened, then extended his hand to Felicity, who sat cross-legged on the floor. She offered her elbow, one of the few body parts not wrapped in gauze, and winced in pain when he pulled her to a stand. Now that the adrenaline had faded, all she wanted to do was crash for days.

"It's time." Tom gave her a little smile.

"The Chinese takeout's here? Let me change real quick." She turned to head into her bedroom, but Tom placed his hand on her shoulder.

"No Chinese. It is time for me to go."

"Where? Do you need me to drive?"

He laughed. "Not necessary. We were victorious. *You* were victorious, in the most astounding way. And now it's time I head back to the Realm of the Gods."

Felicity froze. "*What?*"

"You did it, Felicity, all that I asked and more. You overcame tremendous odds and forged your own path—a smart, bold, seat-of-your-pants path unlike any Acolyte in history. You are truly one of a kind. Never forget that."

Just then, the sun rose over the trees and warm light spread through the trailer. Felicity could only stare in shock at Tom. Were those actual tears welling in his eyes? Or just irritation from his gauze-packed nostrils?

"I'm going to miss you something awful, Tom."

"And I'll miss you, Felicity Renee Cheshire, thirty-second Acolyte of Bastet." He turned and picked up the ritual knife from the banquette table. All the cats had lined up around them, still and solemn. "Take care of your mistress," he instructed them.

Tom looked to Felicity. "I mean what I said, Felicity. I'll miss you forever, and that's a helluva long time." He broke out in a dazzling smile.

Felicity had known this moment would come. Shit, she'd longed for it since the instant the necklace had been bestowed. She'd felt cursed, as if the rich gold and precious stones were a heavy shackle, their weight a reminder of coming failure. But somehow, at some point, she had grown into it.

She might still be a plain woman on the outside—with her singed, beige hair and puff pastry body—but on the inside she shined as brightly as the necklace. Inside, she was a queen worthy of the crown.

Tom gestured for her to turn around. She did, lifted what

remained of her hair, and offered the back of the necklace to him. "Wait." She spun around. "Did you say your goodbyes?"

Tom exhaled. "I did."

"Oh. Even Ronnie?"

"Even Ronnie."

"Oh."

"Turn around Felicity."

"But you can't go back like that."

"Like what?"

"There's cotton shoved up your nostrils. What will Bastet say?"

He looked to the Airstream ceiling as if to ask the Goddess for patience. Then he glanced at her again. "She'll say, *Good job.*"

"As she should."

"You're stalling."

"I am."

"It's time."

Felicity turned around and lifted her hair once more. It was better that he didn't see her cry. She felt him slip the tip of the blade beneath the heavy gold. She heard him recite the ancient Egyptian words with a lilt of sadness.

His voice wrapped around her like a caress. She prepared for the familiar hum of the precious metal and tensed in anticipation. She was about to hear the necklace—finally, blessedly—release.

Or not.

Tom shifted his stance behind her. He repositioned the flint blade. She heard him take a deep breath and recite the incantation again, louder this time.

Nothing.

The necklace did not hum. It did not vibrate. And it sure as hell didn't unlatch. Something was wrong.

Tom tried a third time.

Not a bit of difference.

Felicity spun around. "What's going on? Why won't it open?"

He shook his head, eyes wide. "I don't know. I've never seen this before. Once Apep—or the Acolyte—is dead, the necklace releases. Always. Without fail."

"Apep's dead! We saw him disintegrate! Hell, Tasha's still Hoovering up his scales!"

"Apep's definitely dead."

"And I'm alive!" Felicity inhaled and exhaled to test her lungs. Then patted down her chest, hips, thighs. "See?"

"You're absolutely alive."

"Then what's the holdup?"

"Something's not right, obviously."

"Then we'll fix it!" Felicity realized she'd slipped back into kick-ass Acolyte mode without conscious thought. She'd been changed forever, without a doubt. "Why don't you travel back to the Realm and ask Bastet what we need to do. There's no danger now, at least for another sixty-three years, right? And I promise to take excellent care of the necklace while you're gone. Sound like a plan?"

Tom dropped his hand. He cleared his throat. "Uh, maybe I wasn't clear about one detail." He appeared to lose his train of thought. His gaze traveled around the small trailer.

"What detail?"

He cocked his head and dropped the knife to the tabletop. "The necklace is how I get back to the Realm of the Gods. It's my return ticket."

"Huh?"

"If the necklace will not release, I can't wear it. If I'm not wearing it, I can't leave here and enter there."

Felicity shook her head, confused. "What are you saying?"

Tom grabbed her by the shoulders. For the first time ever, she saw a flicker of panic in his expression. "Until we figure this out, I'm stuck on earth. In Pine Beach. With you. Your posse. *Ronnie.* Your cats…"

Felicity raised a bandaged hand to her mouth, in shock.

Tom was trapped here.

The necklace would stay around her throat for as long as it took to discover what had gone wrong.

She let her hand fall, brushing her fingers along the gold as her mind reeled. Then, she looked up into those now familiar mismatched eyes and said, "We're going to need a bigger trailer."

THE END

The Cat Lady Chronicles continue...

Book 2: CATASTROPHE, January 2022

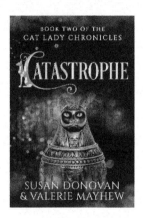

Book 3: CATACLYSM, April 2022

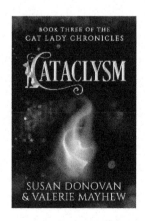

One tough cookie...

Felicity Cheshire has survived cancer, medical bankruptcy, and the world's slimiest ex-husband. Now she's about to be evicted from the broken-down Airstream on the Oregon coast that's home for her and her twelve rescue cats.

One last kitty...

When her car breaks down during a freakish rainstorm, Felicity spies an injured tomcat on the roadside and thinks, "how much trouble can one more be?" A lot, as it turns out. Soon there's a naked mystery man in her bed and her small-town, middle-aged existence careens to *WTF?* territory.

Two weeks to save the world.

With her posse of badass BFFs at her side, Felicity takes a terrifying journey from has-been to hero, where she must face her darkest fears in order to save those she loves. She might even have to attempt sit-ups.

Coming Soon:

CATASTROPHE, Book 2 of the Cat Lady Chronicles
CATACLYSM, Book 3 of the Cat Lady Chronicles

ABOUT THE AUTHORS

SUSAN DONOVAN

Publisher's Weekly has called Susan's books "the perfect blend of romance and women's fiction." She is a *New York Times and USA Today* bestselling author of novels from St. Martin's Press, Penguin USA/Berkeley Books, HQN, Amazon, and Hachette, along with several self-published works. Susan is a former newspaper reporter with journalism degrees from Northwestern University. She lives with her posse in New Mexico.

VALERIE MAYHEW

Formerly a writer of paranormal television (*The X-Files, Charmed*) Valerie is now sowing mischief of the normal kind as a college writing instructor. She lives in Los Angeles with her husband, who writes horror, her children, who can be horrors, and more cats than she cares to admit. Valerie survived four years of the drama program at The Juilliard School, where she received her B.F.A.

Catch up with the cat ladies at:
www.catladychronicles.com

Made in the USA
Middletown, DE
22 January 2022

59338382R00189